African American Life

General Editors

Toni Cade Bambara
Author and Filmmaker

Wilbur C. Rich
Wayne State University

Geneva Smitherman-Donaldson
Wayne State University

Ronald W. Walters
Howard University

COLEMAN YOUNG
AND DETROIT POLITICS

Coleman Young. (Photo courtesy of the city of Detroit.)

COLEMAN YOUNG

AND DETROIT POLITICS

From Social Activist to Power Broker

Wilbur C. Rich

 WAYNE STATE UNIVERSITY PRESS   Detroit   1989

Copyright © 1989 by Wayne State University Press,
Detroit, Michigan 48202. All rights are reserved.
No part of this book may be reproduced without formal permission.
93 92 91 90 89   5 4 3 2 1

Library of Congress Cataloging-in-Publication Data
Rich, Wilbur C.
  Coleman Young and Detroit politics : from social activist to power broker /
Wilbur C. Rich.
    p. c.m.—(African American life series)
  Bibliography: p.
  Includes index.
  ISBN 0-8143-2093-7
  1. Young, Coleman A. 2. Mayors—Michigan—Detroit—Biography.
3. Detroit (Mich.)—Politics and government. I. Title. II. Series.
F474.D453Y677 1989
977.4'34043'0924—dc19
[B]   88-39480
                                                                       CIP

Contents

Illustrations	9
Figures and Tables	11
Preface: Coleman Young and the Political Transformation of Detroit	13
Acknowledgments	15
1. Introduction: Changing Detroit from the Mayor's Office	18
2. Growing Up in Detroit: Learning to Cope with Racism	40
3. The Making of a Black Politician	61
4. The Elections of Coleman Young, 1973–1985	91
5. Decade of Decision: Economic Growth and Change in Detroit	126
6. The Nurturing of Economic Development Projects in Detroit: Money, People, and Commitment	168
7. Affirmative Action and Collective Bargaining under Fiscal Adversity: The Case of Detroit	205
8. The Fiscal Crisis of 1981: Detroit's Brush with Disaster	232
9. Conclusions	264
Notes	282
Index	296

Illustrations

Frontispiece, Coleman Young
Following page 151:
Coleman Young as an infant
Class picture at St. Mary's
Young's mother, Ida Reese Young
Young's father, William Coleman Young
Coleman Young as a soldier in World War II
Young and Paul Robeson
Young testifying before the House Un-American Activities Committee
Coleman Young as an insurance salesman
State Senator Coleman Young and Ken Cockrel
Governor Milliken signing No Fault Insurance Bill
Young with Robert Kennedy, Basil Brown, and other politicians
Portrait of State Senator Coleman Young
Young with Leonard Woodcock, William Milliken, Henry Ford II, and Richard Austin
Young with Richard Hatcher, Robert Blackwell, and Maynard Jackson
Young at a black mayors' forum
David Rockefeller, Coleman Young, and Henry Ford II
Coleman Young and Dr. Benjamin Hooks
Young with President Carter
Young with James Baldwin, Thomas Bonner, and O'Neil Swanson
Rev. Martin Luther King, Sr., Henry Ford II, Coretta Scott King, Coleman Young, and Robert Green
Roger Smith of GM presents a check to the city of Detroit
Coleman Young and Lee Iacocca

Young with Eric Sevareid in 1980
Young and Hubert Humphrey
Jim Wright, Coleman Young, George Crockett, Harriet Crockett, and Arthur Johnson
Muhammad Ali and Coleman Young at the mayor's home
Young checking his schedule
Coleman Young, Michael Blumenthal, and Damon Keith
Young campaigns for Texas Democrats
Young with members of his constituency
Coleman Young and Detroit children
Coleman Young

Figures and Tables

Figures

1. Leadership Styles and Policy Orientation	35
2. Mayoral Election Turnout, 1919–1985	122
3. Job Shifts in Metropolitan Detroit, 1967–1985	133
4. A Model of Economic Decision Making in the Mayor's Office	147

Tables

1. Black Percentages in Subcommunities	24
2. Black Percentages of Detroit Population	25
3. 1973 Election Voting Statistics	106
4. 1977 Election Voting Statistics	112
5. 1981 Election Voting Statistics	115
6. 1985 Election Voting Statistics	118
7. Detroit Welfare Recipients, 1973–1986	137
8. Breakdown of City Personnel by Race, Sex, and Rank, 1974	213
9. Racial and Gender Composition of Detroit Police Department, 1981	225
10. Detroit Budget Data, 1970–1983	239
11. Sources of Budget Deficit, 1975–1976	243

Preface

Coleman Young and the Political Transformation of Detroit

This book challenges the conventional wisdom, which asserts there is an immutable fate for the so-called rustbelt cities such as Detroit, Gary, and Newark. Despite the millions of dollars spent on these cities in federal grants, private investment, and local funds, critics tell us they are doomed. Sinking slowly into the economic quicksand, rustbelt cities are fighting a losing battle to survive, and our struggles to save them may only delay their appointments with atrophy. This prognosis remains, despite encouraging developments such as the recent elections of dedicated ethnic mayors, who are thought to be capable of rallying ethnic spirit and creating interethnic coalitions that might challenge the deterioration of their cities. The decline is inevitable and natural, according to these analysts; the housing stock has been worn or filtered out, factories rendered obsolete, and skilled labor has fled to the suburbs. A rational strategy might be to allow these cities to die so that new cities can be permitted to grow. Conventional wisdom also holds that the election of a black mayor has come at the wrong time in the lives of these cities. Indeed, we are told that the elections of black mayors are triggering, or at least accelerating, "white flight." Whites are fleeing away from high taxes, poor schools, and black neighbors; black politicians are inheriting worn-out infrastructures; and the city halls they are inheriting turn out to be hollow political prizes that offer their constituents only symbolic reassurances.

This study emphasizes the accomplishments of a major American city, Detroit, and its attempts to confound conventional economic wisdom. It argues that the skills, visions, and politics of Mayor Coleman Young have made a difference for the future of the city. Despite intense competition from the city's suburban neighbors for residents, resources, and industry, Coleman Alexander Young has been an effective leader in the face of political obstacles and a wayward economy.

Although an exception does not make a rule, at first glance, Detroit seems to be an unlikely candidate for contradicting conventional wisdom. Yet, a closer look reveals a city that is reshaping itself and responding appropriately to policy choices placed before it. Detroit is being led by an unlikely mayor with a dream of restoring Detroit to the boom town of his childhood. Coleman Alexander Young, a product of the city's East Side, leads the dual worlds of white and black Detroit into a new future. If one looks deeper, one can see the city of Detroit evolving into a new city with a different raison d'être. The unfolding of this, yet another, new Detroit may be the most interesting evolution among rust-belt cities—hence, the need to record the events that will shape this history.

Chapter one outlines the basic strategy underlining Coleman Young's approach to policy-making. The chapter attempts to explain his approach to decision making based on his personality and his environment. Chapter two looks at Coleman Young's childhood and the politics of early Detroit. Chapter three analyzes the socialization of Coleman Young and why he views the world as composed of shifting coalitions and an endless struggle for power and status. Chapter four outlines the four mayoral campaigns of Coleman Young and his opponents. Chapter five examines the processes of decision making as they relate to economic decisions. Chapter six recounts the steps in the creation and maintenance of large economic development projects during the Young administration. Chapter seven describes the development and implementation of affirmative action programs during the periods of fiscal crises. Chapter eight outlines the fiscal crisis of 1981 and its impact on the mayor and Detroit politics.

Finally, the concluding chapter brings together the findings and analyzes how these events have shaped current Detroit politics, and it suggests how future administrations will be affected by the policies of Mayor Coleman Young.

Acknowledgments

This book grew out of a discussion over lunch in the summer of 1983. I met with members of the Board of Directors of the Coleman Young Foundation—Malcolm Dade and Larry Doss—and Arthur Johnson, vice president of Wayne State University, to discuss the project. We wanted to review the first ten years of the Young administration with special attention to affirmative action, economic development, and the fiscal crisis of 1981. At the time I knew very little about Detroit politics and had never met the mayor, and there was already speculation that he might not run again. These rumors proved to be false and the mayor ran and won a fourth term. The biography/policy analysis of the first ten years of the Young administration had to be extended to include his latest election. Nevertheless, I had no idea what I was getting into. First, I knew little about the history of black politics in Detroit or the role of labor unions in its development. Accordingly, a project which was designed to take one year lasted for four.

Throughout the project, Dr. Johnson acted as a mediator between civic leaders in Detroit and me. He wrote personal notes of introduction to individuals explaining the project, and he advised me during the first year of the project. Malcolm Dade, Larry Doss, and William Beckham also acted as facilitators. Malcolm Dade made several phone calls in my behalf and served as liaison with the Young Foundation. The foundation provided support for research assistants, travel, and word processing.

Through the efforts of Malcolm Dade and Arthur Johnson, I was able to interview friends, relatives, and colleagues of Coleman Young. I was also able to interview several city politicians and corporate leaders. I have cited some of their comments in the manuscript; overall, they were most helpful in giving me a three-dimensional image of Coleman Young. A partial list of people interviewed included Robert Spencer, Ron Hewitt, Emmett Moten, Claud Young, Diane Edgecomb, Robert McCabe, Peter Stroh, Max Fisher, Robert Phillip, Augustus Adams, Robert Vanderbeek, Richard Simmons, Bernice Grier, Joyce Garrett, Hubert Holley, Forrest Holman, William Beckham, Remer Tyson, Corrine Gilb, Bob Pisor, Albert Ward, Mel Ravitz, Reggie Witherspoon, Damon Keith, Douglas Fraser, William Milliken, John Mogk, Phillip Smith, Robert Battle, Willie Bell, Sidney Rosen, George Crockett, Larry Horowitz, Horace Sheffield, Tom Turner, Maryann Mahaffey, and David Moore.

A variety of colleagues helped to clarify my ideas either by listening to or by reading parts of or all of the manuscript. I am particularly grateful to Charles V. Hamilton, Martin Kilson, Carter Wilson, Lana Stein, Martin Halpern, Henry Pratt, and Fred Greenstein. My colleagues John Strate and Jorge Tapia helped me with graphics and tables in this book.

I owe a very special debt to my research assistants, Sean Corcoran and Mark Nottley. Sean did most of the preliminary research on chapter six and Mark on chapter seven. A different version of chapter four was published in Michael Preston et al., *The New Black Politics*, 2d edition (Longman, 1987).

The typing of the various versions of the manuscript was done by Paula Sanch and Benji Johnson.

I should like to express my deep appreciation to Mary Jane England, associate dean, and H. Jim Brown, director of State, Local and Intergovernmental Center of Harvard University's John F. Kennedy School of Government, for allowing me to spend my first sabbatical at that institution. The Research Fellow Program at the center provided me with an opportunity to remove myself from Detroit—to get the necessary distance—long enough to complete a total revision of the manuscript.

I also wish to express my appreciation to the staff at the Walter Reuther Library at Wayne State University for allowing me to use their collection on labor history. The Reuther Archives also maintains the papers of State Senator Coleman Young. The correspondence in that collection was critical to my understanding of Coleman Young as a young politician.

Finally, there were supporters closer to home. My wife, Jean Russell, and daughters, Rachel and Alexandra, encouraged me throughout the writing of this manuscript. To all those others not named in this acknowledgment who helped in the preparation of this manuscript, I am profoundly grateful. Of course, I accept responsibility for any errors in it.

1

Introduction

Changing Detroit from the Mayor's Office

In the early 1970s many felt that the prospects for revitalizing American cities were very good, but those hopes waned near the end of the decade as American politics became more conservative. The election of the Democrat, Jimmy Carter, did not reverse this trend, which reached its peak in 1980 with the election of Ronald Reagan, the conservative Republican; then, anticity sentiments were unleashed. It was almost as if cities, and particularly their inner city residents, had become targets of economic retribution. Programs designed to reverse urban decline were labeled wasteful. The beginning of the eighties marked a watershed in the history of American cities. Optimism gave way to retrenchment and abandonment. Population dispersals and the economic recession that began in the late seventies accelerated the decline of many older American cities. The partial withdrawal from cities by the federal government during the decade further divided residents along racial, class, and ethnic lines. The inhabitants who remained in declining urban centers chose to elect new leaders and demand from them a fight for survival, and in turn many of these cities have evinced a gritty determination to survive and compete with their younger counterparts. In order to do so, older cities will literally have to create a new axis within their boundaries and reverse the cancer of decay.

Detroit is a classic case study of a city attempting to reverse the losses it has suffered in recent years. The city's golden era of the fifties and early sixties has given away to a protracted period of economic uncertainty. More than twenty years have passed since Detroit was cited by *Look* magazine as the "All-American City." *Look* no longer exists, nor does the Detroit of 1966, yet Detroit is currently undergoing a political-economic metamorphosis. New housing is being built, a new commercial center is under construction, and the city's revenue base has been restructured. For a decade political leaders have maintained a working alliance with local businessmen, producing an enviable record of relative political stability, and part of the reason for the resurgence of the city lies with the election of Mayor Coleman A. Young in 1973. Political stability has provided an anchor against the precipitous declines of population and resources. In his fight to rebuild Detroit, the mayor has enjoyed the support of local leaders from labor, business, civic, and religious organizations, yet his task has been particularly difficult.

When Coleman Young took office, the city was in a transitional stage. The riot of 1967 had accelerated white flight. The 1974 oil embargo, the year of his inauguration, precipitated the decline of an auto-based economy. The mayor was willing to "Move Detroit Forward," but many individuals and problems stood in his way. The 1973 city charter left the burden of policy directions mainly in the hands of the elected leaders of the city; no organized opposition offered alternatives to policy solutions.

In an essay that appeared in 1973, the same year that Coleman Young was elected, Jeffrey Pressman warned of the limitations of mayoral leadership. Pressman cited seven preconditions for mayoral leadership, including sufficient financial and staff resources; sufficient staff support for mayor jurisdiction over social programs; mayoral jurisdiction over public policy; adequate salary for the mayor; friendly local media; and mobilizable and supportive interest groups.[1]

It has been fifteen years since Pressman's essay on mayoral leadership was published, during which time the changing economic condition has placed even greater constraints on mayoral power. Pressman's observations grew out of a massive study of the Oakland (California) area conducted by the University of California at Berkeley but was extended to studies of other cities. As times have changed, a review of Detroit politics suggests that some additional preconditions might be appropriate, such as: unlimited opportunity for rational political risk-taking; mayoral jurisdiction over visible rehabilitation and revitalization projects; dependable federal and state financial support; potential opposition groups that are amenable to cooptation; and a predilection among inner city constituencies and the audience for different interpretations of political events. These additions seem particularly important for black mayors of predominately black cities and may be applicable to all mayors of large industrial cities.

Were Pressman's preconditions met when Coleman Young assumed office? What has Mayor Young done to enhance the capability of the office to meet the economic and political challenges facing the city? What is the supporting evidence for a transformation of city politics? How does Coleman Young compare with his predecessors in the mayor's office? How does he measure up to the standards he originally set for himself? To answer these and other questions, city policies of the first ten years of the Coleman Young administration were analyzed.

Mayor Young and Detroit as Case Studies

Coleman Young and the decade encompassed by the first ten years of his administration provide a significant foundation for studying black politics and big city politics in the U.S. in the seventies. During 1984 and 1985 several background interviews were conducted for this study, followed by an analysis of secondary data. This research strategy permitted a double check on the sources' memories and infused interpretation of events with the commentary of significant actors. Interviewers also pointed out additional source materials that were not an original part of the planned research itinerary and also were not traditional sources for information on urban politics. Previous work on Detroit politics was so lacking that we were forced to organize the data based on the interviews and direction offered by these sources. This study is not an attempt to test a hypothesis as such, but rather it is a serious attempt to understand the decade of change in the city and the impact of Coleman Young's leadership.

Given our narrow task, there is no attempt to refute the literature on city politics; rather, the intent is to offer another interpretation. The generalizations contained in the study may be amenable to theory-making for black politics and snowbelt industrial cities. In many ways, Detroit is a prototype of such cities. It has an aging infrastructure, a majority black population, and recurrent economic problems. With more than its share of unemployment, welfare recipients, and decaying housing stock, the city is still considered an anchor of the great American industrial empire. Accordingly, many people have a stake in trying to save it, restore it, rebuild it, and improve it.

Among the city's distinguishing characteristics are three that might be particularly striking to the casual observer—that the automobile industry dominates the city's (and the state's) economy; that a black political elite has emerged in Detroit; and that Coleman Young's mayoral leadership has a broad scope. A student of the city's politics might ascertain something more from current speculation about Detroit's future political transformation—the need for economic diversity, a maturation of the black elite, and the need to take a long-term view of the eventual post–Young era. For now, city events indicate not a return to a golden era but the creation of a new city entirely. All of the preconditions for this change must be considered within the context of changing demographics and black politics within the city.

Black Politics / White Reactions

In 1980 Peter K. Eisinger, a political scientist, compared black political takeovers in Atlanta and Detroit. His purpose was to analyze the changes that occur when one ethnic group displaces another. Using nineteenth-century Boston as a prototype, he called the process "ethnoracial transition," which he defined as "the acquisition of formal executive office in a political jurisdiction by a member of a previously subordinate ethnic group that is now backed politically by a new, potentially durable working majority composed largely of or dominated by members of that group." The transition, to be complete, must have durability—that is, retention of the office of mayor over time and a supportive constituency, or "working majority."[2] Eisinger is not prepared to conclude that these conditions have been met in Detroit, but from his review he is able to analyze the consequences of the Detroit version of the politics of displacement. Aside from psychological and strategic (political) adjustments to Young's "takeover," whites have emerged as tolerant and magnanimous. Eisinger attributes this behavior to economic expediency and democratic principles. Hence, the cooperation of white corporate and business leaders in Detroit's revitalization is consistent with Eisinger's description of psychological adjustment behavior. However, the attitudes of white residents in the inner working-class suburbs of the city are another matter. Nevertheless, Eisinger's concluding observations about the newly empowered black leaders seem appropriate.

> Newly victorious ethnic groups, even if they are relatively deprived in American society, do not embark on radical transformations of the social, economic, or institutional structure. They operate

within limits, for example, which preserve the broad established patterns and principles of private ownership, taxation, and income distribution. Change is aimed at the extension of goods to the new group (such as the efforts to encourage the growth of black-owned business) or at most to incremental redistribution (such as the opening of government contracts and employment to greater minority participation). The restraints that govern American politics also mean that new victors work more to enlarge the distribution of respect and status than to replace one system of honor with another.

Although to an observer the minority white voters and residents of Detroit seem invisible, they exist, and generally they support the mayor (in his candidacy for reelection) and the city's political elite—despite the fact that many of them would prefer a less race-oriented brand of politics. Of course, making issues of race absent from Detroit politics is impossible, and herein lies the dilemma of the city's politics. Race-oriented rhetoric is necessary to mobilize an essentially disengaged national minority population. Meanwhile, its use tends to remind white residents of *their* minority status as city residents and predisposes them to believe that they will be ignored in decision making or in policies implemented at their expense.

Although an at-large election system ensures white representation on the city council, and Mayor Young's policy of appointing whites to high ranking government positions also guarantees a certain amount of representation for whites, the white minority senses that its ability to influence the direction of the city has diminished. Some observers regard Young's policy of racial evenhandedness, particularly during his first term, and his generally open attitudes toward whites as magnanimous; others consider the approach to be "good politics." Several have argued that if whites were to regain control of the city's politics, they would never appoint a similarly high percentage of black appointees to top technical and political positions as Mayor Young has done for whites.

Data from the Cavanagh and Gribbs administrations support this view; however, black politics demands that elected black leadership prove no intentions of implementing policies of revenge against whites, nor may it appear a vanguard of an official policy of racial separation and exclusion. Even in the 1980s, the era of the new black politics, black politicians cannot safely ignore their white audience both within and outside the city. Nevertheless, the demographics are on the side of blacks and the transition is theirs.

Detroit: A City in Transition

While it has been losing population to its suburbs for years, Detroit entered the 1980s losing its skilled workers and retirees to other parts of the country, particularly the Sunbelt. With a population of 1,203,339 residents and a city work force of 19,600, the city is a shadow of its former self. As the city population changed, the once-"white only" neighborhoods have become integrated. Blacks live in communities where, just twenty years ago, they were not allowed. The psychological pressure of having black neighbors and the aftermath of the 1967 riot have caused white flight.[3] Table 1 shows the population changes by race and subcommunities.

This table shows black population integration into all the city's neighborhoods since 1970. Communities such as Brightmoor and Redford, strongholds of white blue-collar workers, are among the areas which previously had no black residents and now have gained some. Indeed, some of these subcommunities have lost most, if not all, of their white population since the 1980 census was taken. The hemorrhage of middle-class white residents that began in 1960 increased and was amplified by the movement of working-class whites in the 1970s.

Black Population Percentages in Detroit Subcommunities

In 1970 there were 838,877 whites in Detroit; now there are 444,730. And the city's black population has increased from 660,428 to 758,939—primarily due to births, as there has been a notable decrease in overall immigration to the city. Since 1970 Detroit has lost 20.5 percent of its population. This profound demographic transformation has been accelerated by industrial decline, which, in turn, has prompted the elimination of approximately 4,000 city jobs. I will consider the economic situation of the city in greater depth in chapter five.

The emergence of black politics as a dominant mode of political relations has changed the nature of the Detroit political system. Black succession to offices and governing cliques has been juxtaposed with a lack of discernible black ascendancy to economic control or partnership. Indeed, the Big Three automakers have no visible black officeholders in critical decision-making positions. In the auto industry, as in other industries within the city,

Table 1. **Black Percentages in Subcommunities**

Subcommunity	Population 1970	Population 1980	% Change 1970–80	% Black 1970	% Black 1980
Central	42,668	30,376	−29	83	91
University	37,529	23,902	−36	55	56
Central Business Dist.	6,474	4,064	−37	37	57
Lafayette	16,748	13,766	−18	70	75
Hutzel	20,663	13,069	−37	81	85
Indian Village	8,091	7,664	− 5	36	45
East Riverside	27,909	15,516	−44	51	76
Foch	34,524	18,189	−47	85	92
Jefferson-Mack	23,280	16,657	−28	22	83
Chandler Park	19,652	17,917	− 9	15	81
St. Jean	24,665	15,292	−38	91	97
Kettering	44,611	27,148	−39	92	97
Chene	39,244	23,654	−40	60	70
Airport	39,611	26,762	−32	42	81
Conner	35,922	34,101	− 5		46
Finney	37,320	32,446	−13		17
Denby	24,291	21,158	−13		10
Burbank	30,272	26,124	−14		8
Mt. Olivet	33,985	28,840	−15		13
Grant	13,684	12,392	− 9	3	30
Pershing	27,456	23,703	−14	37	69
Davison	28,750	22,785	−21	39	48
Nolan	30,743	27,793	−10	55	79
State Fair	16,314	16,519	+ 1	2	24
Palmer Park	14,276	13,321	− 7	15	56
Pembroke	26,762	24,784	− 7	79	95
Bagley	24,291	23,178	− 5	76	96
McNichols	21,408	16,342	−24	85	94
Harmony Village	48,756	42,957	−11	71	95
Grandmont	24,330	26,111	+ 7	9	85
Cerveny	21,263	23,530	+10	11	87
Greenfield	29,686	30,090	+ 1	13	81
Evergreen	37,625	35,722	− 5		63
Redford	28,782	24,494	−15		18
Rosedale Park	21,473	20,141	− 6		43
Brightmoor	23,351	19,914	−15	2	19

Source: City Planning Department, 1984.

most high-level blacks are in staff positions—in personnel or public, minority, and legal affairs. Therefore, Detroit lacks an industry-trained black managerial elite, and there is no current prospect of a black being appointed to a critical vice presidency or presidency of any prominent city industry. The lack is significant because it means that available black managerial talent is being

Table 2. **Black Percentages of Detroit Population**

Years	Total Population	Percentage Decline or Increase By Decade	Black Population	Percentage Increase By Decade	Percentage Black to Total Population
1940	1,623,452	—	149,119	—	9.2
1950	1,849,568	13.9	298,875	200.4	16.2
1960	1,670,144	− 9.7	482,223	61.3	28.8
1970	1,514,063	− 9.3	672,605	39.5	43.6
1980	1,203,339	−20.5	758,939	12.8	63.1

Source: U.S. Bureau of Census, 1980.

used either in government or in nonprofit agencies. Hence, when Coleman Young came to office there was a dearth of blacks with experience in managing large projects or making production decisions. Young's first administration would have been an entirely on-the-job training operation if the mayor had not decided to keep administrators left over from previous administrations and to import some blacks from other cities.

The lack of a well-stocked managerial job market or pool early in the Young administration meant some lost opportunity, yet it gave leaders time to examine and mark their course of action. Unlike its counterparts in earlier successions to political leadership, the new black elite continues to be discriminated against and underutilized by the economic elite. Nevertheless, the members of that elite recognize the positive changes made in Detroit within their lifetimes, and they are pleased with the general direction the city is taking. Like their earlier counterparts in ethnic successions, they are very sensitive to criticisms of their policies and policy-making. They are understandably self-conscious and regard most critics simply as nay-sayers or racists. The black elite wants to prove that it can manage a multi-billion dollar corporation in a sound and efficient manner. Proving it to their black constituency, their white audience, and themselves remains a significant task for the city's leadership.

Mayoral Constituencies and Audiences

In most American cities the mayor's position is at the political center. Yet it may or may not be the center of political and economic power. What kind of a mayor an individual makes depends on who the individual is, where he or she came from, and events arising during his or her tenure that one cannot anticipate. Frequently this office succeeds in reducing its occupant to a sentinel of routine municipal administration, but sometimes it can springboard that occupant to fame.

Elected mayors bring to their offices psychological, sociological, and cultural baggage. The office of mayor can bring out the best and the worst of individual incumbents. An accommodating and garrulous individual can turn into a Machiavellian misanthrope. The office can also turn an ordinary person into a symbol of ethnic secession and/or a paragon of moral virtue. This transformation is sometimes orchestrated, but usually it is some political, economic, or another societal event that triggers the process. A mayor elected for one reason, skill, or circumstance may discover that he or she owes his/her successes or effectiveness to some unrelated quality or experience. Few mayors hope to be a mayor "for all seasons."

Obviously, public expectations depend upon the circumstances of the election. Newly elected mayors are often under pressure, for instance, to establish their governing style quickly. During his inauguration, Coleman Young felt it necessary to tell would-be lawbreakers that certain kinds of behavior would no longer be tolerated. He is fond of recalling the moment: "I said that lawbreakers, regardless of whether they were wearing a superfly suit or a police uniform, to hit Eight Mile Road" (that is, to leave the city). He wanted to establish a law-and-order reputation and put the police force on notice that he was the boss. This was a crucial move since both his audience and constituencies were waiting for cues as to what type of mayor they would have for the next four years. The reference to superfly suits keyed his inner city constituencies that he had seen or knew about the movie depicting a black streetwise cocaine dealer who wore fancy clothes and outsmarted the cops and mobs. At that time many black youths saw Superfly as a hero and wanted to dress like the character. The mayor was telling them that he understood that identification but rejected the criminal lifestyle. The reference to criminals in police uniforms meant that he expected the city officers to respect civil liberties and stop using their uniforms as covers to break the law. The mayor was using his own cultural references to make a point and to set a psychological tone.

Mayors must adapt their styles of leadership to events. The ones who manage to do this emerge successfully as great mayors. Detroit's mayors Hazen Pingree, Frank Murphy, James Couzens, and Jerome Cavanagh are remembered as great mayors because they were able to dominate the politics of their times. Alternatively, Charles Bowles, mayor during the Depression, never dominated the office, and he was recalled after seven months. The operative variable is a combination of individual talents, psychology, and events. Demonstrating the requisite leadership qualities enables a mayor to really use mayoral power, which closely resembles other types of executive power.

In the conclusion to his study of presidential power, Richard Neustadt observed that

> Governmental power, in reality not form, is influence of an effective sort on the behavior of men actually involved in making public policy and carrying it out. Effective influence for the man in the White House stems from three related sources: first are the bargaining advantages inherent in his job with which to persuade other men that what he wants of them is what their own responsibilities require them to do. Second are the expectations of those other men regarding his ability and will to use the various advantages they think he has. Third are those men's estimates of how his public views him and how their public may view them if they do what he wants. In short, his power is the product of his vantage points in government, together with his reputation in the Washington community and his prestige outside.[4]

Political leadership, for Neustadt, is the ability to persuade others to accept your solutions for public policy problems. Using one's political clout, threats, and patronage are legitimate leverages in pursuing a given policy. Crises become opportunities for exerting leadership.

Most observers around the mayor's eleventh-floor offices in the City-County building in Detroit will attest to Mayor Young's persuasive skills, but few, including journalists covering the city hall beat, are so familiar with the decision-making process that goes on within the mayor's office. There is a need, therefore, to analyze the formation and context of mayoral and policy decisions to more clearly discern the reason for their successes and failures. The measure of any mayoral leader is his/her reaction to the ongoing and inevitable crises of governance.

In 1969 James Q. Wilson suggested that the behavior of modern mayors was defined by the paradox of having an audience that was increasingly different from their constituency. Wilson defines an audience as "those whose favorable attitudes and responses the mayor is most interested in, those persons from whom he receives his most welcome applause and his most needed resources and opportunities."[5] A mayor's constituency is the city's voters. Wilson included federal agencies, large foundations, and the mass media within his definition of the mayor's audience.

In the past, audience and constituency were identical, or

nearly so. Today, however, the differences are wide and widely apparent. Increasingly, mayors have had to cater to different audiences in the quest for financial resources and the maintenance of their administration's favorable reputation. These audiences not only have resources and access to communication, but they also have the power to define issues and shape a mayor's career. According to Wilson, mayors who seem neighborhood-oriented or constituency-oriented are heavily influenced by their audience. This posture could take the form of a mayor appearing to be the defender of neighborhood and city traditions, while simultaneously making changes demanded by what Wallace Sayre and Herbert Kaufman have called the "money providers."[6]

The white suburban-controlled media miss the mark when they attack black power wielders as if they were merely ethnic politicians. Many reporters underestimate the emotional content of black politics, or, in Detroit's case, the symbolic nature of the Young administration. An example of this misunderstanding was in the reporting on the Vista and Magnum scandals. A review of the coverage of those stories by an Ohio State University Journalism School team reached this conclusion:

> In a very real sense, the Mayor of Detroit and the Detroit media serve different constituencies. The media seem never to have recognized that. The reporters talk about Detroit as a large metropolitan area spreading far from the city center. Coleman wasn't elected by those people. In the view of the Mayor, the media represent an outside set of interests—interests which should be treated with suspicion. Given the social geography of the metropolitan area, there is a racist relationship between the media and the city.[7]

Since blacks have few economic penalties which they can impose on erring reporters or media executives, they use the only weapon they have: criticism is termed *racist*. Indeed, this particular characterization of reporting seems to keep many white reporters in line. There is also a mischievousness on the part of reporters, however, when they cover black mayors. Reginald Stewart, a *New York Times* reporter, observes: "The Detroit newspapers seem to take a certain delight in quoting the streams of vulgarity, but most of what [the mayor] utters for the record would not be printed in the *New York Times* if he was mayor of New York."[8] Unfortunately, this tendency to broadcast the mayor's idiosyncratic style also hampers the media's presentation of otherwise useful criticisms and examinations of city policies.

In other words, nowadays modern mayors have to deliver

more to their audience than to their constituency. Wilson claims that this situation leads to overpromising, unrealistic goal setting and alienation of the constituency by the mayor. When Wilson presented his views, he exempted the increasing number of black mayors who were then being elected in old cities. He believed that black mayors had a guaranteed favorable and sympathetic audience and that they could therefore concentrate on their constituencies' concerns, with little regard to the audience. Much has happened since 1969. Several large cities have elected black mayors, and their audience has mushroomed, threatening fiscal retribution on prodigal black spending in inner cities. Accordingly, there is a need to update and expand Wilson's typology of audience and constituency.

Using Detroit as an example, one can extend Wilson's definition of a political audience to include some additional elements, such as the state legislature, corporate leaders, and a variety of rural/small town/suburban coalitions. Ad hoc awards or rating organizations such as the Junior Chamber of Commerce emerge as evaluators of mayoral performance. (In 1962–63 both the Michigan and national chambers of commerce made Mayor Cavanagh "Outstanding Man of the Year.") Each of these audiences seeks to exact policy changes as the price of its continued financial and reputational support for the mayor.

Support from the state legislature is needed to pay current bills, and the support of corporate leaders is necessary for the maintenance of the city's image as one that is efficiently managed. Moreover, the larger audience is often influenced by decisions made by the local corporate elite. A corporation's decision to build (for example, the new General Motors plant in the redeveloped Central Industrial Park) or its leadership in the development of a large office center, such as the Renaissance Center, has a ripple effect throughout the city economy and in the consciousness of the constituency. Corporate leaders have a stake in the city's infrastructure and tax system. They are generally neither altruists nor guilt-ridden liberals. Instead, they are motivated by their interest in seeing that Detroit remains an environment where business growth is possible. A mayor acting out of step with the corporate elite can suddenly find that his/her city's economy has suddenly ceased to grow. By the same token, a mayor whose term of office stretches into a period when his/her political party is the "out" group in national politics may suddenly discover that the city's fiscal fate is seriously affected by the perceptions of nonresidents. With the advent of instantaneous television coverage of state legislatures and the coeval decline in federal support for urban programs, outstate legislators have become increasingly visible and vocal about city problems.

A remaining element in this expanded audience is the bond market. Cities today cannot pay their bills if they are unable to sell short-term revenue bonds. Investment houses constantly oversee the political stability of cities. Any change in the city's ability to pay its debts can bring about a downgrade in the city's bond rating, accompanied by an increase in the interest rates it must pay for borrowed funds. Although Detroit's reputation as a worthy investment has declined from its prime ratings of the sixties, the city can still borrow money without incurring severe penalties.

Wilson's definition of constituency must also be expanded to include nonvoters. Nonvoters, many of whom are not registered, are a reserved electoral force that can be mobilized on cue by a mayor who is perceived as a race leader. By warning the constituency of the dangers of misrepresentation it faces from outstate and out-of-state politicians and other audience members, a black mayor can better mobilize these nonvoters. Black mayors are expected to play a "watchman's" role, among others, and this distinguishes them from old-time machine politicians, as well as from their modern-day white counterparts. Hence, their constituency contains both active and reserve electorates, and accordingly, actions by the mayor must be scrutinized for both psychological content and signal intent. Mayoral initiative and leadership are critical to the care and maintenance of the silent reserve voting bloc. Black mayors have tended to treat this group much like a part of their audience, but many have provided uplift rhetoric as well, which encourages the silent voters. In 1969 Professor Wilson cautioned about rising expectations among a constituency. As it has happened, black mayors have had to spur the desire for psychological "catharsis" among the newly empowered constituency, both voters and nonvoters. Although most blacks do not wish their white counterparts any physical harm, some want them to feel the experience of being political outsiders.

Mayoral leadership, then, has to be measured by the opportunities created and visions proffered because of it. Coleman Young had to work harder than his predecessors to convince his black constituency that the assumption of political power does not mean absolute control of events. Political power is partly endogenous, and apparent power can lead to actual power. In short, a mayor's power is enhanced by the perception that he or she *is* powerful; the more successful he or she is, the more successful

Introduction 31

he or she can be. A successful mayor must establish the very criteria on which he or she is to be evaluated so that style, language, and how one approaches issues follow from choices the mayor makes about the goals of his or her administration.

Variety of Models of Mayoral Leadership

Milton Kotter and Paul Lawrence's study of mayoral leadership remains the best review of mayoral leadership in the sixties and seventies.[9] Kotter outlined five different models of mayoral leadership—the first of which was the *power broker model*. This type of mayor, said Kotter, uses power as capital. Edward Banfield's *Political Influence*, a study of Chicago's Richard Daley, exemplifies the power broker approach to the study of leadership.[10] The late mayor Daley used patronage to maintain power and influence with the subbosses of the Chicago political structure. Daley invested his influence much like a shrewd financial investor—in the most promising subleaders. Frank Murphy, Jerome Cavanagh, and Coleman Young have each exemplified some of the qualities of a power broker, but none could be described as "the Daley of Detroit."

The second type of approach to the study of leadership recognizes the *public entrepreneur*. James B. Cunningham described this approach in *Urban Leadership in the Sixties*,[11] and portrayed the entrepreneur as creative, energy-oriented, and one who takes risks. He or she was also described as open to new ideas and possessing organizational ability and promotional ingenuity. In many ways Young's predecessors Oscar Marx and Albert Cobo resemble the entrepreneur. Marx qualifies for having constructed the Detroit Receiving Hospital and the municipal court building and for appointing the first woman to a commissionership. Albert Cobo's creative financing of the Civic Center and Detroit's expressways certainly characterizes him as an entrepreneur. The nonentrepreneur would be more cautious, meticulous, and protective in initiating new policies and projects.

The third approach, the *coalition building model*, characterizes the career of Richard Lee, mayor of New Haven, and Robert Dahl's *Who Governs?* represents this breed of consensus-oriented executive who tends to seek compromise.[12] Mayors Murphy and Cavanagh could be considered the functional equivalent of New Haven's Mayor Lee. The key factor in policy success within this model is the creation of a workable coalition of interests. This was the most popular model among political scientists during the sixties and seventies, because it was well suited to the then-dominant paradigm of urban politics and pluralism.

The *personality model*—Kotter's fourth approach to mayoral leadership—still has its adherents. Indeed, many studies of mayors are examinations of their personalities.[13] Mayor Edward Koch of New York believes that personality matters, and so he has written his autobiography while still in office, and, according to some biographers, the great mayors of New York have also been charismatic personalities. This view of leadership relates to the intellectual school that advocates the Great Man theory to explain leadership. Detroit's Coleman Young is certainly a charismatic personality; he creates an agenda, seizes a crisis, and dazzles both his audience and his constituencies. Yet there is more to his leadership style than pure charisma. To understand his leadership, one must consider the unique window of opportunity given to him because of the circumstances of his election.

Charles Levine's *Racial Conflicts and the American Mayor* argues that after the riots of the sixties, mayors of large cities operated under conditions of social polarization. Blacks and whites saw new policy as a zero-sum game. Since programs are often interpreted by their psychic effects on the self-image of contesting groups, the distribution impacts of new proposals come under close scrutiny, proposals are evaluated for their opportunity cost (what other program might better benefit either the black or white communities?), and the long-run political consequences of an innovation are carefully analyzed (will a new program ultimately strengthen one side at the expense of the other?).[14] Levine concludes that in polarized communities three types of mayoral leadership can be identified.[15] The so-called bystander is a mayor who avoids conflicts or initiative and simply observes. The second type is the partisan mayor who is willing to take sides in a conflict, centralizes politics, opts for limited changes, and builds exclusive racial coalitions. The third—the hegemonic style—involves complete domination of the political process. Building a political machine might be a way to exclude the opposition racial group. The mayor uses social appeals for mobilizing voters and is free to implement his policy preferences. In a racially polarized city, this will mean integration of one race at the expense of another. After a review of Gary, Cleveland, and Birmingham's mayoral politics, Levine concluded that a contingency theory of leadership (that is, different situations require different responses) seems most appropriate for the variety of social and political situations facing mayors.[16] In other words, leadership to Levine is a consequence of the environment.

The leadership model that guides the present study is really a combination of the previously mentioned models. It asserts that the leadership or management style is dictated by the environment (contingency, entrepreneurship, and coalition-building) and by the psychological predisposition of the individual (Great Man theory). The office does not make the man so much as the man makes the office. An election cannot change a man, but it can alter political conditions. A single election can change a city's politics for decades. In the nineteenth century Mayor Pingree, a Republican, put together the first coalition of "Yankee" and foreign-born ethnic voters and permanently changed the political context. He also promoted the notion of municipal ownership of city railroads and that issue dominated mayoral campaigns until 1922.

The present study also takes the view that an individual brings to office a set of values and habits that shape decision making and his or her worldview. Like the rest of us, mayors are products of their socialization. They admire certain types of leaders and despise others. They pattern their speaking styles and support organizations after models they regard as effective and efficient. The office of mayor does not convert or transform an individual into some Dionysian or Apollonian personality; it simply provides a potent vehicle for self-expression. The differences one sees in modes of behavior and reactions to the political environment provide yet another way of organizing types of mayors.

Eudaemonism and Mayoral Leadership

Eudaemonists, according to one observer, are individuals who are stimulated by challenges that involve a low probability of success.[17] They enjoy conflict and draw strength from encounters. Eudaemonists enjoy life and the opportunity to take risks. Society usually finds ways to channel the natural instincts of eudaemonists, and politics offers one socially acceptable channel for individuals—black and white—to engage in vicarious eudaemonic behavior. Because there is an added stake for blacks, as the minority race, in political eudaemonism, a black constituency shares more deeply in a black mayor's missteps, victories, and frustrations. It resents each new occurrence of media criticism of its hero, and it identifies with *its* hero as it imagines him attacking the forces of evil.

Coleman Young seems to be a prototype of the eudaemonist.

Tom Green, a journalist, agrees with this assessment and asserts that "Coleman Young understands politics and he plays it like a showdown poker."[18] Young also understands what is at stake in the political process. He can tolerate an incredible amount of uncertainty while playing the game, which makes him a better player than some of his less patient opponents. Aside from patience, Coleman Young is a terminal optimist; he represents the strength that many blacks believe they lack. Blacks identify with his style and with his emotional outbursts. They enjoy stories of his one-on-one battles with the giants of industry—the mayor fighting for Detroit while the others are composing obituaries. They sympathize when he asserts, "I don't like phony a—— people. I take unconscious pleasure in shattering them with language."[19]

Mayor Young seems to have a thirst for conflict. He takes on the media, the city council, and presidents of corporations and the country; there are no exempt categories or individuals. He presents the very same agenda in talking to national Democratic party leadership as when he addresses a civic meeting in a local church.

Coleman Young is effective because his constituency supports him, and audiences enjoy what might be characterized as his flamboyant style. White constituents and other white observers tend at times to feel left out because often they are unable to relate to his manner. All too often they have been acculturated to expect blacks to be more "Apollonian" in temperament—as seekers of racial harmony who are conciliatory in manner and who exercise rhetorical restraint.

Many believe that the black leader's role is to serve as a model of passivity and extreme morality, but Coleman Young is anything but that. To many whites he comes across as "uppity," outspoken, and militant, but, in the black community, it is those very adjectives that boost his reputation. His confidence enables him to pursue eudaemonic risks, behave pugnaciously if the situation calls for it, and mete out instant retribution when that is due. His mayoralty stance provides his constituency with a regular diet of vicarious eustress and offers his audience the reassurance that someone is emphatically "in charge."

Risk-taking is an unusual use of power, which is rooted in the belief that power cannot be depleted—that there is an endless supply. The joy of exercising power is thus triggered by its value as a risk and as an endless resource in a game of chance. To win and raise the ante, like in a poker game, is to be willing to take a gamble.

Leadership Style	Partisan-Oriented	Reform-Oriented
Risktaker	I	II
Caretaker	III	IV

Figure 1. **Leadership Styles and Policy Orientation**

It is important to remember that class, age, culture, and race are independent variables in the study of eudaemonism. In addition, it is necessary to consider the proper interaction of personality in an uncertain situation. In Coleman Young's case, his willingness to assume risks that other politicians have avoided allows him to stay at least a step ahead of them. He has displayed this daring by building the Joe Louis Arena in 1980; showcasing Detroit for the 1980 Republican Convention; suing the U.S. Census Bureau over the 1981 Detroit census because of an undercount; clearing Poletown for the GM plant; taking over the construction of the People Mover; and proposing a city tax increase during a recession. Becoming a risk-taker rather than bowing to those counselors of moderation who permit themselves to be governed by circumstances—such as changing demographics—depicts for us an iconoclast who deliberately chooses the rocky road. No job less challenging than mayor of Detroit could have allowed Coleman Young to be Coleman Young. He is an unsettling paradox, a sharp mind with no college refinements, a builder with no single design, and a politician with no higher office ambition. Potential political opponents are continually thrown offguard by these contradictions. These qualities also make Coleman Young an effective mayor.

In order to understand the importance of mayoral risk-taking, it is necessary to contrast this behavior with that of a caretaker mayor. A simple matrix helps us ascertain the differences among mayoral leadership types (see Figure 1). Risk-takers who are party oriented (cell I) devote considerable time to constituency and party matters. Convincing the constituency that political parties do matter requires that a black leader play a major role in party activities. This may explain Mayor Young's decision to support Jimmy Carter of Georgia after the presidential candidate's ethnic purity remark in 1975, his refusal to attend the Jefferson-Jackson dinner in 1981, and his early endorsement of Mondale in 1984. In contrast to some other black elected officials, Young was willing to say publicly that the Reverend Jesse Jackson could not win the nomination and that a vote for him was a wasted vote.

A skillful mayor, especially a black one with a black constituency, can juggle several interests at once. To do this, he must *assume command, project a vision,* and *prevent internecine strife.* Young has mastered the art of coalition-building, social commentary, and party brokering—skills that are necessary to mobilize the economic, political, and moral resources of the community. He has done this within the context of party loyalty in a city with a relatively weak party infrastructure. Lacking a group of subcommunity leaders, as well as the power to dispense patronage enjoyed by the legendary Richard Daley of Chicago, Coleman Young offers himself and his career as political stakes.

Risk-takers who are reform oriented (cell II) put their political careers on the line in the attempt to reorganize and restructure government. Many reformers hold the central conviction that the municipal government must be cleansed of its evil influences. For them, a well-managed city assumes a high moral purpose, and in some cities, reformers have gone to the extent of repudiating partisan politics entirely. They feel obligated to attack patronage, nepotism, and corruption. Fighting corruption and sin generates publicity, but it also creates legions of enemies. Party activists and other politicians tend to loathe crusading reformers. They see them as mere "showboaters," angling for media coverage rather than tending to the shepherding function associated with party development.

Reform mayors love to experiment, stir up departments, and endorse grandiose plans. The more resistance they receive, the more convinced they are that their course is right. They are prone to actions that upset other politicians and attract audiences. It is not unusual for such mayors to become the favorites of the local media, which usually agree that the mayor's intentions are good but probably unrealistic.

Caretaker mayors who are party oriented (cell III) often become the servants of local political groups. Typically, they are very careful not to offend any powerful group leaders or coalitions, and in trying to accommodate a maximum number of interests, they allow government to become the site of internecine conflict. Policy fragmentation is not uncommon for these politicians, nor is the sense that they must serve their "patrons" and adopt a certain attitude of indebtedness.

Caretaker mayors who are reform oriented (cell IV) preside over ongoing changes in government. The media are generally supportive and tend to excuse any failure by the mayor with the view that the mayor is attempting to implement ideals in a real world that is unsympathetic to his or her goals. Caretakers are seldom trailblazers; instead, they are the camp followers of the reform movement. Although elected on reform tickets, they never seem to take bold action or actually implement a reform agenda. Detroit's Mayor William Mayberry (1897–98), a protégée of Mayor Hazen Pingree, never lived up to his mentor's standards of reform, and he is remembered as a caretaker. After leaving office, many such mayors return to private business, and others frequently fade slowly into obscurity as judges or to other positions that can be retained easily from term to term.

Caretakers in cells III and IV tend to concentrate on what is, not on what could be. However, reform-oriented caretakers are more amenable to innovation than their party-oriented counterparts. As housekeepers of sorts, they strive to deliver services efficiently and maintain the stability of city neighborhoods. Roman Gribbs started Neighborhood City Halls, for example, to give neighborhood residents greater access to local government. In presiding over the city rather than articulating a new mission for it, caretakers seek to strike a balance between competing interests. These mayors are more concerned with the audience than with the needs of their constituents, because often audience and image control their narrow political ambitions. These mayors usually receive good reviews while in office, but in the longer course of history, they often find themselves relegated to footnotes.

In the last twenty years, Detroit has made an important transformation. Rising from its 1968 likeness to post-war Dresden, the city has gained a new lease on life. Despite the fact that it has lost 20.5 percent of its population since 1970—most of which is due to white flight—the downtown skyline has continued to change. Despite many setbacks, small shopkeepers still bet their savings on the city's revival and its potential for economic growth. The automobile industry, backbone of the economy of southeastern Michigan, seems to be recovering from its worst recession. Although that industry will never again offer the cornucopia of blue-collar jobs it once did, it can still act as a magnet to attract other supporting industries. Everyone concerned with the city's recovery seems to recognize this, and city officials have tried to consult the auto industry in planning economic development.

Coleman Young has been in the forefront of Detroit's economic transformation. He has sought to paint a vision of a new

Detroit, one born out of an old yet solid industrial base and moving steadily into the emerging service economy. He has acted swiftly to check the losses of the city's assets to the suburbs. He built Joe Louis Arena to keep a white sport—hockey—from leaving the city. He made the politically hazardous move of asking people to tax themselves, and he persuaded city workers to accept wage freezes so that he could avert a major fiscal crisis. In yet another controversial situation, he forged ahead to clear a neighborhood, Poletown, to make room for a new Central Industrial Park and a General Motors plant.

None of these feats was accomplished without controversy, risk, and a host of opponents and doubtful second-guessers, and perhaps a less determined man would have tried to take an easy route and cut his losses. Avoiding criticism and racial stereotyping and relying on the mercy or wisdom of the press—these are not the goals of Coleman Young. Instead, he welcomes confrontations, challenges, and even uncertainty. He has shown that he can stand his ground, smile enigmatically, and move aggressively or unpredictably as he feels necessary. Refusing to fit into any mold, shaking off praise, remaining undisturbed by the reactions of those who sycophantically attach themselves to him, and punishing and rewarding his fellow politicians—all of these are apt descriptions of the mayor's style, yet they tell only a part of the story of his success.

The present study examines Coleman Young as a product of Detroit and as one who has been willing to take on the powerful in America. It tells about his leadership, but more specifically about reactions to it. And if it serves its purpose, it should also tell us something about America's fear of unleashed and unshepherded black political power.

Why does this country fear those black politicians who want to take part in enjoying power for its own sake? Why, for instance, has Detroit's mayor stirred such controversy on a national scale and attracted such wide attention? To many he is a leviathan, while to others he remains an enigma. Detroit's recent history has become, in a very real sense, the saga of Coleman Young. Rather than question whether the city could have made its vast transition without him, perhaps it is more useful to ask why and how Young happens to be leading the city's march, and doing it with great aplomb.

In many ways, Coleman Young has transcended the stereotypes of black leadership, and, in carrying out his role as Detroit's mayor, he has managed to sidestep the demands of a peculiar ethos for black politicians, as well as the intrusion of white racism. Clearly, the mayor has undertaken his own personal quest; like any other, it will be triumphant or quixotic.

Detroit has a special kind of risk-oriented politics, all too often perched at some precipice—which is what makes the city's politics fascinating to watch and describe. In observing and unfolding the politics of its mayor, Coleman Young, and acknowledging the fears his administration generates in various realms, one gets a better sense about the role of black leadership in America and, particularly, the unique response of one black leader to the needs of an aging city.

2

Growing Up in Detroit
Learning to Cope with Racism

Most journalistic analyses of black mayors tell the reader little about their political backgrounds. When they first arrive at their mayoral campaigns, according to the newspapers and journals, black mayors seem to lack any relevant background; when they win the race, life begins. This approach could be called a "persona theory" of black politicians—that is, with them what you see is all there is. Such a person is portrayed as clearly one-dimensional, leaving the reader or viewer with the impression that any other aspects of the incumbent's life are simply not worth knowing. On the other hand, of course, the media can be counted on to dig up incriminating negatives—peccadilloes, divorces, scandals, and conflicts of interest—if there are any. But none of these incriminations truly sharpens the picture of a black man, in particular, who has been drawn to politics. Being called to politics is in reality analogous to being called to preach—a fact sometimes surprising to the chosen as well as to the flock. Since politics is an area in which choices must be made, the flock, or the electorate, must make a final selection.

What separates successful black politicians from unsuccessful ones? Why was Coleman Young rather than one of his cohorts elected as the first black mayor of Detroit? What particular circumstances gave him a comparative advantage over his competitors? What events and attitudes shaped his views about politics? What are the differences between the 1940s Young and Young in the 1980s? To answer these questions, especially the last one, requires an understanding of black politicians in general—some organic theory that considers these black leaders as products of evolution and political socialization.

Political socialization can be defined as the process of teaching citizens their roles in the political process. The learning starts early within the family and continues throughout one's lifetime. Every day citizens are bombarded with political messages. In the case of Coleman Young, his father kept a political house. According to Young's siblings, their father held regular informal talk sessions in his living room or "behind the cases" (clothes bags in the cleaning shop) to discuss politics with fellow workers from the post office.[1] The elder Young followed political events, particularly city politics. Young Coleman and his brothers supplemented their political diet with regular Saturday visits to the local barber shop. In the early days the black barber shop served as the center where political ideas were exchanged. Black nationalists, Marxists, and Christian Fundamentalists were allowed to argue their case in this marketplace of ideas. The most striking political messages that the Young boys heard were that political ideology determines political and economic relations. At the same time, they were also getting messages from the political system itself and from the local political leadership—messages that were largely negative. Yet the Young children had become at least partially insulated by more positive countermessages; they had been taught that efficacy was possible through political activism.

In America political messages are segmented according to race and class. Blacks and whites often hear the same messages but derive far different interpretations, and the contrasts can be neatly traced to differences in socialization patterns. A white man who grew up in Detroit during the same period of time as Coleman Young may have an entirely different view of political events. He may attribute different causes for the city's decline and espouse different solutions. Political scientists Joel Aberbach and Jack Walker's post–1967 riot survey of Detroiters, for example, found that black and white residents viewed the "Black Power" movement very differently. To whites it was a sign of racism, while to blacks it was not.[2] In America whites have been socialized to believe that anything that advocates blackness is a threat to them. Blacks, on the other hand, believed that it was the attitudes of whites that was, and still is, a major impediment to black mobility. Hence, what Coleman Young, as a black man and mayor, thinks about the city's future is at least in part a reflection of his socialization as a black man.

Migration at an Early Age

Coleman Young was born in 1919 in Tuscaloosa, Alabama, to William and Ida Reese Young. He was the eldest of five children. Being black in a small southern town was not without its perils then. Economic stagnation was visible everywhere in the agrarian South, especially in the smaller towns, and the Ku Klux Klan (KKK) were active threats. Except for the wealthy, Alabama in 1919 was not a very pleasant place—for either black or white. Because it was basically a rural state, Alabama had very few job opportunities for its citizens. Tuscaloosa, a town of 11,996 residents—thirty-eight percent of whom were black—was best known for being the home of the University of Alabama. Like most small southern towns, it exported its white and black youths to northern industrial cities, where they could find work; yet, one notes the migration of blacks especially. For example, Tuscaloosa since 1910 has increased its population by three thousand, but in that time it has lost five percent of its black population. Blacks have been forced to go elsewhere to find work. The agriculture-based economy simply could not support Tuscaloosa's rapid population growth.

In 1919 the black man was alone. His president, Woodrow Wilson, had by then resegregated Washington, installed race signs, and used reduction-in-force to push black civil servants out of their jobs. The governor of Alabama, Thomas Kilby, was a typical southern chief executive of that time—short on enlightenment and long on race baiting. The local leaders of towns like Tuscaloosa did very little to provide jobs for their black citizens or to protect them from the Ku Klux Klan.

In 1919 the Ku Klux Klan was nearing the zenith of its political influence. In expanding its membership, it had managed to convince whites, especially the poor and those of the working class, that blacks were the enemy. The Klan not only committed outright violence against blacks—with impunity—but it also played a key role in selecting white state and local politicians. Some state legislators and executives spent their entire terms developing ways to separate the races permanently (the invention of Jim Crow laws, for example) rather than trying to bring them together.

The political world of Coleman Young's childhood was one of racial violence and social upheaval. Blacks were forced to be supplicants to an economy and way of life that was the epitome of uncertainty and instability. Black parents feared the wrath of the Klan and taught their sons to repress their anger in order to avoid confrontations with whites—that unfortunate social relation having been handed down by history. Adult American blacks' belief in the political system and their roles in it must have been shaken by the events following Reconstruction a half-century before. The failure of Reconstruction took a devastating toll on blacks across the South. When the Democratic party regained power in those years, it was with a policy of "white only." Blacks were robbed of the franchise to vote and constrained by a plethora of Jim Crow laws. In the 1901 Alabama Constitutional Convention, whites blatantly furthered their advantage by permanently crippling the black public school system with a biased funding plan.[3] These events invariably played a part in the political socialization of Coleman Young's father, William, a veteran and a Republican. In 1923 Young reacted to the violence, economic uncertainty, and political instability of the U.S. South by leaving Tuscaloosa. Like other black immigrants, Young saw cities such as Chicago, New York, and Detroit as employment meccas and places to escape from social repression. Certainly in retrospect one might ask, But were they?

Black Politics of the Twenties

Beginning early in the century, the automobile makers, or what David Davis has called the "gasoline aristocracy," dominated white and black politics in Detroit,[4] and as a result, Detroit politics developed a staunch antiunion reputation early on. After World War I, immigrants came to Detroit in search of jobs. Naturally many sought housing within their ethnic communities. Because the city ward, or district, system allows each city subgroup to identify with its city council member, local politicians began to use potent ethnic identifications to build an ethnic political machine strong enough to dominate city politics. The possibility of powerful ethnic groups presented a clear threat to the patricians who then ran the city—by prohibiting partisan elections, the reformers successfully limited the council to nine, and they separated municipal from state and national elections and insisted on the creation of more positions for appointed officers.

The new capitalist class of the twenties had dramatically stunted the growth of ethnic-oriented political machines like those in New York and Chicago. In 1912 Leland Olds, founder of the Detroit Citizens League, led the fight to depoliticize city elections and create a new city charter, which was passed by 32,256 to 4,554 votes, a small turnout for such a critical measure. The *municipal reform movement*, patterned after similar movements in other cities, called for a coalition of white Protestants (WASPs) united against the incoming Catholic ethnic groups, such as the Italians, Irish, and Poles. The Good Government movement also enlisted the assistance of leading Detroit churches and local academics. The Charter of 1918 was designed to represent government by businessmen for businessmen.[5] Lent Upson, later a dean at Wayne University, was brought to the city from Dayton to create the Bureau of Municipal Research (BMR), and immediately he began to make inventories of the city's assets, services, and voting behavior. Upson, whose BMR board was dominated by business, was presented to the public as an honest broker of political issues on the Detroit agenda.

While Upson kept tabs on city officials, Henry Ford made it an avocation to "take care of" blacks. In 1923 John Ragland observed: "to be employed by the Ford Motor Car Company seemed to be the growing achievement of all comers to Detroit."[6] The great automaker, Henry Ford, provided a whole range of welfare services to workers, and in 1914, he promulgated the five-dollar day. In the twenties the automobile industry was fast becoming the anchor of America's industrial expansion. The year 1923 was "almost a universally prosperous year"[7] for the industry. Ford made a million cars in the first six months of the year, more than it had in all of 1922. Edward Kennedy, the historian, called 1924 and 1925 the Golden Age of the automobile. By 1926 Ford had 100,000 workers, of which ten percent were black—roughly half of all black workers in the industry.[8] Ford also used his reputation for hiring blacks to sponsor formative activities in black politics; he organized his efforts around the black churches. Not only did he contribute money to them, but he used the black churches and their ministers as recruiters for his plants. Black ministers became power brokers in the black community. By channeling his contact through them, Ford elevated their position in the community and buffered his class and industry against unions and socialist politics. Ford knew he faced an ongoing struggle for the hearts and minds of black workers; he feared the threat of Bolshevism and Jewish radicals and sought to insulate black workers from their influences.

The church and its clergy represented the most stable institutions and leaders in the small black community (40,838 or 4.1 percent). Followers of Marcus Garvey and heads of Negro fraternal orders and small business associations were no match for the ministers. They were the ones to determine who got what, when, and how in the black community. Their potential rivals—black business and civic leaders—did not have a patron to supply them with support, political information, and financial resources, as the black ministers had the powerful Henry Ford as a sort of sponsor. In other words, the coalition between Ford and the black ministers was the beginning of clientage politics in Detroit. This breed of politics inhibited the development of an independent black leadership and the entry of blacks into the official Democratic party. Shelton Tappes has made a similar argument about Ford's influence on black politics in Detroit:

> There was really no sophisticated, organized Negro political activity at the time. White politicians usually made appeals to the black voters but little came of them and few blacks were in a position to work in politics. Those who did were almost forced to be Republican and work for Republicans since they were the only party which had clubs in the black community. There were ministers, the three most prominent were Reverend Peck, Father Dade and Father Daniels, who were highly thought of in the black community and were the type of people whites had a way of selecting to be black leaders.... These and other influential ministers had *entrée* to the white community and with the establishment. When things got tough, blacks looked to them for help. If anybody could get you a little relief, they could.[9]

Contrary to Tappes's assessment, there *was* a sophisticated organized Negro politics in Detroit, and blacks were not forced to be Republicans. Those who were had grown up in the "party of Lincoln." Ford simply funded the maintenance of Republicanism among blacks. A working coalition of black proletarians and Protestant patrician Republicans was probably appropriate for black politics of the twenties and thirties. Labor historian B. J. Widick would later call Ford's domination of black politics "plantation politics." And it was. It worked so well in fact that it was not until the collapse of the economy in the 1930s that the Republican hold on blacks was finally loosened. Only then did the ministers reject their capitalist patrons and join forces with the unions. At that time black politicians worried more about an odious form of white politics lying outside the formal structure of parties and votes.

The Ku Klux Klan was very active in Detroit in the 1920s. The competition for housing and jobs among white immigrants and blacks made for hostility—thus, good recruitment grounds for the KKK. The organization grew rapidly in the 1920s and recruited openly throughout the white community. Leaders like Manly Caldwell were able to recruit thousands for the so-called

Invisible Empire. By 1923 the KKK had aggregated enough members and sympathizers to take an active role in city politics. Its members lost in their attempt to unseat city councilmen, but they managed to push their own candidate for mayor in the election of 1924. Their candidate, a write-in candidate named Charles Bowles, came within 10,000 votes of defeating John Smith, the Republican party candidate. This close defeat not only demonstrated the political clout of the Klan and its sympathizers but enabled the group to broaden its membership base. It continued to grow until 1926, when its numbers reached 32,000. Kenneth Jackson, an historian, plotted the organization's movement and the development of its leadership and concluded that the Klan ceased to exist as a political force in 1934.[10]

One can only speculate about the impression the Klan must have made on the black community in the 1920s—at its zenith. Many blacks had left the South to avoid the Klan, only to come to a city like Detroit to see the hate group's northern brethren burn a cross on the lawn of the city hall in 1923. Since jobs were relatively plentiful in the North, the real struggle for blacks was finding housing; it was a problem for all classes of blacks. In a celebrated 1925 case, Dr. Ossian Sweet, a black physician, moved into a white neighborhood and was jeered unmercifully by his neighbors. Sweet was accused of shooting a white demonstrator and was arrested for murder. Clarence Darrow defended him in his murder trial, and Sweet was acquitted.[11] The violent reactions to the case alerted southern black immigrants to their common plight in the new city. Coleman Young was too young to understand the turmoil going on throughout his childhood, but the events of the twenties doubtless had an effect on his father. William Young had just arrived in the city, and he found it engulfed in racial tensions. Detroit's version of the Klan was similar to that of northern Alabama. It grew on the fears and negrophobia of poor and working-class whites. A year after the group's serious bid at the mayor's seat, tear gas had to be used on a KKK demonstration—emotions and violence had gotten too far out of control. Indeed such a scene provided an intimidating welcome for a black family escaping southern racism and terror. The elder Young worked as a night watchman at the post office and as a tailor; he was able to overcome his social environment and managed to build a small business in the city. While he was away at his regular job, his wife operated the family dry cleaning shop. William Young did the tailoring, and young Coleman helped clean and press clothes. William's jobs, along with his veteran's pension, afforded him a certain independence and social status not enjoyed by other blacks who worked in the auto factories, who were trapped in the lowest jobs available. Historian Robert Dunn described the jobs available to blacks as some of the "dirtiest, roughest and most disagreeable work."[12]

In an interview with oral historian Studs Terkel, Coleman Young recounted what life was like with his parents. His father, William, was a Republican until the Depression, when he switched to FDR and the Democratic party, like most blacks. Coleman's sister Bernice recalled the conversion and said that her father knew the Democratic party was full of white southerners. But, he thought, there were indeed so many poor whites that anything the party did for them would help blacks.[13] Coleman Young describes his father as an avid reader, a militant, and an American who served in World War I. Coleman said,

> He read every damn thing he could lay his hands on. My mother was a school teacher. He was very militant. She was the stable one. She worried about me because I was my father. He was constantly in some argument. He wasn't a big man, but I've seen him beat guys twice his size by picking up a bottle or scissors or anything at hand. He hated white people until he met a guy who treated him as peer. A Catholic. We all converted to Catholicism.[14]

As for his mother, Young has described her as a "neat person" who insisted that the children use good English. Coleman recalls that he himself acted as her lieutenant in taking care of his siblings: "I became a sort of disciplinarian, a stool pigeon. (Laugh.) An enforcer for my mother (laugh)."[15]

Young also recalls the norms of the black community: "I knew three aspects of black life. I knew the working-class part. I knew the slicker, the gambler. There was also a middle-class part that I became alienated from." During an interview with Young, he rejected the color consciousness of blacks that puts a premium on light-skinnedness. By rejecting the values of what sociologist E. Franklin Frazier has called the "black bourgeoisie"—color consciousness and conservative politics—Young's ideological view has remained consistent with his radical lifestyle—part inherited, part self-created.[16]

Despite his disclaimers, Coleman Young had a basically middle-class upbringing in many ways. There were differences, however, between the Youngs and their neighbors. The Youngs converted to Catholicism, unlike most of their Protestant neighbors, and they were not a part of the developing automobile industry. Even during the Depression the elder Young was somewhat insulated from the despair of many families, because of his pension, his post office wages, and income from the cleaning shop. In an interview with Terkel, Young suggests that his family was an outsider in the neighborhood.

Religion, Race, and School

Coleman Young's school days are critical to understanding the making of this political man. The negative reception of some of his white teachers to his precociousness reinforced the racial messages he received from his parents and alerted him to the duplicity of the educational system. The entire school experience managed to stimulate him intellectually and scar him psychologically. The lessons learned were both personal and political.

Coleman Young began elementary school at Capron, Barstow, Dussfield, and Miller Public Schools and switched to St. Mary's, a Catholic school. As one of the few blacks in either school, he learned to compete with whites early in his life. In the twenties and thirties, Catholic schools were more dominated by Catholic theology than they are today. Described by some as theocentric in nature, the Diocese of Detroit employed few lay instructors (only 10 percent)[17] and the organization made little attempt to emulate the public schools in its educational approach.[18] Families sent their children to Catholic schools precisely for their religious teaching and discipline.

Coleman Young was a good student in elementary and junior high. After returning to the Miller School (ninth and tenth grades), he graduated from Eastern High School. Despite a scholarly record, he was refused scholarships at the University of Detroit High School, Catholic Central, and LaSalle High School. Young described one incident in which a friar tore up his application right in front of him, and citing his first racial incident, Young describes how he was dismissed from a Boy Scout excursion to Belle Isle because he was black. As a way perhaps of humiliating the boy, the man took Coleman's scout cap off to expose his hair in front of all of the white scouts. Perhaps it is not the functional equivalent of young Franklin Roosevelt's rejection from the Porcellian Club at Harvard, but the experience remains as one of those unpleasant memories that stays within one's psyche and contributes to a strong personality. Every black person in America has a similar encounter with racism. Only the content and setting are different in each story. These encounters can either break a person's spirit or they can stiffen one's resolve to circumvent or fight the system. Young Coleman recalled his first confrontation with racism: "[A]fter that, I became more alert. That's probably part of my history in becoming a radical. I had so many rebuffs along the way." Coleman Young went on to graduate second in his class at Eastern High School only to be blocked again by his principal from attending both the University of Michigan and the City College. Young recalls the meeting with the principal. "A week before graduation, the principal called me in and said: 'We have four scholarships, two to the University of Michigan and two to City College. You got your choice.' I said University of Michigan, of course. He says: 'Do you have a job? Money for your board?' I said: 'No, I thought the job went with the scholarship.' He said: 'No.' I said: 'In that case, I'll go to City College.' 'Too late,' he said, 'that's been taken.' I found out another black kid had been done the same way the year before. I got screwed and resented it very much. Almost subconsciously, I'm beginnin' to take on an adversarial role toward society."[19] In the 1930s a young black teenager taking an adversary posture toward society faced a job market which was shrinking as a result of the Depression.

Black Politics and the Great Depression

In Detroit the collapse of the American economy hit blacks especially hard. Widick claims that unemployment among Detroit blacks reached 80 percent during the depths of the Depression.[20] They had been lured to the city to work in the growing automobile industry, but now many who worked at menial jobs in the industry were laid off. The city's economy was in chaos, and workers everywhere found themselves on relief. The soup lines were a common sight, and so was fierce competition for the few remaining jobs. Needless to say, racial tensions were high, as they always are in times of scarcity. Coleman Young was eleven years old when the stock market crashed. Bernice Young recalled, "We were fortunate. We worked through the Depression. It was not unusual to come home from lunch and find a stranger eating at the table."[21] As a young child, Coleman was insulated from the economic horrors of the Depression, but not from the stories of racial violence and police brutality that happened simultaneously. As the economy waned, violence toward blacks increased. It was not uncommon for the police to rout blacks who were standing in groups, and if they caught one, take him to a sandpile by the river and beat him. A horrendous example of police brutality occurred when white policemen killed James Porter, a black man, in his home in the hot summer of 1933. Stories of hateful and bigoted white policemen would continue to haunt young Coleman's life.

Young's teenage years took place during the era of Roosevelt's New Deal. FDR was not a liberal on the race question, yet he was highly regarded in the black community. The New Deal, with its pragmatic proactive ethos, taught Young several lessons. For one thing, he learned that government could be a positive force and a valuable employer. During this era many blacks got their first government jobs in such agencies as the Civilian Conservation Corps (CCC) and Works Progress Administration (WPA), and the New Deal saw blacks begin to play small but visible roles in the national administration.

Politically, the thirties were much like the twenties for blacks. Their political power, albeit limited, was invested in the leading ministers of large black churches. Henry Ford continued to use the black church as a screening device for black employees. Ministers such as reverends Horace White, Robert Bradbury, William Peck, and Everard Daniel became power brokers in the black community. Ford also financed and supported blacks in the Republican party. By 1930 Charles Roxbourgh was elected to the state senate. Although he did not get reelected, the effort behind his bid reflected yet another example of the rise of bloc voting by blacks. Despite the relatively high profile of black politicians in Detroit in the 1930s, their impotency was clear. Reverends White, Daniel, Bradbury, and Peck were the "big brokers" in the black community, yet in 1933 they could do little about such things as police brutality.

The election of Franklin Roosevelt in 1932 changed the fortunes of local black Democrats. Republican influence was waning, and the Democrats were wooing black voters. A. J. Stoval, a political scientist, cited 1932 as the beginning of the rise of local blacks within the Democratic party. Harold Bledsoe was appointed chairman of the "Black Committee" of the party. Along with Joseph Craigen and Charles Diggs, Sr., Bledsoe began to recruit blacks to the party.[22]

Recruiting was a difficult task, because there were so many cleavages within the black community. In 1934 Aaron Toode, the journalist, wrote in *The Crisis*—official organ of the NAACP— that blacks were divided along social class lines in terms of their lengths of residence ("old-timers" versus "newcomers").[23] Nevertheless, by the mid-thirties, blacks were able to aggregate their political power, and in 1936 they elected Charles Diggs, Sr., to the Michigan Senate. Diggs, a mortician and owner of the House of Diggs, a funeral home, was the leading politician of his time. The Diggs family, which lived near the Youngs, organized the black section—the east side of the city—to vote. Diggs's election was one of the high points of black politics in the thirties.

Meanwhile, the Republican grip on black ministers and the black vote was slipping. Ignoring the advice of Republicans, blacks tended to vote for the reelection of FDR. They were emboldened by the efforts of black unionists in the CIO sit-down strike of the late thirties and now paid greater attention to shifting local political power to unionists and the Democratic party. Any informal grumbling about the efficacy of the old Republican/black coalition went public with Horace White's article entitled, "Who Owns the Negro Church?" published in *Christian Century*.[24] Encouraged by the NAACP leadership and black unionists, White attacked the alliance between blacks and the Republicans—and Ford. Ford reacted by investing more in building a sound infrastructure that would satisfy black Republicans. Donald Marshall and Willis Wards of Ford's black affairs department created the Wayne County Voter District Association to encourage participation by Ford's employees in the Republican effort. The organization was not solid enough, however, to survive mass defection.

By 1939 the black leadership had switched its alliance, partly in response to Reverend White's stinging critique, but also because of the Democratic party's support for the successes of the CIO in the turbulent sit-down strikes of 1937 and in its advocacy of fair treatment for black workers. Reverend White, Reverend Charles Hill, and State Senator Diggs signed a leaflet condemning the use of black strikebreakers at the Chrysler Corporation. They declared: "If Negroes are to have jobs they must have them in cooperation with all workers."[25]

Black leaders were attempting to alert working-class blacks to the growing power of labor.[26] If blacks wanted to continue working, they had to come to terms with their changing political environment, and if they wanted to participate in this new political reality, they also needed to register to vote. In a survey of class and voting behavior between 1930 and 1940, it was found that only 51.9 percent of poor blacks and 62.1 percent of middle-class blacks were registered to vote. This rate was below the 70 percent average for blacks and below all classes of whites, including the foreign-born.[27] To black leaders, the meaning was clear; If they wanted a role in the new politics, they would need to mobilize the black vote.

Meanwhile, the city of Detroit continued to operate on shaky fiscal grounds. Detroit was a city in social and financial turmoil, remaining in debt mainly due to tax delinquencies and the inheritances of a growing relief roll—the result of mismanagement of the city's administration and its economy. Despite earlier defaults, the recall of an incompetent mayor, Charles Bowles, the reduction in salaries of city employees, and, in some months, paying employees with scrip, the city leadership struggled desperately to meet the needs of a large, new population on relief.

For working-class Americans, especially blacks, the arrival of the New Deal was truly a blessing. The New Deal saw a shift in black party allegiance to the Democrats, produced the first executive order on fair employment, and increased the visibility of a new black leadership class. The NAACP's Walter White became a spokesman for the new black consciousness. Mary McCloud Bethune, a black educator, was given a presidential appointment to the National Youth Administration, and her appointment was considered a major breakthrough in the black community. White and Bethune became role models for black youths. Black people were talking about a new politics for the thirties, and new personalities were beginning to compete for power and influence in this New Deal politics. However, nationally, the NAACP and Urban League maintained their influence and practically dominated black politics in Detroit. Black politics of the thirties was a struggle to get blacks their fair share of economic recovery work. Those who had jobs in the automobile plants fought to keep and insulate themselves from the effects of the Depression.

After graduation from high school and losing his chance at a college scholarship, Coleman Young entered the Ford Rouge Plant as an electrician trainee in the late thirties only to find there the same racism he had discovered in high school. After his training, the job went to a white foreman's son, and Young found himself doing the same jobs as other blacks before him. His assignments, however, led him to meet the men who were trying to organize a union. Young became a union organizer and achieved enough visibility in that role to be fired from the plant. In 1937 Young was forced to defend himself after one of a group of burly workers, sent in to roust union organizers, came after him. As he later recalled, "I wasn't going to let [him] get his hands on me." He grabbed a steel bar and hit the attacker. When he left the Ford plant, Young took a job at the U.S. Post Office. He continued to organize workers as the nation entered World War II.

Despite the War, Racism Continues

Coleman Young entered the army on February 3, 1942. The U.S. Army of 1942, an officially segregated force, treated blacks as ancillary manpower. The indignities that they suffered as second-class citizens in civic life were continued in uniform. A racist American army was fighting a racist Nazi army, and most blacks found they were forced to join maintenance and service units. Many were cooks, truck drivers, and supply workers. Denying blacks a combat role was yet another way of stigmatizing them as second-class citizens. The NAACP had fought for years to have blacks play a combat role in war. Walter White, executive director of the NAACP, and A. Phillip Randolph, president of the Brotherhood of Sleeping Car Porters, had petitioned several times for a combat role for blacks. But it was denied, because white soldiers did not want blacks in their units. President Roosevelt refused to integrate the service despite appeals by Negro leaders.

President Roosevelt finally relented somewhat by allowing blacks to form segregated combat units. Coleman Young became a part of the famed Tuskegee Airmen, trained at Tuskegee, Alabama, to be pilots, navigators, and bombardiers. Young finished Officer Training School at Fort Benning, Georgia, and was commissioned as a second lieutenant in the infantry, and he trained as a bombardier in Midland, Texas. He was stationed at Freeman Field in Seymour, Indiana, and never saw combat. Young best remembers his tenure in the army for his participation in a sit-in at the all-white Officers' Club. He and some fellow black officers were arrested, but Young managed to get the message out through a black orderly, who alerted the black newspapers to what was going on. Daniel "Chappie" James, a pilot-courier (who later became a general), secretly sent messages out of the camp. Young recalled, "They were trying to isolate us so they could court-martial us. I managed to get the case in the headlines of the black newspapers. I wrote letters to the Adjutant General's office. They sent an investigation team to the base. They wanted to find the leaders. The most interesting thing was that not one of the 101 individuals gave names." As a result of the failure of the investigating team and the negative publicity generated by the racial incident, the group of protesters was subsequently released. This protest could be cited as Young's first purely civil rights activity, although he had already clearly established himself as a "race man"—that is, militant within the black community and the labor movement.

Black Politics after World War II

During the war blacks became further entrenched in the Democratic party. The death of President Roosevelt did not slow the migration of blacks to the Democratic party, and they became part of a new social and political realignment. After the 1943 race riot and Mayor Jeffries's inept response to it, blacks united with the UAW to oust Jeffries from office.[28] In 1944 Horace White became a member of the Michigan House of Representatives and local Democrat activist Louis Martin, editor of the *Michigan Chronicle*, was given a staff job at the National Democratic Party headquarters. The growing prominence of black politicians in the Democratic party made switching parties easier for other blacks.

In the forties, as at other times, there was a saying in the black community that conditions for blacks always improve after a war. After World War II the country was in an upbeat mood and several hundred black veterans, including Coleman Young and most of the future black leadership class, returned to Detroit and to the automobile plants. If the war taught them anything, it was that bigotry was ubiquitous and that the Democratic party's policy of racial gradualism was no longer applicable to the more rapidly changing black condition. As early as the mid-forties, black leadership was signaling to their white counterparts that gradualism was being interpreted as a containment strategy and a ploy to prevent black empowerment. Black leaders wanted a seat on the city council, but their white allies felt that they should wait until blacks had more than ten percent of the population. Detroit's black population continued to grow again after this war because many southern black veterans left the South to find jobs in the automobile plants.

Meanwhile, the influence of the labor movement, particularly the UAW, grew in Democratic party affairs. By coopting the formal structure of the Wayne County Democratic organization, the unions, with their full-time organizers, money, and communication capacity, helped strengthen and liberalize the local Democrats' weak party structure. The CIO Political Action Committee (COPE) found itself in charge of the candidate selection process around 1947. The union/party alliance was critical to the development of black politics for it assisted the creation of a new black leadership group that could challenge the clergy-dominated or old clientage politics of the thirties.

Many black labor leaders performed a racial function for the unions. As the sociologist William Kornhauser discovered, few, if any, of these leaders actually had an administrative function in the general labor leadership structure.[29] Rather, their roles included monitoring and directing the political activity of the black membership and the larger black community. To do this, it was necessary for labor activists to get themselves entrenched in precinct delegate politics and thereby become power wielders in the black community. Since they shared the same civil rights agenda as the black clergy leadership, this proved to be an easy task. The money, manpower, and political communication system necessary to organize, once provided by Henry Ford under the old clientage politics, was now being provided by Walter Reuther and other labor leaders under a new system of clientage politics. By carefully manipulating the clergy with church donations and other acts of patronage, the new black labor leaders gained dominance as the voice of black politics. The emergence of this black labor leadership distinguishes Detroit's politics from those of other northern cities that were without a strong black/labor coalition. For Detroit's black leadership, clearly, the forties was a period of sorting out and consolidating.

The Truman administration, which followed Roosevelt's death, was seen at first as a continuation of the New Deal. Indeed, in its platform for the 1948 elections, the National Democratic Party adopted a civil rights plank, and Truman had signaled his commitment to civil rights by integrating the armed forces. In retrospect, these gestures were more than just symbolic, as they served to consolidate the party's hold on the black vote. They made it easier for black leaders to mobilize voters for the local Democratic party, and the effects of this mobilization drive were felt first in state elections. The black vote helped to elect G. Mennen Williams as governor, and in turn he appointed several leading blacks to state positions.

Black immigrants, many of whom had never voted before, were eager to participate in party activities, and they accepted the authority of their labor leaders. Although Detroit's leaders could not deliver the local patronage of their counterparts in cities like Chicago and New York, they were believed to be more effective at the state and national level. They were what Daniel Thompson, a sociologist, called "racial diplomats."[30] This is not to say that they were without opposition. Many blacks criticized their gradual approach, yet whites and blacks joined in labeling the opposition as troublemakers, communists, and militants. Many of their opponents lost their jobs in the automobile plants, and by the end of the decade, their critics were effectively purged from the labor movement and from any positions they held in the local Democratic party.

An important correlate of the postwar political developments affecting blacks and labor was the shift away from an apolitical posture by the black bourgeoisie. According to Frazier, who coined the term, this group tended to withdraw from the political realities of blacks and indulged instead in conspicuous consumption. A fantasy world that included debutante balls was created in an attempt to mimic white society, from which these middle-class blacks were excluded. In Detroit this group called itself the Cotillion Club, taking its name from a similar Philadelphia group. First established in 1949 as a social club for black businessmen and professionals, in time the group became a major social organization in the city. Its first president, John Roxborough, was a prominent attorney whose uncle managed Joe Louis, the boxer. In a recent *Detroit News* interview another one of the founders, Jesse Thomas Hougabrook, recalled that the group was able to organize a debutante ball within the first year of its organization, which was quite an achievement. The group gained instant visibility, and black politicians began to take notice. To invite politicians to become members was not unusual, but the decision to directly involve the club in politics was uncommon among such clubs nationwide. Hougabrook believed that the decision of the Cotillion Club to become political was made because the conditions of isolation and discrimination generally experienced by black Detroiters were extreme. He said:

> You have to understand that when the Cotillion Club was formed there was nothing black in Detroit. The Police Department, the Fire Department, was segregated to the hilt. Black people couldn't move across Woodward Avenue. No black access to Highland Park. No black access to the northwest section. No black access to Boston Boulevard.[31]

The Cotillion Club became a political base for blacks seeking greater social mobility and for ambitious black politicians. Charles Diggs, Jr., solicited the club members for support in his 1950 race for the state Senate, and the club sponsored the first black fund-raising ball at the Gotham Hotel. Diggs was elected in 1951 to the state Senate and in 1954 to the U.S. Congress, and the club continued its involvement in politics and claimed credit for William Patrick's election to the Common Council in 1957.

The actual involvement of Detroit's black businessmen in politics contrasts sharply with Frazier's caricature of the black middle class. The behavior of the so-called E lites represented the growing politicization of blacks in general. Men who would not run for office or accept political patronage of any kind understood that in the next decade racial progress would depend upon the efforts of black organizations. The E lite group, though influential, was upstaged by more aggressive black labor leaders who, like their counterparts in the twenties and thirties, had white support.

Nevertheless, in the 1940s and 1950s in Detroit, if a man wanted a political career, he got his apprenticeship in the labor movement. By his own account, Coleman Young's tenure in the labor movement shaped his political career.

Summary

The politics of the twenties was a style of clientage politics in which black ministers acted as brokers for the Protestant Republican class that dominated city politics. In this particular political universe, Henry Ford was the star; black ministers revolved around him. Martin Kilson, a political scientist who characterized this kind of relationship as clientage politics, claimed:

> clientage politics was almost exclusively the political method of the Negro middle class—a bourgeois affair. The black bourgeoisie ideologically portrayed clientele politics as "race politics," presumably beneficial to all blacks, though in reality it was of benefit more to the elite than to urban Negro masses.[32]

The working coalition of Republicans and black ministers was broken by the Depression and the subsequent conversion of blacks to the Democratic party. After the economy collapsed and unions gained a foothold in the automobile plants, black leaders began to reject what Widick has called "plantation politics."

The emergence of a new clientage politics, this time directed by organized labor, allowed blacks greater leeway in defining their own agenda. If the Republicans practiced "plantation politics," the Democrats' oversight of black politics could be termed "paternalistic." In supporting the emerging black leadership, practitioners of the new clientage politics were also committed to isolating the so-called racial blacks and forging a coalition with pliant white liberals. Whether in a system of old or new clientage, black leaders have been expected to monitor the black community for possible political deviations by black leaders and voters. White labor leaders demonstrated their support by defending black civil rights claims, funding the assimilation of black labor activists into precinct-level politics, and contributing to the black churches. In the process, organized labor also created a new black leadership class, which finally emerged as a rival to the influential ministers of the late forties and throughout the fifties. After some initial adjustment problems the two groups learned to work together. In the late 1950s, with the emergence of the black civil rights movement, the black labor/ministers coalition began to show its strains. The civil rights movement created yet another group of leadership claimants, community leaders and black nationalists. At that time, black ministers and labor unionists at first resisted then integrated the more militant civil rights claimists into their expanding black power elite.

To filter Coleman Young's life through the various changes in black politics is to attempt a valid biographical representation. Recognizing the significance of his father's conversion to the Democratic party and Catholicism for his own life imbued Coleman Young with the notion that a dogma can outgrow its usefulness. Young himself abandoned Catholicism when he felt that it was no longer useful to him. While Coleman Young's family was not actively involved in the politics of the twenties and thirties, like most American blacks, they were at least interested and discussed political matters. Coleman Young acquired an interest in political ideas and his strong belief in the equality of the races from his father especially. From his mother he learned the value of public goodwill and concern for those less fortunate.

While black ministers were making deals with automobile makers and serving as spokesmen for other blacks, such interactions were not shared by the average black person. A young black man still encountered racial indignities on and off the job. Coleman Young's early experience with racial discrimination led him to be more "alert," and he made a decision not to get mad but "get smart"—to understand power. He directed his anger not at the white workers, who insulted him directly, but at the capitalists, whose employment and economic policies contributed to racial conflict. Being able to decipher the true antagonists probably saved Young from taking part in mindless, perhaps violent, confrontations with whites. To Young being alert meant watching and learning from whites; it was nothing other than political acumen, which also meant it was cautious to differentiate between unscrupulous whites—whether or not they wore clerical collars or policemen's uniforms—and supportive whites, regardless of any personal politics. Clearly, by the time Coleman Young lived through the Depression, the New Deal, and a segregated army, he had also rejected the old clientage politics, with its inherent limits for blacks. By early adulthood, Young's success in organizing other blacks—both on the job and in the army—had convinced him that he could indeed stand out and even triumph over a new fledgling breed of clientage politics.

In *Leadership, Love and Aggression*, Allison Davis examines the lives of three great American black leaders—Frederick Douglass, W. E. B. Du Bois, and Martin Luther King, Jr.[33] In Davis's view each of these men dealt with his anger and aggression in different ways—and they looked at the matter of race in separate ways as well. Davis develops a typology of leaders based on the "manner in which they handled their own aggression." According to Davis, the *sadistic* leader feels a need to control and exploit others; he or she holds an unsatiated lust for power. The *masochistic* leader is the opposite; he or she is willing to subordinate him or herself to the system in order to survive in the political world. He or she must swallow indignation and anger, no matter how justified. The final type, the *reality-oriented* leader, is motivated by principles and goals. In pursuing personal and political security, this leader also accommodates a sturdy self-regard. Allison put Frederick Douglass in this final category of leaders, because, she claims, he fought for self-preservation but did so with dignity. In seeking some power and justice, he did not subordinate himself to anyone, nor was he prone toward mindless violence. Coleman Young resembles Douglass in the manner in which he has handled aggression. He emerged from childhood with aggressive and self-assertive drives, which were certainly strengthened by his exposure to the racial violence that has been so much a part of Detroit's history.

Young's alienation from the black bourgeoisie is significant in examining his personality along the lines of Davis's typology. Rejecting the lifestyles and inhibitions of the black bourgeoisie probably assisted Young in escaping the style of a masochistic leader, who certainly would have been more ambivalent toward whites. Young was never prepared to subordinate his views in order to be accepted by whites. His lack of a college education—an omission not of his own making—also helped him to avoid being seduced by the black bourgeoisie politicians of the forties and fifties—who invented their own conservative model of the "qualified Negro." Yet, despite any hostile attitudes, Young mostly felt ambivalent toward the black bourgeoisie. He was not a Cotillion

Club type, yet he felt the need to prove himself to its members. He deflated their approach to Detroit politics and ridiculed his 1977 mayoral opponent, Ernest Brown, who presented himself as the model of their elitist style of politics. Coleman Young's self-created brand of politics has outlived the careers of William Patrick and Charles Diggs, Jr., two of the most visible of the Cotillion, or E lite, politicians. In retaining the identification of his proletarian roots, he has managed to forge a kinship with the class that has kept him in power. The working class make up the voting majority, and they have been willing to support Young's economic development projects. His supposedly macho rhetoric and lifestyle help to reinforce his relationship to the working class.

3

The Making of a Black Politician

The process of selecting potential black leaders is not the work of a conspiracy, but rather it is a normal part of maintaining the political system. The leadership of the political system conscripts, appoints, and elects those men and women who it believes will promote the national interest—both white and black. In the case of black self-starters, the political system can terminate, coopt, or sponsor a career once it is under way. Thus, opportunities for untutored, unsponsored, or unreliable politicians to enter the inner circles of political power are remote. Without the inner circles' endorsement, a would-be claimant would likely remain an outsider. Although outsiders do play roles in the political system—primarily as critics—rarely are they in the critical areas of policy development and implementation. As critics, outsiders nonetheless serve a useful role, since commentary helps those on the inside to better examine alternative solutions.

Coleman Young has been both an outsider and an insider. And although his development has clearly been unique in many ways, his political life in many ways parallels the evolution of other black politicians in America. The young Coleman Young differs from the mature Coleman Young, though both have had legitimate grievances against a political system that incessantly relies on racist sentiments to keep blacks at a social disadvantage. In Detroit politics of the seventies and eighties, Young must be credited with anticipating the fundamental changes required of a black politician, because of the city's declining economy and its poor social relations, and for reasserting the role of risk-taker into public policy decisions. Having experienced the perspective of an outsider contributed to Young's understanding of mass expectations and needs. He has been able to gauge what it takes to arouse and placate the masses. Alternatively, he has learned what the business and political elite are prepared to do for the city and how, thereby establishing his status as an insider. In effect, he has undergone two processes of socialization—elite and mass socialization.

Arguably, Young's career reflects a larger political era in the making—one in which the issue of race was of declining significance to politicians and what arose was a black political elite capable of dealing with nonracial issues such as economic transformation. How and why Coleman Young has chosen to lead this transition for Detroit can partly be explained by the socializing agents of his adult political life.

The first stage of Coleman Young's socialization as a member of the political elite came during his career as a union organizer and aspiring labor leader. The formative period of the United Auto Workers (1930–50) provided him with an excellent opportunity to watch whites and blacks create and share political power. As a result of his involvement in the labor movement, Young learned important lessons about building coalitions, distributing patronage ("pork chopping"), and reacting rationally to even heated confrontations.

The second stage of Young's official training came as a local community politician. Although his early efforts at entry into municipal politics were failures, he persisted, and, apparently, he learned from each loss. When he at last won an elected office, he discovered what was necessary to stay in office.

Coleman Young and the Labor Movement

Perhaps the single most important socializer for Coleman Young was his experience in the labor union movement. In 1919, the year Young was born, Henry Ford used black workers to break a strike. The legacy of strikebreakers died hard, but not as hard as racism, which was surely present within the emerging union organizations. In 1933, while Young was in high school, a group of Negro unionists formed the Federation of Negro Labor (FNL) and played a founding role in organizing the postal union with which Young was later associated. During the thirties, when the union movement was in its organizing and consolidating period, its leadership was considered far more radical than it is today. A young man could watch labor leaders defy the giants of the auto industry, and he could see picketing, strikes, and violence in reaction to the industry's unjust practices. Company owners considered union organizers conspirators and anticapitalists, and those who infiltrated the plant to educate the workers received a mixed reception from black workers. The early labor movement consisted of communists, socialists, and progressives; some early labor organizers even espoused civil rights for the black community. Their pro-black rhetoric made other top union leaders sound moderate. Newspapers of the 1930s, however, made little distinctions among labor leaders; they simply labeled them radicals.

When Coleman Young became affiliated with the union, such an association meant being against the status quo. Union organizers were not content to organize for better conditions and higher pay; they were actually attempting to build a whole new political force in America. Political ideas that were debated within the labor movement helped to educate blacks in the various *isms* of the world. The labor movement was as much a place for the exchange of ideas as the black church. Labor movement debates allowed Coleman Young to build on the rudimentary knowledge he had gleaned from political discussions and arguments held during his youth at the local black barbershops.

With his induction into the labor movement, Young met black labor organizers like Hodges Mason, Horace Sheffield, Robert Battle, Marcellus Ivory, William Oliver, James Watts, Frank Edwards, Tom Wilson, and Shelton Tappes, the first Negro secretary of a local. In 1937 Young became an organizer for the UAW, which was then a part of the CIO. The years 1936 and 1937 were critical for the UAW. After a series of sit-down strikes, culminating in the so-called Great Sit-down strike at General Motors in 1936–37, the UAW won official recognition on January 11, 1937.

The CIO was considered the most radical of what were then struggling federations of unions. The initial success of the UAW lifted morale throughout the entire union movement. The CIO's national president, John L. Lewis, visited Detroit and personally helped negotiate the GM and later Chrysler union agreements. The Ford contract was signed four years later. In 1938 historian Benjamin Stolberg saw a great future for the CIO—particularly the UAW:

> The U.A.W. is one of the great triumphs in the history of American labor.... It is a social movement in the widest sense, and derives

its strength from the new outlook on life which it gives the workers.... In short, the union is more than a mere collective bargaining agency for the automobile workers. It has become their form of life. It is for this reason that the U.A.W. is here to stay.[1]

For black members the union was indeed a critical forum for their struggle. Yet, while the union espoused equality and worker unity in principle, it practiced racial discrimination in the election of its leadership. B. J. Widick suggested that Ford Local 600 was a highly valuable training ground for blacks, yet there were no blacks in top leadership positions—neither in policy-making nor administrative roles. The Negro caucus lobbied hard and long for equal representation in the early days of the union. Some blacks believed that white members opposed any black leadership, particularly for a full-time position, because it was seen as an upgrading of blacks in status. In the forties there were so-called hate strikes against black promotions in the factories. Despite the New Deal, the plenitude of jobs brought by war, and a healthy economy, race relations improved little in the forties. In Detroit racial violence continued to be a part of the city's image.

The 1943 race riot occurred, in part, because both blacks and whites were fearful of each other. Historians Alfred McClung Lee and Norman Humphrey attributed the riot to competition for jobs (in defense plants) and housing.[2] The riot marked a change in the city's black politics. Blacks were fed up with their isolation.

The aftereffects of the riot affected union convention politics. As in most unions, convention elections expose the fractional politics within the organization. In 1943, the left wing of the UAW—led by Richard Frankensteen, George Addes, and others—and the Negro caucus tried to get the convention to support the idea of creating a black position on the executive council. The proposal was vehemently opposed by the union's right-wing leaders, led by Walter Reuther and Richard Leonard. Reuther and Leonard argued that a specifically black seat would be based on a "Jim Crow" approach to politics. Their position was consistent with socialist rhetoric, which argued that the "black problem" was not special but a part of the overall class struggle. For blacks the fight for a black seat was an effort to get beyond the labor union practice of providing blacks with merely symbolic jobs as vice presidents who held no power—also known as "tipping the hat."

For those on the UAW's left, the creation of a black seat was consistent with their position on equality generally, but clearly their stance divided them from the emerging right wing of the UAW. The proposal's defeat embarrassed the Negro caucus leaders and rankled the rank-and-file members. Reuther's forces, in an effort to mitigate the Negro caucus, agreed to hire a black consultant to study racial discrimination within the union. The UAW recruited George Crockett, a black lawyer employed by the federal Fair Employment Practices Commission (FEPA), to conduct the study. Crockett recommended the establishment of a Fair Practices Committee, which the union agreed to. The new committee consisted of six members, including individuals from both the right and the left. The compromise worked mainly because Crockett, serving as executive director, made the committee a functioning unit. In the process he became the most visible spokesman for black labor in Detroit. Despite the good work of the committee, in subsequent conventions the CIO refused to act on the question of black leadership in the union.

In 1945 Coleman Young returned from the service to find a newly integrated work force, but the fight for black representation still going on inside the union. Young recalled having been surprised by the sight of a black motorman:

> Blacks and women were all over the place. Blacks were conductors. These workers were scheduled to lose their jobs as the returning veterans reclaimed their seniority. We, in the left wing of the union [CIO], proposed that blacks and women be given "average seniority" [that is, whatever was the average years of seniority within the plants] to allow them to keep these jobs. As the plant expanded, more workers could be added. If we allowed the veterans to recover their full seniority, the plants would revert to an all-male plant.[3]

The proposal failed, and veterans recovered their positions.

Young had returned to the labor movement during a power struggle between the right and left wings of union organizations. The struggle for control of the union pitted old allies against left-center forces. Thirty-three years old and fresh from the Air Corps, Young joined the struggle as an organizer and member of the CIO's left wing. After being reinstated in his post office job, he became a representative for the public workers' union. This post lasted only a short time, because Young took a leave in order to devote himself full-time to union organizing. He became very active and visible in Wayne County's CIO politics, which was dominated by individuals associated with the left. The larger Michigan CIO, on the other hand, was dominated by the right wing.

In the 1946 convention the black caucus decided to use a new tactic to get a full-time paying position for a black in the union leadership. Their proposal involved creating an entirely new position, bringing up the number of full-time positions from two to three. At that time only the president and the secretary served full-time. Surprisingly, Reuther's right-wing faction went along with the proposal. Instead of taking on the Negro-left coalition on the convention floor, they decided to run their own slate against the left-center coalition, which supported Tracy Doll for president, Sam Sage for secretary-treasurer, and Coleman Young as director of organization. Young recalled that he was surprised to have been picked and speculated that it was perhaps because veterans were popular. "We veterans were heroes for about six months," he said.[4] Perhaps the Negro caucus selected Young because he was not as closely identified with the union's factional politics as the more experienced Hodges Mason. Young's candidacy may also have been helped by his not being in the more turbulent UAW. A more plausible explanation, however, is that Young was a "comer" who was also an articulate and skilled organizer. The election was a spirited one with the Doll slate winning in what turned out to be not a two but a three-slate race. The third one, nonaligned, emerged partly as a reaction to Young's left-wing politics.

The election of Coleman Young to the directorship of organization within the CIO was a major victory for the Negro community. Instantly, he became a spokesman for blacks. When his union gave a testimonial banquet to celebrate the victory, Mayor Jeffries and the top black labor activists attended. Young's tenure as director was marked by his leadership in the petition drive to repeal the 1947 Callahan Act, which was Michigan's version of subversive control legislation.[5] It required labor organizations and leaders under the influence of foreign governments to register as foreign agents. It also required them to make their records public. Although labor groups claimed they had collected enough petition signatures to repeal the act, the secretary of state would not certify them as valid. Young was also instrumental in getting the CIO involved in the fledgling civil rights movement in Detroit.

By 1946 factional politics within the UAW had reached a peak. Walter Reuther challenged left-winger R. J. Thomas for the presidency, and though Reuther won the election, he did not gain control of the executive committee until the 1946 convention. Meanwhile, Reuther was consolidating his position. Despite the fact that Thomas received a majority of the black vote, Reuther reacted by building his support among the black caucus and by promoting his reputation as a foe of racial discrimination. Nevertheless, he was still on record as having opposed the creation of a black seat on the UAW executive council. In the 1947 convention Young and others increased the pressure for a black leadership position by again raising it on the floor. Young joined the anti-

Making of a Black Politician 67

Reuther forces and challenged Reuther to a reelection. He actually seconded the nomination of Douglas Fraser of DeSoto Local 227, the left-wing candidate running against Reuther forces. In turn, Fraser seconded Young's nomination for the directorship of CIO against Bunny Hopkins. Both Fraser and Young lost the election; the stars of the left wing had begun to dim.

In 1948 left-wing factions of the local CIO endorsed Henry Wallace as the Progressive party candidate for the U.S. presidency. The national CIO had endorsed Harry Truman. This was the last straw. Reuther and others complained to the national CIO that the organization was out of control and asked the national leadership to take over the state organization. The national office sent Adolph Germer to investigate Reuther's charges. Finding that the council had relatively good relations with the membership of most locals, Germer decided to use a different tactic to get control of the council. He urged several estranged locals to reaffiliate with the council in preparation for the great showdown election of the 1948 convention.

The 1948 convention will likely go down as one of the most significant meetings in Michigan labor history. After a noisy debate over the credentials of the newly affiliated locals who would be casting votes, Germer assumed control of the convention. Arming himself with a telegram from the National CIO office, he declared himself the administrator of the union. The Michigan CIO was now in receivership. Reuther had won, and his forces had purged the left-wingers, including Coleman Young.

Young recalled the incident. "They bloomed me and others," he said. "I had to walk the gangplank. The labor unions had joined the Red Scare. It became a part of the McCarthy movement. He [Germer] blessed the 'rump Convention.' Walter Reuther was a pragmatic politician but he never gave up his red-baiting."[6] Young also credits Reuther for coopting the best and brightest individuals within the UAW, regardless of their prior connections to the right or left. He cites Frazier's appointment as administrative assistant to Reuther as an example.

After being purged from the union's politics, Young went to work as a full-time director of the Henry Wallace campaign in 1948, and after Wallace's defeat, he continued to work for the Progressives. In 1950 he opened a dry cleaning establishment with Jack Raskin, a former white leader of the Civil Rights Federation. The Progressives struggled to stay alive during the next four years, which were stormy ones marked by the "red scare." In 1952 the party nominated Vincent Hallinan for president. According to Young, "This was the last dying kick for the party."[7]

A parallel development in Young's career occurred with the organization of the National Negro Labor Council (NNLC), an association of Negro caucuses from various trade union organizations that was organized to get blacks appointed and elected to the governing boards of their unions. The council also took on the task of fighting job discrimination. It developed into a national organization with its headquarters in Detroit, and according to Young, the Detroit chapter included many black labor leaders. Young himself served as executive secretary of the national organization.

Under Young's leadership, the council was credited with forcing Sears, Roebuck and Company to hire black clerks in Detroit. Along with this success, the council gained a reputation as a hotbed of black radicalism and militancy. Its militancy was first condemned by the UAW and later investigated by the House Un-American Activities Committee (HUAAC). In a press release on October 22, 1951, the UAW warned unionists against the leadership of the NNLC, labeling the organization a communist front. In the press release the union cautioned its membership:

> The Detroit Negro Labor Council actually works against the best interest of all the American people by attempting to destroy genuine civil rights movements and increasing inter-group tension. . . . During the last year the Detroit Council has sabotaged the sincere and genuine efforts of a Detroit citizens' committee, including the CIO, the NAACP and other liberal groups, to bring about the enactment of a local fair employment practices ordinance.[8]

The press release was designed to disassociate the union from the council and its leadership. It acknowledged that the head of the National Negro Labor Council was an officer in the UAW-CIO, but it never mentioned Coleman Young by name: "the man is acting as an individual and . . . the UAW-CIO does not support in any way either the Detroit council or the formation of the national group." Disassociation and isolation were some of the tactics used by the union against black militants. Another tactic was red-baiting.

Black Radicals and Reds

The role of the Communist party in the development of the UAW and other industrial unions requires more elaboration by scholars. Those who remember the beginning of unionism in America believe that understanding the Communist party helps one understand the personality conflicts, factionalism, and ideological struggles that took place during the inception of industrial unions in America. Roger Keeran's *The Communist Party and the Auto Workers Unions* is perhaps the most comprehensive look at the role played by the party in the early period of the UAW. Keeran devotes only a few pages, however, to discussing the party's influence among Negro workers. Some would argue therefore that his review is not a complete history because it is one-dimensional. It lets us know that blacks were communists and that the party was very successful in recruiting them.

The real impact of the party, however, was that it taught an ideology that helped many black radicals shape their thoughts about the black condition. The communists earned their respect in the thirties, forties, and fifties when they alone stood up for black civil rights in the unions as well as in general society.[9] Party leaders were in the early unemployment marches when other whites only gave lip service to efforts to fight race discrimination. Black radicals saw these leaders as potential allies and valuable sources of information. The communists capitalized on their relationship with black radicals and sought to make unbridled advocacy of racial equality a distinguishing feature of their movement. Keeran's research suggests that the party's intense recruiting and advocacy paid off. In the 1940s blacks made up forty percent of the party membership in Michigan. Keeran credits the party for bringing blacks to unionism, saying:

> Communist influence among black workers at Ford dated back to the 1930s, when Clarence Oliver had organized an Unemployed Council in Ecorse. Communists and such members of the National Negro Congress as the Reverend Charles Hill had played an important part in recruiting black workers to the UAW. During the war, Ford Communists favored public protest to force the upgrading of black workers, most of whom were concentrated in the foundry. At this time, the two most open Communists in the Ford plant were black workers, Nelson Davis and Joe Billups. Another black Communist at Ford's, Art McPhaul, who was elected UAW district committeeman at Ford's in 1943, openly sold the *Daily Worker* and other Communist literature in the plant. McPhaul later recalled that one year during the war he sold 400 subscriptions to the *Daily Worker* in the plant and that of 785 workers in his department, 450 read the Communist paper regularly.[10]

From all accounts communist influence was ubiquitous among civil rights organizations and labor unions, which were aided in their recruiting by racism in the auto industry and in the UAW. Party members were welcomed into these groups and in turn sponsored the careers of many labor activists, blacks and whites. Their presence in black organizations gave them an integrated image, but it also made it easy for opponents of black mobility to twist the motives of these organizations. Consider the plights of the National Negro Congress (NNC) and the National Negro Labor Council. Because they had left-wing support, many black leaders felt it necessary, politically, to disassociate themselves from the group. In 1940 A. Phillip Randolph refused to run for reelection as president of the NNC because of these linkages, and Young, who headed the NNLC's Detroit chapter, was thus very intimately involved with the group, and as a result, was accused of being a communist.

Throughout his career reporters have speculated about Young's connections with the Communist party. When one reporter asked him about it directly, Young replied, "It is because the National Negro Labor Council drew support from leftist unions. That's how I became tagged as a Communist." He never denied that he knew people who were members of the party or that he learned from or was helped by people who were accused of being members. Indeed he regarded singer/actor Paul Robeson and historian/educator W. E. B. Du Bois as having the most influence on his intellectual development. Having being denied opportunities to perform in concert halls because of his left-wing politics, Robeson sought concert outlets in churches and union halls. He also gave several benefit concerts to aid the union movement. During a concert in Peekskill, New York, threats were made on Robeson's life. Wherever he traveled, local activists provided security, and during his trips to Detroit, Young and others acted to protect him. A friendship developed between Young and Robeson that lasted until the singer's death. Robeson's trials and tribulations with the government represented a profile in courage for most blacks, and, besides, he was the first black superstar that Young had ever met. Young admired Robeson for his courage, his intelligence, and his integrity.

Whereas Young and Robeson shared a personal friendship, the relationship between Young and Du Bois was more like that of teacher and student. Young met Du Bois, a Harvard University graduate and NAACP official, as part of his work in the Progressive party. In 1949 Du Bois spoke at the Music Hall in Detroit. "I got a chance to talk to him," Young recalled later. Du Bois told him about colonialism in Africa and how the white man has twisted the true history of Africa's civilization. During his lifetime, Du Bois was arguably the leading authority on black history. Throughout his lifetime, he remained an advocate for civil rights and for the teaching of Negro history. Du Bois was not only a guiding force behind the NAACP but also a radical intellectual of international fame.

Apparently, the lives of these two men are critical to understanding the early role models for Coleman Young. Robeson and Du Bois were called communists, but both stood tall and fought for black civil rights despite any political obstacles. They were persecuted, denied jobs, and vilified by the media. Young could not have known that his own career would follow a similar path, nor could he have known that a radical background would be a badge of honor in the years to come.

Meanwhile, the erosive effects of red-baiting were taking their toll on black radicals. Many young careers were mangled by the charges of being a communist. Senator Joseph McCarthy had captured a frightened nation with the red scare. The federal government passed several measures to combat subversion. In 1947 President Truman promulgated an executive order requiring loyalty oaths of government employees and ordering the attorney general to prepare and keep a list of subversive organizations. Congress passed (over the veto of the president) the Taft-Hartley Act, which forbade communist participation in labor unions. The McCarran Act (Internal Security Act of 1950) established a Subversive Activities Control Board. It was designed to designate communist front organizations as well as those infiltrated by communists. Once the groups were identified, they would be forced to register with the board, supply the names of their members, and turn over their financial records. Any future publications by such groups would be labeled communist propaganda. The McCarran Act also stipulated that any labor union with communist members would lose all rights under the national labor laws. Those identified as communists could not serve as union officers.

In 1951 the National Negro Labor Council was branded a communist front organization by U.S. attorney general Herbert Brownwell. The organization was placed on the subversive list. Young remembers the period as a time when "you were guilty until proven innocent." Red-baiting in America had reached epidemic proportions.

In 1952 HUAAC called on Coleman Young to testify before the committee—a tactic used to ruin many Americans' reputations. During the McCarthy era, simply being called before the committee could put one's patriotism into question. The tactic was particularly effective against intellectuals, entertainers, and well-known liberals. Members of HUAAC would invariably ask the question: Are you or have you ever been a member of the Communist party? They would also cite names and ask whether the person on the stand knew them. Many refused to answer questions, others pled the Fifth Amendment, and still others demanded that their First Amendment rights be adhered to. No appeals seemed to work, and the committee became a cruel circus. Its energies disrupted and destroyed the lives of many innocent individuals, but on occasion it confronted someone who was not afraid of it. This proved to be the case with Coleman Young. Young attacked the proceedings as a witch-hunt and refused to answer questions. He repeatedly used the First and Fifth Amendments to the U.S. Constitution as his defense, and he used the occasion to mock the committee, such as correcting the committee's counsel, Frank Tavenner's, pronunciation of *Negro* and denouncing Jim Crowism in the auto industry. Young recalled how angry he was at congressman John S. Wood of Georgia: "I did research on him and discovered that his district was 75% black and only about a half dozen of them could vote. I charged him with holding his seat illegally. How could he challenge my patriotism?"[11]

The HUAAC hearing was a serious crisis for the NNLC as well as for Young. Young charged: The "McCarran Act drove the NNLC out of business. It allowed the Attorney General to declare an organization subversive and you had to prove that you weren't. It reversed the presumption of innocence until proven guilty. They wanted me to disclose the names of the members. I couldn't do that. I would have exposed the cream of the labor movement."[12] A tape recorder was slipped into the hearing during Young's performance, and he became a hero in the black community. He said later, "I took those Mother F——— on. Several labor leaders approached me after the hearing about running for the state senator. I waited ten years to do that."[13]

Meanwhile, the white leadership of the labor movement was busy distancing itself from Young, and he discovered that he could not get a job in the plants. Although he was associated with the NNLC until 1955, he took a less prominent role in black politics during the last part of the fifties.

Black Politics in the Fifties

If the forties were a period of consolidation in black politics, the fifties became a decade of striking changes in race consciousness and political mobilization. The U.S. Supreme Court ruled favorably in *Brown v. Board of Education*, and in the South, the Montgomery Bus Boycott and the Freedom Riders challenged white supremacy and won. In the *Brown* decision, the high court declared that "separate but equal" schools were inherently unequal. This ruling confirmed suspicions in the black community that whites had all along been violating the U.S. Constitution in making laws that segregated the South and restricted black activity in the political arena. The ruling also increased black dissatisfaction with all forms of petty Jim Crow laws. The bus boycott and the sit-in signaled changed attitudes throughout the black community. In Detroit the new militancy undermined the policy of racial gradualism then advocated by the Democratic party. Local black leaders began putting pressure on the party for more black representation in party affairs and more opportunities for black elected officials.

The big event of the fifties was the election of state senator Charles Diggs, Jr., to the U.S. Congress from the 13th congressional district. The Diggs family had been involved in politics since the thirties. Charles Diggs, Sr., had been elected state senator as early as 1936, serving until 1944; however, he was convicted of bribery in 1948. The election of the younger Diggs to Congress was a milestone for black Detroiters and a major breakthrough for blacks nationwide. Diggs, Adam Clayton Powell (New York), and William Dawson (Chicago) became important symbols of black political power in the cities.

The elections of Diggs and others were signals that black political power was beginning to assert itself in those districts numerically controlled by blacks. Yet, a seat on the city council remained elusive. Cities like Chicago and New York had black city council members. Why not Detroit? The at-large election laws were still blocking black progress despite a 200 percent increase in the black population, which now stood at 16 percent of the city's total population. In the early fifties black mobilization was impeded by the red scare. Blacks who spoke out became targets for blackballing. By the mid-fifties a certain political inertia was broken by the mobilization of blacks in the South. Blacks were risking their lives for the right to vote and participate in sit-ins. Could the South become the showcase for black mobilization? Northern black leaders, especially Detroit's, with its strong labor element, had no choice but to assert more forcefully black aspirations lest they be upstaged by the new black militancy coming out of the South.

An additional spur to changes in the black leadership's position was the increasing popularity of Albert Cobo, a conservative mayor, with many white voters. Cobo rejected both black and labor demands, and the union political machine was no match for Cobo. In 1949 he defeated UAW-endorsed George Edward and won reelection until his death in office in 1957. His popularity can be traced to his support for urban renewal, expressway building, and other public works projects—contributing to his support by white homeowners' organizations. In 1957 the union decided to follow the white voters and endorsed his successor, Louis Miriani, a fellow conservative, for mayor.

The election of Louis Miriani proved to be a serious problem for black leadership. Although it was supported by labor, the Miriani administration was essentially insensitive to the rising aspirations of the black community, and in time the mayor received much criticism from blacks. Some of the complaints had to do with treatment by city police; some criticism came from city-sponsored neighborhood block clubs. The mayor chose to ignore the complaints, but, nevertheless, he responded to the potential threat from black groups by shifting the block organizing group, led by a young white planner named Mel Ravitz, to the housing department. Within this new conservative setting the organizing team met its demise, yet the infrastructure was laid for a black voter mobilizing effort. Meanwhile, Miriani managed to keep labor support while ignoring black leadership. His unqualified support of the police endeared him with elements of the white community. The so-called Patrick Amendment, which would have empowered the Commission on Community Relations to investigate complaints about the police, was introduced in the council. Conservative council members defeated the ordinance by a close 5-4 vote. It appeared that Miriani was heading toward reelection. Accordingly, the black leadership began organizing against him.

Some of the white leadership of the CIO could empathize with the frustrations of the black working-class leadership. Nevertheless, to keep control of the Democratic party and to keep white voters in the fold, they could not afford to be forthright on the race issue. Wilson has observed:

> The CIO in Detroit acts, in part, as a political machine with two important differences: it has relatively few tangible rewards with which to attract workers and supporters, and it is out of power in the City. Being out of power, and forced to rely on inducements other than material, it has become skilled in raising and agitating various issues which appeal to many of its constituent elements.

This, of course, does not deny the evident sincerity of the union leaders who espouse these causes.[14]

The union's endorsement of Miriani for mayor created a crisis for the new clientage politicians. George Crockett reflected on that period:

> The Negro community being more or less wedded to the Democratic Party, as opposed to the Republicans, went along with the UAW-Democratic coalition. And then you get the feeling (by you I mean the Negro) that the UAW feels it has, more or less, the Negro community in its pocket. It is no longer concerned with how the Negro thinks—it feels it can tell the Negro what you support and what you shall not support. And they continue to do this, down throughout the Miriani campaign. Well, Miriani's record on the issue which was pretty close to stop and frisk now, was so bad, Negroes would not sit still for that. When the UAW said, "We endorse Miriani," the Negro said, "This is the parting of the way."[15]

The Cobo and Miriani tenures as mayor served to strengthen the conviction of those black leaders who felt they must develop a separate organizational posture from that of the unions, yet many blacks were opposed to any kind of open break with white union leaders, albeit symbolic, because of their strong commitment to coalition politics and their relatively weak population base. The two sides finally agreed on a compromise. Blacks would develop a black organization within the labor movement, and white labor leaders would work harder to get member support for qualified black candidates.

In 1955 blacks elected the first black, Remus Robinson, to serve on the Board of Education. The election was an important victory for blacks since it meant that a certain "qualified Negro" could attract white votes, and blacks would turn out to support black candidates in at-large elections. The term *qualified Negro* became a watchword throughout black politics; the search was on to find a black leader who could appeal to white voters. To whites the term signified a well-educated and generally conservative black. A qualified Negro candidate for the city council had to be acceptable to both the black middle class and the labor movement. In this regard, the black civil rights movement in the South presented the UAW leadership with image problems. Since there were no blacks on the union's executive board, it could not claim to be a progressive organization. The courage of southern blacks created unrest among black UAW rank-and-file members in Detroit, and they began to put pressure on the white leadership for more black representation in the union decision-making process. Walter Reuther relented on his opposition to black labor leaders organizing separate black political clubs.[16]

In 1957 thirteen black labor activists, including Horace Sheffield, Frank Holly, John C. Brown, Elizabeth Jackson, Hubert Holley, and Robert "Buddy" Battle, organized the Trade Union Leadership Council (TULC). The council grew out of a need in the labor movement to assert the black agenda, get a black on the executive board, and end job discrimination. In 1959 the group came to national attention by defending A. Phillip Randolph when he was verbally attacked by George Meany, the AFL-CIO president.[17] In 1960, the Negro American Labor Council (NALC) was organized as a national umbrella organization for groups like TULC, and Randolph was elected president. The Detroit TULC became a cradle for black political development within the labor movement and the general black community.

TULC grew from a two dollar dues organization with five hundred members to a peak of thirteen thousand. After obtaining a class C liquor license and opening a restaurant/bar, it became one of the only black labor–led political clubs of its kind in the state. Despite internal disagreements and personality conflicts, the organization became a sound forum for political education and mobilization during the campaign to unseat Mayor Miriani.

The first task, however, remained the election of a black to the city council. To the chagrin of many blacks, the UAW decided to support the incumbent in the mayoral race. Yet, they were divided on a choice for the 1957 council elections. The AFL supported George Edwards; the Teamsters, Charles M. Diggs (not related to Charles C. Diggs, Sr.); and the UAW, Bill Patrick. Indeed, UAW president Walter Reuther personally endorsed the Patrick candidacy—an action designed in part to take some of the sting out of the union's support for Miriani. TULC engineered labor's endorsement of Patrick and mobilized the black/liberal coalition in his behalf. Patrick won, and his victory was a major breakthrough for the black leadership, for it demonstrated the increased sophistication of political activists on a larger scale than simply within the first congressional district. Now, almost invariably, black aspirants for citywide office needed to get support from TULC to be successful candidates. Patrick's victory also improved the sagging image of black labor leaders; it served as proof that they could deliver white members' votes. The 1960 census count also strengthened the image of this group, for it showed that blacks now made up twenty-nine percent of the population.

With those figures in hand, black leaders could be more than mere supplicants to labor leadership.

Black Politics of the Sixties

By the sixties the black community was in complete revolt against all barriers to their full citizenship. Many black Detroiters had relatives in the South and answered their call for black mobilization nationally. Driven by the South's successes, the new black leadership found a constituency for change in Detroit. In 1961 lawyer George Crockett was elected president of the Cotillion Club and appointed his law partner Robert Millender as chairman of a newly formed political action committee. Allied with disaffected white liberals, they mobilized the black community to defeat Miriani in the 1961 election. Blacks directed their own campaign, which was called "5 + 1." Black voters were told to vote for just five councilpersons and for Cavanagh. Voting for only five members for the city council meant those candidates would receive at least enough votes to survive the primary. Bloc voting prevented blacks from scattering their votes among candidates, thus allowing the conservative candidates to win. Aside from Cavanagh's victory, the election yielded another voice for black concerns, Mel Ravitz, a white liberal activist who had worked in the black community as a block club organizer.

The period of the Cavanagh administration was a critical time for black politics in Detroit. Blacks remembered election night as the sweet fruit of coalition politics. On that night the newly elected liberal mayor visited the TULC club to pay his respects and thank members for their support. Then he offered something no other white candidate had—three positions in the new administration. Hubert Holley remembered the night and recalled that TULC had not been aware that the mayor's office had a total of 107 appointed positions. He himself turned down a position, but Ted Morgan accepted and went to the Department of Public Works; Willie Baxter took a post as a commissioned secretary to a city department.

The Cavanagh administration exposed black leaders to all aspects of municipal inner workings. The new mayor promised to recruit and hire more black police officers and other members of the city bureaucracy. The coalition of liberals and blacks was presented to the nation as a model of racial cooperation. Cavanagh received several awards and became a major force among urban mayors. From the outside it appeared that blacks were at the zenith of their political influence. In 1961 Nelson "Jack" Edwards, a black man, was elected as a member-at-large on the UAW executive board. Besides Edwards, there was a liberal president, John Kennedy, a moderate Republican governor, George Romney, and a liberal mayor, Jerome Cavanagh.

Inside the black leadership, there was a growing belief that the white labor leadership was trying to prevent them from getting a second congressional seat. In 1962 the U.S. Supreme Court had ruled in *Baker v. Carr* that one man–one vote was to be the principle for redistricting state legislatures. Two years later the court again ruled in *Westberry v. Sanders* that congressional seats were to be drawn on a one man–one vote basis. For blacks these rulings were significant and meant that their concentration in the inner city was no longer a liability but represented a great potential for electing more blacks to state government and Congress. Surely, blacks also had to feel encouraged by the turnout of blacks in support of the one man–one vote issue; approximately 200,000 people rallied for the Martin Luther King march of July, 1963. Detroit's rally at Cobo Hall was also a signal of the new black political consciousness.

In 1964 TULC led a fight against the UAW's efforts to block the establishment of a second black-dominated congressional district. The UAW plan for redistricting called for the black population of 400,000 to be combined into one district. The Cotillion Club also joined the fight to create another district. Robert Millender, a black lawyer and a man with a skill for reading census data, drew up an alternative plan that gave blacks a majority in two districts. Millender's plan called for black voters to split into two districts of 200,000. According to George Crockett, the district lines were negotiated in his law office. Black leaders made a deal with state representative Henry Hogan, a Republican, to support Hogan's plan for redistricting, which strengthened his party's chances for a seat while retaining the essence of the Millender plan.

The vote on the Hogan plan proved to be one of Detroit's black leadership's toughest fights. There were eleven black representatives in Lansing, and since most of them were strong labor people, eight voted against the plan. Nevertheless, it won by 57-54, and again the black leadership had defied white labor and won. The fight was not over, however, as labor decided to back Richard Austin for the seat. The black leadership had decided to back John Conyers, Jr., son of John Conyers, Sr., a UAW activist. The race proved to be a bitter one that threatened to divide the newly empowered TULC leadership. Sheffield and Battle supported Austin, while others supported young Conyers. The fight was fought without the benefit of local dailies because both Detroit newspapers were on strike. This proved to be an advantage for the black leadership, which created its own local community paper (*Vanguard*) and carried on the debate within the black community. Whites in the district backed Austin, but Conyers won by a mere 108 votes—a great victory for blacks. Michigan became one of the first states since Reconstruction to have more than one black congressmember.

After Conyers's election, attention turned again to the city council. A special election was held in 1961 for the seat left vacant by the resignation of William Patrick. Jackie Vaughn ran and lost to conservative Thomas Poindexter, head of the Greater Homeowners' Council. Once again the city council was all white. Several blacks looked toward the upcoming 1965 municipal elections and hoped to run, and the black leadership needed to make a choice. They decided to support the candidacy of George Crockett, much to the chagrin of Walter Reuther. The AFL-CIO balked at the choice and refused to support either Vaughn or Crockett. They voted instead to support the conservative councilman Phillip Van Antwerp. Horace Sheffield and Robert "Buddy" Battle, founders of TULC, also campaigned for Van Antwerp, and their endorsement caused another crisis in the labor-black coalition.[18] Voting returns showed that Crockett and Vaughn received very few votes in the white districts. Van Antwerp won 234,718 votes to Jackie Vaughn's 92,032. The election temporarily split the leadership of the TULC.

Detroit's white voters were not impressed by Vaughn's educational credentials or by Crockett's skills as a lawyer, and thus did not support either candidate. Blacks, on the other hand, did support white candidates. This disparity prompted a proposal by a group of black ministers, called the Interdenominational Ministers' Alliance (IMA), to boycott the white candidate in the general election. A "Vote Black" campaign was sounded by Reverend Albert Cleage, leader of the Black Christian Nationalists, who said, "Vote 4 and no more." The UAW decided, after some maneuvering, to support the endorsement of the AFL-CIO. (The UAW operated under the CIO's Committee on Political Education [COPE] until their disaffiliation in 1969.) The boycott campaign was later joined by the NAACP and the Wolverine Bar Association. TULC came to the rescue of the labor movement by condemning the boycott and declaring that it was not in the best interests of the black community. The boycott movement was crushed, and for the moment politics returned to the familiar clientage style. Emil Mazey, secretary of the UAW, who had once demanded that Walter Reuther fire TULC leader Horace Sheffield, now praised the activities of the group as consistent with unionism.[19] The general election saw Nicholas Hood, a black minister, win a seat with white support after the endorsement of the two dailies and the AFL-CIO. In 1966 George Crockett was persuaded to run as judge for the Recorder's Court. Despite objections by labor, he won the election. Later Jackie Vaughn became a state legislator, and Marc Stepp became a vice president of the UAW.

In 1969 Millender reread the census data and extrapolated that the undercount of blacks in 1960 meant that there was indeed a chance of electing a black mayor. The advance estimates indicated that blacks made up 45 percent of the population; Millender reasoned that they had been undercounted by 10 percent. Richard Austin was selected as the standard bearer for the race; he was liked by both labor and white voters, and he was popular in the black community. Indeed, black voter registration went up. In a recent survey, Denise Lewis showed that blacks had by then clearly narrowed the registration gap observed in earlier studies.[20] In a campaign that everyone thought he could win, Austin lost by one percent of the votes. A decade that had at last brought new members to Congress, city councilpersons, and state representatives ended with an unexpected defeat for blacks. There was no indication at that time that Coleman Young had played a major role in any big decisions concerning candidates during the sixties. No one could have envisioned that the star of the 1970s would be a state senator by the name of Coleman Young.

In the latter part of the 1960s, black politicians and citizens were dealt several crushing blows, including the 1967 riot, the assassination of John F. Kennedy, Martin Luther King, Jr., Robert Kennedy, and Malcolm X. Each of these leaders represented an important symbol in the black community. The Kennedy brothers were epitomes of white liberal politics and the new post-Truman Democratic party. Martin Luther King represented a new breed of black leader prepared to confront the powerful white leadership on all issues concerning black civil rights. For blacks Malcolm X represented the opposite end of the spectrum, sounding the call to black nationalism and race pride. The 1967 riot was perhaps the most important event for black politics in the sixties. Coming as it did after the historical 1965 Voting Rights Act, the race riot signaled significant problems going on in the development of black political power. In 1965 George Henderson put the frustrations of the black underclass quite succinctly in his review of life in Detroit. He observed, "It is not the American dream that is repulsive to poverty-stricken [Detroit] Negroes, but their inability to achieve it. Until something better comes along, disadvantaged [Detroit] Negroes will continue to be disgruntled *Americans.*"[21] Whereas the clients of the labor unions and the black middle class were being elected and appointed to offices, the underclass struggled with poverty and the police. Herbert Locke's chronicle of the riot indicates that disturbances started in reaction to a routine police raid of a blind pig, an illegal after-hours nightclub. One event followed another, and the black community found itself in full revolt. Arson, violence, and mayhem filled the streets of Detroit. Mayor Cavanagh and Governor Romney concluded that the situation was out of hand and asked President Johnson for federal troops.

Some blacks lost their lives, and others were arrested before order was finally restored. The riot created more questions than it answered. For instance, why Detroit? And who were the rioters? What were their grievances? Was it in fact a revolt against the established leadership? The president created the Kerner Commission to study the riot and why it occurred, and the black leadership began to examine itself.

In his study of the 1967 riot, Herbert Locke denied that it was a revolt against established leadership. The leadership, he claimed, tried to stop the riot. Locke concluded that "What the press failed to understand was that this failure was no more an indictment of Negro leadership than the antics of Breakthrough, a local right-wing white organization, or the Mafia are indictments of white leadership."[22]

Despite Locke's disclaimer, white leadership, under the direction of Joseph L. Hudson, Jr., chairman of Hudson's department store, acted to improve communications with the black community. They feared that Breakthrough and its leader, Donald Lobsinger, could become a factor in creating more white racism. Accordingly, they established New Detroit, Inc., a coalition of white corporate leaders and black leaders. The new organization also included self-declared spokesmen for the grassroots black community. New Detroit, designed to be a forum for articulating the black agenda, became a lobby stung by a legislative defeat for open housing in 1967, and a defeat of 5-3 on a school aid bill. The organization did not emerge as a rival to the black political leadership.

Meanwhile, the developing black leadership was assessing post-riot damages. There were several political casualties. Among them was Mayor Cavanagh, who undercut his black support in a bitter primary fight for a U.S. Senate seat against G. Mennen "Soapy" Williams, by then a hero in the black community. The precipitous decline of Cavanagh's reputation as a liberal problem solver came quickly after the riot. One year he was seen as one of the best mayors in the nation, and the next he appeared helpless and hapless in the face of open rebellion among black residents of the city.

In March, 1969, the New Bethel incident occurred, in which there was a confrontation between the police and members of the Republic of New Africa (RNA), a black nationalist group, at the New Bethel Church. One policeman was killed, hundreds of individuals were arrested, and several were wounded. The black community was enraged. Cavanagh's political stock went down further because he displayed what looked like weak leadership in that situation. George Crockett emerged as a hero by intervening and releasing many of the prisoners. The mayor never recovered, and black politicians began planning for the post-Cavanagh era as they screened candidates for the 1969 mayoral election. Cavanagh announced in June that he would not be a candidate for reelection.

The black leadership was busy dealing with a challenge from the so-called grassroots leadership, all of whom claimed to be the "real" voice of the black community. In asserting that the established black leadership had not adequately addressed the problems of downtrodden ghetto dwellers, these challengers struck a chord among inner city residents. Although they did not have an established political base, their rhetoric was consistent with that of the Black Power advocates who argued for black nationalism and self-help. Individuals such as Edward Vaughn (Pan African Congress), Kenneth Cockrel (League of Revolutionary Black Workers), Milton Henry (Republic of New Africa), and Reverend Albert Cleage (Black Christian Nationalists) emerged as challengers to the more established black leadership. Reverend Cleage (also known as Jaramogi Abebe Agyeman) attacked black leaders and emerged as spokesman for the Black Christian Nationalist (BCN) movement. Cleage created the Black Slate as an arm of his church, now called the Shrine of the Black Madonna, and also founded the Freedom Now Party. In 1968 Cleage attempted to organize a coalition of the new leaders into an organization called the Federation for Self-Determination, though it never achieved its goal of consolidation. A flyer circulated in the black community summarized its organizational problems, reporting that "clannishness, lack of clear-cut purpose, lack of money, intergroup haggling and personal ambitions of members were among the reasons given by various observers for the demise of the organization."[23]

Coleman Young maintained an interest in the black militant groups. In 1973 he attended the National Black Political Convention, which brought many of these group together. He and David Holmes walked out of the convention after the group became mired in separatist rhetoric. Though Young was heavily criticized for this move, he held onto his grassroots, radical values.

The Emergence of Coleman Young as an Elected Official

Coleman Young's training in elected politics started like that of many black leaders, as a campaign manager. His first candidate was Reverend Charles Hill, pastor of Hartford Baptist Church and a founder of the National Negro Congress, which was a prolabor civil rights organization. Hill tried several times for a seat on the city council in 1945 and 1949. Although Hill never won a seat, his campaigns offered Young important lessons in the process of electioneering. In 1948 Young himself ran for a state Senate seat as the candidate of the Progressive party and lost. Despite his visibility in the fifties, Young refused an offer to run for the state Senate again in the early part of the decade. Nevertheless, he stayed in politics as an official in the Progressive party.

To many of Young's observers, the period between 1955 and 1960 remains a mystery. By his own account, in those years, Young worked as a cab driver, dry cleaner operator, meat handler, and insurance salesman, yet it was a period of financial uncertainty and personal difficulty, to say the least. Coleman Young's personal life started to unravel. He was married and divorced twice—to his first wife, Marian McClellan, from 1947 to 1954, and to his second wife, Nadine Baxter, from 1955 to 1960. Both marriages were childless, and, of the two, his relationship with Marian seemed to have had the more important role in Young's political development. She took care of Young during the period of intense red-baiting in America, when he bounced from job to job, finally finding stable work as an insurance agent. Young's second marriage was an emotional roller coaster throughout. His mother died in November, 1959, and they were difficult years; according to Young, personal turmoil never took him completely out of politics. He still talked politics with customers and friends, and he maintained friendships with many progressive whites in the labor movement.

The Eisenhower era (1952–1960) did not eliminate red-baiting, nor was it politically uplifting for blacks. After reaching its peak, however, the anticommunist movement began to lose its momentum. Many American communists were shocked by the 1956 revelations of Nikita Khrushchev, the Soviet leader, concerning Stalin's demonic leadership, and they abruptly left the party. Progressive party members drifted to the Democratic party during the Stevenson and Kennedy campaigns for the presidency. Other radicals channeled their energies into the black civil rights movement in the South. Meanwhile, with the election of a black to the city council, black politics in Detroit were catching up with other northern cities.

Young made another entry into Democratic politics in 1959 as a candidate for the city council. He admits that to make this bid in an at-large election with little money or support was quixotic, but at least he received votes from Detroit's East Side. This support encouraged Young to begin building his political base in the East Side. When he ran as the Democratic candidate for the Michigan Constitutional Convention (Con Con) in 1961, Young won without labor support. (Some labor leaders still considered him "a dangerous red.") The convention convened to rewrite Michigan's state constitution and afforded Young an opportunity to interact with the power wielders from all parts of the state. Young served on the Taxation and Finance Committee and gained a reputation as a tactician as well as a defender of the poor. Although, according to Young, the Taxation and Finance Committee was not his first choice, it was nevertheless a worthy learning experience. "Dissecting the Constitution," he says, "is the best education in government. I convinced a lot of people that I didn't have horns. I had great ability."[24] Coleman Young was one of two political stars to emerge at Con Con; the other was George Romney.

When the Con Con was over, Young sought work with the Credit Union League, though, as he recalls, the red-baiting followed him throughout the fifties. Someone in the labor movement called the FBI to try to prevent the Credit Union League from hiring him. They put pressure on the league, but he credits Sam Karsman, whom he met in 1946, and Bob Vanderbeek, president of the League Insurance Company, with standing up to the labor pressure. Vanderbeek recalled, "We knew his background. We were used to hiring controversial people. I asked the board if they could take the heat from the publicity. They said yes and we hired him." Young helped to prove himself by making the second highest score on the company aptitude test, and he proved to be an excellent insurance salesman. After a few months he was put in charge of the Family Group Life Program, a new mail-in policy being promoted by the company. Vanderbeek recalled, "Coleman would go into towns that had never seen a black guy and they would buy the policy."[25] It quickly became obvious to the company that Young had a future in insurance, but the young man had different ideas.

In 1962 Young ran for a sat in the Michigan House of Representatives and lost by seven votes. Con Con had revived his name, but the UAW still opposed his candidacy. Young complained that three black candidates had been put on the ballot to split the black vote. Two years later he ran against Nelis J. Saunda for the state Senate seat and won the election by a 2-1 majority. Almost immediately, he gained the association of some key labor leaders. Gus Scholle, president of the state AFL-CIO, hired Young as union representative for the intervening months before he took office in Lansing. Young joined Basil Brown of Highland Park and became Michigan's second black state senator. He shared an apartment with Brown and Stanley Novak, a white legislator and prolabor politician.

The Lansing Years

As a state senator Coleman Young quickly asserted himself as a leader. In 1966, two years after his election, he was unanimously elected by his colleagues as the Democratic minority floor leader, whose role is to count votes, alert senators of the party's position on bills, and mediate differences among party members. The job took him away from the particular interests of his urban constituency and got him involved in all aspects of party deliberations. Politicians elected to these party positions are called upon to know as much about insurance rates in Grand Rapids as the socioeconomic problems of the East Side of Detroit. Minority leader George Fitzgerald gave Young great latitude in his job. Says Young: "He left decisions up to me."

While he was senator, Young introduced a bill (Public Act No. 370) to increase benefits to families on Aid for Dependent Children (ADC) and allow a single parent to work thirty-two hours per week. He also sponsored a bill to protect residents from urban renewal projects. The urban relocation law guaranteed occupants or tenants relocation to a standard dwelling in an area of their choice before the city could proceed with condemnation. He also sponsored a bail bond law, which permitted individuals to pay 10 percent of bail to the court rather than to a bondsman. If the accused was found innocent, he would receive his money back. The bill also provided that time in jail awaiting a trial would be credited at five dollars a day to any fine the court might levy. Young's efforts, by his own account, were made to ease the burden on the poor. He sponsored a bill to repeal the tax collector's first claims on the estates of the poor.

On one occasion Young joined the antibusing forces in the Senate as a tactical move. As the issue was reaching a peak, Young recommended that the Senate go all the way and outlaw all busing. Rural lawmakers were not prepared for a complete ban because their constituency used buses to get their children to school, and the bill died suddenly.[26]

During his tenure in Lansing, Young was elected chair of the Senate Elections Committee. As chair, he advocated extending registration requirements and changing the time before a person could be eliminated from registration rolls for nonvoting from two to four years. He also supported allowing eighteen-year-olds the right to vote. Governor Romney vetoed the bill to extend the time for nonvoting, but, in campaigning for it, Young gained a reputation for advocating progressive legislation.

Young also maintained his career as a labor supporter. He was one of the chief sponsors of Michigan's Public Employee Relations Act. The act was designed to grant exclusive certification of elected unions as bargaining agents for public employees. It also provided checkoff privileges for employees, which authorized payroll deductions for union dues, and although it prohibited strikes by public employees, it did provide for binding arbitration in case of an impasse in negotiations.

Perhaps Young's most controversial actions were the sponsorship of the state's open housing laws and the introduction, at Cavanagh's behest, of the first Detroit city income tax bill. He also played a major role in enacting the state's abortion law, and he supported the Macauley bill, which exempted licensed physicians performing abortions in licensed hospitals from any criminal liability. Young also played an important role in the enactment of state consumer protection laws and laws for the decentralization of Detroit schools.

Clearly, the Lansing years served as an apprenticeship for Young—his second. He was given the opportunity to show that he could manage party affairs and stay clear of left-wing politics. Whether his politics changed is unclear, but Young used his ten years in Lansing to rethink and refocus. And these years allowed him time to earn IOUs among his East Side constituency.

While Senator Young was busy with constituency casework and leadership duties, a new type of politician emerged as a response to President Lyndon Johnson's so-called War on Poverty. Johnson's war became the politics of poverty. White and black politicians were busy making a name for themselves by fighting poverty, but the 1967 riot came as a rude interruption to certain fledgling careers and a turning point for others. Young had consistently warned white elected officials that the behavior of the white police in the black community was potentially an explosive situation. Many blacks wrote to Senator Young in hopes that he could do something to combat police brutality and racism. In a letter to his constituency, Young outlined his position:

> I have been one of those who has urged a complete shakeup of the police department from top to bottom including a full integration of Negro police officers at all levels of command and emergency steps to recruit new Negro patrolmen immediately. I also feel and have demanded that the whole approach of the police department in terms of "standard riot control procedures" be drastically revamped.
>
> The current procedure, as you know, amounts to laying siege to the Negro community by the police department and because of the lily-white composition of the police department, amounts to a Negro-white confrontation which, in my opinion, is a provocation for further violence rather than a step aimed toward a reduction of violence.[27]

Young's advice, along with that of other black leaders, was not heeded.

The intensity of the 1967 explosion of black anger had not been anticipated or predicted by the black leadership, yet most, if not all, black leaders were expected to be able to pacify the black community. In his study of the incident, Herbert Locke does not include Coleman Young as one of the leaders who played a role in pacifying the black community following the riot, although Young claims he did: "I was a spokesman for blacks in the assembly of leaders who spoke before the Wayne County Chamber after the riot." This group addressed itself to rebuilding Detroit. Young attributes Locke's omission to an incident involving Young's effort to help a constituent get a liquor license. He explains:

> I had a constituent who was a felon. He wanted to open a party store and was trying to get an SBA loan. The city had some inflexible rules against ex-felons owning party stores. I went down to

talk to Herbert, an aide to the police commissioner, about the case. We went to visit the man. On our way back Herbert kept talking about "we." I finally realized that I was talking about the black community and Herbert was talking about his "we," i.e., the police, which was different from my "we," i.e., the black community.[28]

Conclusions: Politics as a Vocation

One of the most fascinating aspects of Coleman Young's life has been his ability to remain engaged in Detroit politics for nearly fifty years and make a living at it. Max Weber, the German sociologist, differentiates between politics as a vocation and as an avocation. Weber defines the latter as an "occasional" politician: "Politics as an avocation is today practiced by all those party agents and heads of voluntary political associations who, as a rule, are politically active only in case of need and for whom politics is, neither materially nor ideally, 'their life' in the first place." Certainly Coleman Young has interacted with such occasional politicians, but in his own life he has made politics a vocation. He says,

> There are two ways of making politics one's vocation: either one lives "for" politics or one lives "off" politics. By no means is this contrast an exclusive. The rule is, rather, that man does both, at least in thought, and certainly he also does both in practice. He who lives "for" politics makes politics his life, in an internal sense. Either he enjoys the naked possession of the power he exerts, or he nourishes his inner balance and self-feeling by the consciousness that his life has *meaning* in the service of a "cause." In this internal sense, every sincere man who lives for a cause also lives off this cause. The distinction hence refers to a much more substantial aspect of the matter, namely, to the economic. He who strives to make politics a permanent *source of income* lives "off" politics as a vocation, whereas he who does not do this lives "for" politics.[29]

One could argue that the reason Young has made politics his vocation is that it is the only thing he is good at. Because he is also adaptable to change, and has in the process developed a hard shell of pragmatism, he has found himself especially well suited to politics. His political career was filtered through an incredible set of fundamental changes in the labor movement. He survived the ego wars of Detroit's black politics and changes in the civil rights movement. Having watched the socialist wing of the labor movement, led by Walter Reuther, join the red-baiting campaign, he discovered that ideology is often a means not an end to politics. Young endured the red-baiting campaign and revived his career as a politician—this time running for office without the help of labor friends and winning. It was only after he won the nomination for mayor in 1973 that some labor leaders joined in to support him. Yet, the labor movement was one of his greatest teachers. Coleman Young was enough of a student to know that racism and mindless power struggles among his white colleagues were no different than in other organizations, even though the labor unions tried to set themselves apart by their demands for economic equality. Coleman Young learned the lesson of labor organizing—how to build coalitions, negotiate, and compromise when necessary. For him a good organizer and leader must understand his constituency and be prepared to put his career at risk in representing and pushing for its concerns.

The years in Lansing taught Young to appreciate the perceptions of outsiders toward Detroit, and he acknowledged that the people who could truly save Detroit from collapse in the 1970s were outsiders—even just as far outside as Dearborn, next-door to Detroit and the home of Ford Motor Company—for they controlled the money needed for revitalization. Accordingly, the Coleman Young who had once attacked the automobile companies and their hiring policies now had to reach an accommodation with the new manager of the industry if he hoped to govern and keep jobs in the city. While ideology works in speeches and within intellectual circles, it provides little guidance for governing a city with a declining population and without the resources to supply jobs for the general population, and Young knew this. Accordingly, if he was going to remain in office, he would have to move beyond any compelling *isms* and make some dramatic changes for the city. This meant becoming what Allison Davis called a reality-oriented leader, one who concentrates his/her energy on keeping the city from becoming a ghost town.

The transition from the young Coleman Young to the mature Coleman Young has been most difficult to understand for those who have interacted with both. They see an idealist who has been transformed into a professional politician, and many people dislike the mature Young. Those who tend to view politics as an avocation still talk about the old days and illustrious past struggles. They remember when Coleman Young was one of them, and they fear that he has abandoned the ideals he shared with them.

Coleman Young's political education took place in a rapidly changing social environment, and his experiences helped him to gain a broad personality, capable of acknowledging a number of points of view. Young claims to know several types of black lifestyles—the middle-class, the slicker, and the gambler—and admits being alienated from the first, the middle-class, which is consistent with his personal values and his behavior in office. Young says he has always admired the gambler most and has used strategies learned from risk-taking in making political decisions. More importantly, he has never allowed white rejection or his own ambitions to deter him. When he lacked proper direction, he improvised, and he seized opportunities when they appeared. Obviously, he is a man of passion. He remembers painful incidents in his life but allows himself to laugh about them. He also remembers his enemies and friends. He has learned to appreciate loyalty and competence in those serving under him. However, he will not hesitate to terminate the job of a subordinate who crosses the line. Young recalled that, in the labor movement, "if you were given a pork chop [a patronage job] and you went over the edge of the pork chop, that's your ———.[30]

Young does not dispute the importance of mentors in his life but regards ambition, risk-taking, and luck as the real secrets to his success. Clearly, he resents the treatment he received during the days of the red scare, but since that time his views about the labor movement and its white leaders have mellowed. Prior to his election to the state Senate, no one would have predicted Coleman Young would have become the dominant black political figure of the seventies. Black leaders such as Robert Millender must have noticed something in Young's tenacity and perseverance that inspired them to take a leap of faith and support him for the mayoralty. Young himself took hold of the torch and ran with it.

4

The Elections of Coleman Young 1973–1985

Detroit's electoral politics have largely been ignored in scholarly research and writing. Outside commentators have casually dismissed the city's political system as simply a labor-dominated one. In the past Detroit mayors and council members have not approached the notoriety of political figures in Chicago; when one thinks about politics in the Midwest, one usually means Chicago, which has long possessed a political machine, as well as the larger-than-life figure of Richard J. Daley as mayor. In many ways Detroit under Jerome Cavanagh and now under Coleman Young can make equally illuminating and noteworthy claims of political intrigue. Although Cavanagh had a reputation as one of the nation's most progressive urban mayors while he was in office, no books have been written about his administration. And this is true for other Detroit mayors as well. As Coleman Young approaches the zenith of his political influence, a more careful scrutiny of his electoral mandate is certainly warranted.

The fact that Young is black becomes important when one considers his impact on the city's overall political agenda. Not only do his elections provide insight into the city's social conditions and transitions; they also herald the rise of a new political elite and forecast future urban politics. Young's continuing political success is not due to a faithful and unchanging electorate. On the contrary, the composition of Detroit's voters has been distinctly different in each of the four elections he has won. Young's margins of victory on his three reelections have included large numbers of new voters and new voting blocs. His four campaigns actually reveal important qualities in both the elements and dynamics of change in Detroit.

In comparing Detroit's politics with Chicago's, the issue is not whether Coleman Young is the functional equivalent of Richard Daley, but rather what is the nature of his impact on Detroit's political party development, coalition building, issue formation, and political socialization and resocialization compared to the other leader. The state of Detroit politics transcends its local dimension because it affects how black politicians are perceived nationally, although the voting behavior and public opinion of city residents are critical.

The Meaning of Elections in Detroit

In Detroit, as in other cities, mayoral elections are presumed to be simple mechanisms through which voters' preferences are expressed. Politicians like elections because, through them, their mandates can be legitimated, voters like them because they empower the citizen, and parties welcome them because they energize their political organizations. Elections are far more complex than mere choices between two parties' candidates. When Detroit's blacks acquired a statistical edge in voter registration, it was logical that the city would elect a black mayor. The 1973 election came at a time when voters recognized a need to reconsider the social and economic meanings of their city. "Rethinking Detroit" implied the abandonment of many outdated concepts about city life, as well as the needs of residents.

In order to properly evaluate Detroit's last four city elections and what they reflect about the city's concerns at different times, it is necessary to establish a baseline for comparison. The election of a black over a white in a close election, particularly at a time when black voters had become the majority of the electorate, suggests no particular change in the ethnic succession theory. But reactions to Young and his policies reflect a number of unresolved feelings that Americans, both black and white, have about the use of political power by blacks. The 1973 election was a classic demonstration of those fears and reservations, as a black man directly challenged a white opponent. In a subsequent election, the voters were given a different set of choices—between two black candidates. The latter election was more than a contest between two political styles; it showed that definite voting patterns were developing.

A possible baseline for examining Detroit's elections over the decades would be according to the winning margins within election districts during the primaries. Urban primaries perform several functions; they air conflicts, eliminate minor candidates, measure support levels among candidates, and shape the debate for the general election. Since Detroit is heavily Democratic, the primary is where the city's real battles are fought and elections are essentially decided. Incremental changes in the socioeconomic status of voters revealed by the primary are in fact quite striking, and each election is clearly a unique event.

In citywide elections, black politicians depend on high voter turnout in the inner city districts. The simple arithmetic of the situation suggests that it costs less to recruit an inner city voter than to convince an undecided voter from the periphery. The fact that black politicians benefit from having inner city voters is considered their competitive edge in winning primaries.

Elections weave voters, candidates, and political parties into a web of relationships that constitute a blueprint by which future policy agendas are shaped. If we view Coleman Young's first mayoral election in this way, then we can begin to shed some light on the history of Detroit in the early seventies. What was at stake in the contest for mayor of the nation's leading auto manufacturing center? Was the election part of a larger trend toward electing black mayors? Cleveland, Gary, and Newark had all elected black mayors; mayors Stokes, Hatcher, and Gibson had already demonstrated that blacks could manage multimillion-dollar municipal budgets, perform ceremonial duties, and provide sound leadership for city services, including public safety, as competently as any of their white counterparts.

In Detroit it was clear that the leading issues concerned economic development, crime, and affirmative action, although the informal agenda had to do with the impending black takeover of the city's major political offices. Would Detroit become an all-black city? The 1970 census showed that blacks were 7 percent short of having population parity with whites. Yet, among Detroit residents, whites were still registering and voting in higher percentages than blacks. Black politicians who had served their political apprenticeships under the Cavanagh administration or in labor unions were aware that they must gain white support in order for a black candidate to win the mayor's race. In the 1969 election they had searched for, and found, a personality that could appeal to white voters. A candidate screening committee was set up, and it was chaired by Robert Millender. The committee screened several individuals and announced that five were qualified and acceptable—William Patrick, Kenneth Hylton, Reverend

Hubert Locke, councilman Robert Tindal, and Richard Austin. Richard Austin, a black professional accountant, was finally selected; he proved to be an appropriate choice, and the political differences between him and Roman Gribbs, his white opponent, went unnoticed in the preelection debates. Austin lost the election by 5,194 votes—a mere 1 percent. His experience showed black leaders that any future black candidate must combine Austin's acceptability to whites with the capacity to strike a compelling pose with those inner city voters who had not been mobilized by Austin. A future candidate would also need strong "law and order" credentials to offset potential charges of softness toward extremists and criminals. In order to get elected, a black candidate had to assuage white voters' fears of black crime.

White flight, which had been initiated by the riot of 1967 and exacerbated by various school busing decrees, became a most significant contributor to changes in the composition of the electorate. Stop the Robberies, Enjoy Safe Streets (STRESS), a special undercover crime program of the police department, began to incite the wrath of inner city residents because it indicated to them a view by officials that all inner city people were criminals, and they became more and more convinced that white officials could no longer be expected to protect black interests. By arousing such sentiments, STRESS did most of the work of mobilizing the electorate for the emerging black political elite. The remaining task facing these politicians was to analyze the Austin campaign to discover the weak turnout areas within their natural constituencies. They were given a bonus by the census data, which showed that whites were leaving the city in record numbers and projected an edge for blacks in the number of registered voters by 1973.

The Austin Campaign and Its Aftermath

On paper Richard Austin should have been unbeatable. He was a popular politician, a good party leader, and an experienced administrator. Austin was a certified public accountant (CPA), and had been a Con Con delegate, chairman of the Wayne County Board of Supervisors, and a county auditor, and he had developed a reputation as a competent professional who happened to be black. The time seemed right for this type of candidate. Walter Reuther thought the time was right for a black mayor. The UAW Community Action Program (CAP) operated the only citywide precinct level organization in the city. Detroit black politicians had elected two congressmen and several judges and common council members; they were regarded by their peers in other cities as great organizers. Since many had been trained as labor leaders, they faced no clergy-politician class against which to contest for power. As it turned out, Austin lost a very close mayoral race to a white candidate. Analyzing the Austin race assisted blacks in planning for a second attempt at the mayoralty. The Austin campaign set a standard for planning in subsequent election campaigns.

The Austin race was influenced by several significant factors. The 1967 riot had divided the white and black communities regarding the character of police services and crime prevention. Several federal court rulings mandating busing in the Detroit school system had served to emphasize and enlarge differences between the two communities. The affirmative action plan of the city's personnel department was gaining momentum at that time, and white police officers were among the strongest opponents of the policy in the city. During the Austin mayoral race, difficulties then being experienced by Cleveland mayor Carl Stokes in obtaining cooperative police department administrators were receiving wide attention in the press. Police morale and civilian control were becoming increasingly potent concerns in urban governance, and public speculation arose on the issue of whether or not a black mayor could control a white police department. And there were the old political misunderstandings within the labor-black coalition. Blacks had played a secondary role in white administrations in Detroit for a number of years. Many voiced their belief that they could best help their constituencies by continuing to work with white liberals, through their influence with the white officeholders. Such power, they reasoned, would evaporate, or be severely diminished, with a black officeholder. In avoiding titular authority, black politicians could escape the consequences of mistakes and allow their white liberal associates to take the heat from the media and black constituents. Some black politicians were simply not ready to abandon their institutionalized subordinate relationship with white politicians. In other words, in 1969 Gribbs's election would not change things, but an Austin victory would bring uncertainty.

Richard Austin ran a creditable campaign against Wayne County sheriff Roman Gribbs. A poll taken during the last week of the campaign and released one day before the election showed Austin leading Gribbs 42 to 39 percent, but it also showed a significant percentage of those "undecided" (18 percent).[1] Gribbs reacted to the poll by charging that Austin had a black radical on his campaign staff. He claimed that Frank Ditto, who had allegedly disrupted a public school class, was an Austin aide. Austin denied the charges, but the tactic served to impress whites with the need to vote for "their own"—that Austin was black and, therefore, unreliable. Since conservative Mary V. Beck's write-in campaign offered a comfortable stopping place for the undecided, it was imperative that Gribbs retain the white votes he had obtained in the primary. He also needed a small percentage of the black vote. On election day he actually received 6 percent of the black vote—from a less-than-overwhelming voter turnout by blacks. Although the black turnout in this election consisted of 70 percent of registered voters, it was still less than the 80 percent that Detroit blacks had given Lyndon Johnson in 1964. On the other hand, it was also a substantial increase from the 50 percent turnout of black voters in the 1965 election. Despite the impressive turnout for Austin, and his increase in white voting percentages from the primary (from 9 to 18 percent), he simply could not overcome the high number of white voters in the election. Whites simply outvoted blacks; the Beck campaign was not really even a factor in the election.

Austin's loss in 1969 was considered a setback for the emerging black political elite. Politically, they had done all the right things, and yet they had lost. In any close race, the losers often find it difficult to resist blaming someone. In retrospect, some claim that Young did not pull his load in the race. Young's own version of his minor role in the Austin campaign was that he was not asked to play a role in the campaign. He says, "I went down to the Austin headquarters and asked to help. I didn't know they had a small room in the back where they decided strategy. I was told to get out the vote in my district. I felt it was insulting. I asked, what can you do for my district? There was no consultation. Austin lost because the numbers were not right. He also took the black vote for granted."[2] Following the loss, Robert Millender, who had served as a political strategist in the election, was reported to have said, "I counted wrong." The next race would require more planning, more resources, and—most importantly—a different kind of candidate. Plans for 1973 began immediately after the election.

Black Politics of the Seventies

Detroit's black political strategists spent the next four years determining who would be the "right" candidate. The person must be someone who was able to excite those segments of the black community that are normally apathetic toward politics—the very poor—enough to get them out to the polls at a rate of 80 to 90 percent of registered voters and win these districts overwhelmingly. He had to be clearly in favor of "law and order," knowledgeable about Detroit politics, and prepared to take on the mammoth task of rebuilding the city.

Many individuals saw themselves as the proper choice, but the key to a successful candidacy would be to reassemble the Austin campaign organization around this quite different kind of person. Austin's campaign manager, Millender, who was also the behind-the-scenes political advisor to most of the city's black politicians, was openly courted by all of those hoping to run. Not only was he a skilled reader of the Detroit electorate, but now he also had the experience of having conducted a narrowly lost citywide election campaign. For this reason, Edward Bell and Mel Ravitz both saw Millender as one who had power enough to confer a legitimation that each of them needed. Bell wanted to claim Austin's mantle, while Ravitz hoped to reconstruct the old labor-black coalition.

Millender reviewed all requests for his assistance and finally decided on Coleman Young. Young recalled that he had to convince Millender that he could win. He said, "Everybody had to reevaluate their positions. Mel Ravitz and Ed Bell were already out there."[3] Millender, the master strategist, began to put together a campaign staff and outlined the endorsements needed. On the labor side of the election was Robert "Buddy" Battle, vice president of UAW Local 600 and president of TULC, who left the UAW to support Young. Millender and Battle gave their support to the Young candidacy and mobilized the community in his behalf. Their efforts constituted a recognition that Young possessed the personality, drive, and political acumen needed to win the election; they were not mere acts of "king making."

In order to elect a black mayor, black leaders had to get their political house in order. The first congressional district, represented by John Conyers, Jr., was divided by fractional politics. One group supported Murray Jackson, activist and educator, and another pushed for Richard Austin. The internecine struggles of the district were driven by personality conflicts, ideological disagreements, and interest clashes. After an impasse had developed, Jack Edwards, a UAW vice president, and John Conyers recruited Hubert Holley, who was considered an honest broker, to lead the district. According to Holley, he agreed to accept the "leadership [role] only if both sides agreed to accept me."[4] They agreed, and the first congressional district enjoyed fourteen years of stable leadership under him.

The thirteenth congressional district, Coleman Young's home district in the East Side of Detroit, was a much older community with a more complex variety of factions. During the years prior to Young's candidacy, the district was also characterized by leadership instability. The leadership problems, in part, stem from the group inability to integrate competing clergy, labor, and civil rights activists. The internal politics of the district happen to be so labyrinthine that, as a candidate, Young, an otherwise favorite son, had to be shepherded through the political maze.

Although the first and thirteenth district organizations acted independently and occasionally endorsed different candidates, they tended to agree on mayoral candidates. Since politics and chemistry have been vastly different within the two districts, endorsement meetings tend to be extremely stressful for all those concerned. Various factions are expected to defend their turf as well as to compromise. The Young candidacy presented a difficult problem for both districts since the precinct delegates were heavily composed of the union-affiliated delegates and new clientage practitioners; many of them were not prepared to defy their white labor patrons.

After the UAW executive board had endorsed Mel Ravitz, many delegates wanted a coendorsement to free them up to work for Young. The board refused this request, however, and reported a unanimous vote. Having failed to get coendorsement, Young supporters had to lobby hard in order to get Young the congressional district's support. As they had done in 1961, black labor leaders departed the UAW and used their political IOUs to secure the endorsement for Coleman Young. Once the endorsements were secured, they started marketing Young as a candidate.

Presenting Coleman Young's Credentials

In contrast to his predecessor, Austin, Coleman Young had developed some unusual credentials for a mayoral candidate. During the previous campaign, Austin's opponent, Gribbs, incessantly referred to Austin's background as a certified public accountant and called Austin a "bookkeeper." Young's background, on the other hand, included a variety of jobs and organizations. Having been an automobile worker, a labor organizer, campaign manager, and elected official, he personally knew most of the key political activists, both black and white, who would be instrumental in gathering support. He had established credibility with both white and black radicals; as a labor leader years before he had aligned himself with the left wing of the unions. He also had credibility with the newly emerging civil rights militants. Indeed, his reputation as a black leader was in part based on his involvement in the civil rights campaigns. If he had ever lost touch with the concerns of his fellow East Side residents, he regained it during a decade of not holding a steady job. He recovered from the adversity of HUAAC and unemployment and returned to politics under his own steam, and he recovered from rejection by the labor unions and went on to become a champion of the labor bills in the state legislature. In Lansing he developed a reputation as a consummate politician. His intellectual strengths included a sharp mind and an intuitive sense of timing, and his versatility permitted him to talk with equal ease to downtown businessmen and residents of the East Side ghetto.

Young's roller coaster career reflects his penchant for taking risks; he has been on the unpopular end of several controversial issues. During his encounters with reporters, the issue of Young's leftist background has often been raised. On one occasion he asserted, "I am not now and never have been a member of any organization that was subversive or whose design was to overthrow the United States in any way."[5]

During his tenure with the state senate, he was elected to leadership in the state party, and in 1968 he was appointed as the first Negro Democratic party national committeeman. He also served as party spokesperson on a variety of nonracial issues. A successful comer in politics must be able to read the issues and also direct attention to himself. Young had no intention of retiring in the state Senate and searched for issues that would further his ambitions, and as early as 1968, rumors were circulating that Young would challenge Mayor Cavanagh in the next election. In an interview with reporters then, he said, "I've been with Jerry [Cavanagh] until recently, but one thing I've against him is that he has been capitulating to the Police Department lately. The question is: Who is running the police?" The reporter later declared Young "the black man's political showpiece."[6]

In 1971 the *State Journal* had published an interview in which Senator Young mused about politics in general and reacted to reports that he was interested in running for the U.S. Senate.[7] In an early interview, he had predicted the election of a black governor for Michigan.[8] Coleman Young was signaling that he was ready for larger responsibility. The media sought his views on everything from no-fault insurance to state politics. Young had achieved the kind of reputation and visibility needed to mobilize inner city voters. Interviews from that period clearly portrayed both Young's ambition and his conviction that blacks should not limit their political horizons. To achieve visibility and credibility, Young answered broadcast editorials and blasted race discrimination in the Detroit Police Department. He also led a drive to include ethnic history in Michigan's public school curriculum. Throughout his Lansing days, Young had also been careful to maintain his contacts within the Detroit black community and the progressive white community.

In order to conduct a citywide campaign, Senator Young needed the support of party regulars and labor leaders, as well as a strong campaign staff. In 1969 Young was prevented from running for mayor by a state law that blocked his candidacy because it prohibited state legislators from running for another office until the expiration of their elected terms. He recalled, "This time I started early so that I had time to take the case to the Appeals Court." Again, he lost his challenge to the constitutionality of the law in the lower court. The court interpreted the Michigan Constitution as prohibiting campaigns for other political offices by members of the Michigan legislature, prior to the expiration of their terms in office. The ruling was later reversed by the state appeals court, but, in the meantime, the publicity surrounding the case helped boost Young's image as a fighter in the working-class black community. Many interpreted the initial court ruling as an attempt by whites to keep Young from running for mayor of Detroit; they reasoned that whites were afraid of a Young victory. If Young had any chance of winning, he needed an all-out effort from black voters and the Black Slate helped provide this.

Mobilization for the campaign started early, and many believe that the place where it began was in Robert Millender's basement. Millender became Young's campaign manager and Malcolm Dade, Jr., the day-to-day coordinator. Dade had previously served as an aide to former Michigan senator Phillip Hart. Veteran political activists William Beckham, Jr., and Leon Atchison joined the team. The greatest asset of the campaign, however, was the candidate himself. As a gifted extemporaneous speaker, he could turn a phrase under fire, and it would be quoted by the press. He campaigned for white votes but also made it clear that he was not particularly concerned about attempting to be acceptable to all voting groups. Besides, the available data showed that he had demographics and voter registration on his side. Nevertheless, Young was not so sure of his chances. He recalled, "I was late. I had no money. I did not have s—— except the right to run. I got 25 people together and they agreed to cosign a $25,000 loan for me. Then I decided to roll the dice. I purchased 30 minutes of time on Channel 4 and called a news conference. I gave a 3 minute opening statement and then opened up for questions. I figured that if I came out of that I would do alright. Otherwise it [the collapse of his candidacy] would come early and painless."[9] It worked, and Young became the black to beat.

The 1973 Primary

The various candidates for the 1973 mayoral primary reflected the changing nature of the Detroit electorate. The major candidates were Edward Bell, a former judge and prominent lawyer; John Mogk, a law professor at Wayne State University and specialist in housing matters; Coleman Young, a state senator and former labor leader; Mel Ravitz, a Wayne State University professor and president of the city council; and John Nichols, a former police chief. Each man had a target constituency for the race.

Before Young's entry into the race, Bell had hoped to build on the labor-liberal coalition organized by Austin in the 1969 election. He had resigned his seat on the circuit court bench to spend a year building the campaign team he felt would make him the city's first black mayor. He had solicited support among the black political elite, and had recruited Dennis Archer, a former Wayne County campaign chairman of Austin's successful 1970 secretary of state race. In addition, Archer was a widely recognized Democrat, which would help to offset Judge Bell's Republican party background. John Mogk was depending on his reputation as a housing expert. In those days, Detroit was a prime area for the Department of Housing and Urban Development (HUD) housing scandals. Coleman Young already had strong support in the inner city neighborhoods and among elected black officials. He was also hoping for a split in the white vote among the three white candidates and viewed Ravitz and Nichols as his strongest opponents. While he did not have as much money as the other candidates, he had the support of an angry group of black labor leaders who were still reacting to the UAW's endorsement of Ravitz.

Mel Ravitz represented the "liberal" community and progressive elements within the city. He built his career as an advocate for the poor. In 1953 Ravitz had started working as a "staff sociologist" at the Detroit City Planning Commission. The director asked him to organize and develop neighborhood block clubs as a part of the agency's Neighbor Conservation Program. Neighborhood residents were taught political mobilization and, particularly those in poor communities, became a political network. In a 1968 survey of black and white families, blacks were found to be five times more likely to belong to a neighborhood or block club than whites. When these black clubs began to pressure Mayor Miriani with various demands, he transferred the Community Organization Division to the Housing Commission. The Ravitz team found few friends there, and their activities were effectively terminated. Seven years as a civil servant had yielded Ravitz a reputation as a friend of the black community, and he moved quickly to capitalize on that reputation by declaring himself a candidate for city council. He was the only nonincumbent selected by the TUCL 5 + 1 campaign for Cavanagh. His election cemented his reputation as a white liberal, and during the 1964–66 period, after Patrick resigned from the council, Ravitz became even more important as a communication link to the black community.

Ravitz wanted to run for mayor in 1969 but was asked by Walter Reuther not to enter the race. Reuther thought that the UAW now had a chance to elect a black mayor instead, and according to Ravitz, Reuther made a personal promise to consider him for the job at a later time.[10] Reuther died in 1970, but his black supporter Marcellus Ivory, director, Regional IA, UAW, led the fight for a UAW endorsement of Ravitz for mayor in 1973. The struggle over the Ravitz endorsement was a crisis in coalition politics. Ravitz had paid his dues and bided his time and had been promised an endorsement from no less than Walter Reuther. Yet Coleman Young had friends on the UAW executive committee. Indeed, it had been reported that Young received votes in the straw vote but Ravitz got more actual votes. It is a practice of the executive committee to vote again for the purpose of arriving at a unanimous vote. Ravitz recalled, "[Ivory] went to the mat on that vote for me."[11] The black labor leaders supporting Young had failed to get coendorsement from the UAW, and what emerged was a schism within the black leadership.

Despite such problems, Ravitz was optimistic and hoped to build a coalition of labor and progressives. Having received the endorsement of the UAW and also of some black labor leaders, Ravitz was unbeatable on paper, yet he was defeated. Ravitz believes two factors damaged his campaign: the entry of John Mogk as a second white liberal candidate and Mogk's endorsement by the *Detroit Free Press*, who, according to Ravitz, "knew that Mogk could not win." Even today, Ravitz remains puzzled by the newspaper's endorsement, but he also believes that he miscalculated the racial polarity of the city.[12]

John Nichols led the primary vote, as he was able to claim

most of the white working-class vote. His campaign was primarily directed at white voters, with some limited efforts to solicit votes among elderly inner city residents. He essentially conceded the inner city vote to Young.

Ravitz and Bell faded during the campaign, and their vote totals in the primary were 52,708 and 25,767, respectively. Nichols won the primary, carrying a total of 96,767 votes. Young came in second with 63,614.

The Nichols / Young Confrontation

The final bilateral contest for the mayoralty was classic theater for Detroit politics. It pitted a liberal-labor leader with a reputation for radicalism against a law-and-order candidate with thirty-one years' affiliation with the Detroit Police Department. Many whites saw the race as a last stand before the takeover by an onrushing black majority. The 1970 census showed a dramatic increase in the number of black Detroit residents eligible to vote. Black voters outnumbered white voters 228,800 to 220,000—a historic first, and at that time most commentators were expecting a record turnout of all voters. Although whites were losing their edge in registration, few saw the need to form a coalition with blacks. They supported Nichols because of his tough talk on crime. Senator Young's task was to present himself as a reasonable individual who was not attempting to drive whites from the community. His strategy was to shift the debate from crime to economic development. Although he was opposed to STRESS, a notorious police decoy squad, he had to validate a position as a supporter of law and order.

Nichols' tactic was to concentrate on his record as a crime fighter and what he called his "administrative approach" to city problems. He claimed that Young took a legislative approach, saying, "The administrative approach is to get things done, while the legislative approach means more studying and government by consensus while problems mount up."[13] During campaign appearances, he repeatedly called attention to his experienced background and Young's lack thereof. He also went after the votes of senior citizens. During his campaign, his organization sent 11,000 letters to the elderly. Michael Murray, coordinator of the Nichols campaign, conceded the inner city vote to Young: "Young is going to turn out those voters anyway. Our polls show we have the best shot at the older vote on the issue of crime."[14]

In the two so-called great debates, one in the *Detroit Free*

Press and the second on television, each man attempted to project an image of know-how and authority. In the *Free Press*, Nichols was asked why blacks should vote for him, and his reply sounded the keynote for the remainder of the campaign:

> NICHOLS. I would hope that if there's one white man out there who's going to vote for me simply because I am white, that he would stay home on Election Day. I don't think that the criteria should be how much we can appeal to each other's ethnic group, but rather how much we can appeal to the broad base of citizens. I would hope that the senator shares this belief in that we should be selected for what we stand for and not for who we are or what our accidents of birth may have made us in terms of skin pigmentation.
>
> YOUNG. I have no problem with that general approach. I have said before that I'm running on a program. I espouse no position which is good for blacks which I don't consider to be good for whites and vice versa. I hope to be judged and I expect to be judged based on my programs.
>
> I'm not naive, I know there is polarization in this city. I'm seeking to close that polarization and to unite the differences between the races. And I believe that based on my experience, again in the legislature, the labor movement, and across the spectrum of my public life, I have been able to appeal to all groups.[15]

Herein lies the essence of the 1973 campaign. Nichols could afford to disavow race-oriented support, while Young had to appeal to all groups. For him the strategy was to project his willingness to be evenhanded—hence his pledge to run a 50/50 administration. Young repeatedly denied that his election would represent a black takeover. He said, "I am trying to field a team that has balance—racially, ethnically and politically. A lot of people think that this is a black takeover. But that is not pragmatic." His main target was STRESS. "We want professionals, not Keystone Kops," he said.[16]

Young's strategy of asserting a strong anticrime posture combined with a reform orientation was effective. He was able to characterize Nichols as a single-issue candidate with few economic plans for the city's future. According to *Detroit News* polls, Young led Nichols throughout the campaign.[17] In the first poll of likely voters, taken in September following the primary, Young led Nichols 46 to 33 percent; in early October, the lead was 48 to 42 percent. Just before the election, the percentages were 48 to 43 among likely voters. In the same poll, figures for all voters (regardless of voting intentions) were 47 to 41 percent, 50 to 39 percent, and 52 to 40 percent, respectively. Among the undecided Young held his own; he lost only one percent among likely voters and three among all voters. By the November poll, it was clear that whites needed to turn out a rate 6 percent higher than blacks to equalize the ballots, but the Nichols campaign was not generating that kind of interest among white voters. The problem was compounded by the inexorable increase in black voter registration. It was believed that the 58,000 new registrants that fall were mainly black, so Nichols faced an almost insurmountable task. The 1973 election returns illustrate even greater problems.

Table 3 depicts Young's victory in thirteen of twenty-three districts. Nichols and Young each had three districts in which they won over 90 percent of the vote. In one of these districts, Young achieved a "mixed" vote (that is, 10 to 50 percent white). The significant result was that there were no districts in which either of the candidates scored a marginal win. The district that came closest was divided 59 to 41 percent. Young won by a city-wide total of only 16,741 votes. His relatively narrow margin can be explained by absentee votes. Nichols received 24,529 absentee votes, while Young only received 9,186 votes. It is difficult to determine the true composition of this vote, but it is quite unlikely that poor people or newly registered voters would cast absentee ballots. The overall low turnout (56 percent) did not hurt Coleman Young.

The election results showed how much black politicians had learned since 1969. They now knew how to target their appeals, and they had their man campaign in white districts, even though there was an equal risk in those areas of losing votes as there was in gaining them. This tactic was more than a symbolic gesture, because it helped to show a commitment to both white and black voters that the candidate intended to conduct a fair administration. During and after the campaign, the newly elected mayor reiterated his commitment to a 50/50 administration.

Young's victory was a triumph for bloc voting. Black voters registered their anger at STRESS and at the economic direction of the city in the polling booths rather than on the streets. Young's three-day inaugural celebration marked a new arrival for black voters in Detroit, for now *they* were in charge in the person of Coleman Young. Young responded to their confidence by promising to maintain law and order. In his 1974 inaugural address, the new mayor invited the criminal element to "hit the road."

As the band played, singer Diana Ross performed, Judge Damon Keith spoke, and the crowd cheered for Young's success, the

Table 3. 1973 Election Voting Statistics

District	Raw Vote Totals Young	Raw Vote Totals Nichols	Percent Turnout	Winning Percentage	Ethnicity of District
3	9,117	3,154	43.1	74.2	white
4	3,867	15,084	49.8	79.5	white
5	1,758	21,182	56	92.3	white
6	1,689	22,349	58.6	97.4	white
7	5,869	10,415	50.3	63.9	black
8	16,068	1,209	53.6	93	black
9	10,133	3,035	48	76.9	black
10	7,361	2,724	49.1	72.9	black
11	5,499	3,025	36.7	64.5	black
12	13,319	1,774	48.9	88.2	black
13	12,411	8,314	57	59.8	white
14	14,954	5,445	52.9	73.3	white
15	23,404	3,025	36.7	64.5	black
16	4,485	17,506	47.4	79.6	white
17	5,781	15,275	53.5	72.5	white
18	1,379	18,635	48.5	93	white
19	5,984	13,396	53.4	69	white
20	18,939	1,927	54.4	90	white
21	15,274	5,055	53	75	mixed
22	17,622	975	52.8	94.7	black
23	15,632	910	43.3	93.9	black
24	6,451	2,600	47.3	71.2	black
25	1,907	11,910	52.2	86	white
26	5,567	2,755	55.6	66.8	mixed
Totals*	224,470	191,679			

*Absentee ballots not included.
Source: Detroit Board of Elections Commissioners.

city was reacting to the recession of 1974. The first black mayor of Detroit had inherited a politically rich city but an economically poor one. In his first four years of office, he would have a fiscal crisis in 1975, a near riot, a police confrontation over layoffs and residency rules, and the threat to close Chrysler's Jefferson Avenue plant.

There were other events that took place far beyond the mayor's control. The federal government came to a standstill as the 1974 Watergate scandal preoccupied Congress and the media. The U.S. Supreme Court found that cross-district busing was not required by the Constitution, which meant that whites could escape integrated schools by moving into one of the suburbs. Their relocation increased pressure on remaining whites to help integrate the system. Needless to say, the acceleration of white flight created additional problems for the city's tax base.

Meanwhile, construction of the Renaissance Center, locus of

the new Detroit, hit a financial snag. The project's leader, Henry Ford II, had to scramble to find new investors in the middle of the venture. Automobile production was at a twenty-three-year low, and unemployment was near 10 percent. To top it off, the American Motors Corporation (AMC) announced that it planned to move its headquarters from downtown to Southfield, a suburb contiguous to Detroit. The mayor reacted quickly to this announcement. He stated that AMC "was not subtle about moving from Detroit and we weren't subtle about changing the bidding specification [for city vehicles] to exclude AMC." This type of quick response would prove to be a trademark of the Young administration. Along with ending STRESS in three months, leading a delegation to Washington to make a case for city revitalization before the president, settling the sanitation drivers' strike in four days, and creating the Economic Growth Council (with former leaders of the automobile industry, Lynn Townsend and James Roche of Chrysler and General Motors, respectively), Coleman Young began to implement his agenda of remaking the city.

The first term of Young's administration was a time of testing not only the mayor but also his staff. The normal problems of integrating a campaign staff and the established bureaucracy experienced during any change of administration (particularly those involving ethnic succession) were exaggerated by the media. Those who were charged with following orders, the permanent bureaucrats, resisted the tone, pace, and ethos of the new administration. The first weeks and months were similar to the first part of the Stokes administration in Cleveland. The media spent its time searching for signs of dissension within the new administration. The mayor was constantly interviewed by the press, each reporter getting the same assurances that this administration did not represent a black takeover and that the mayor would not tolerate criminality from blacks or whites.

Meanwhile, the mayor was assembling his governing team. He appointed Elliot Hall as corporation counsel, Mary William as director of the Department of Recreation, Ronald Hewitt as director of Community and Economic Development, Herman Dudley as director of City Engineering, Laura Mosely Jackson as director of Public Information, Agnes Bryant as director of the Human Rights Department, Georgia Brown as director of the Model Neighborhood Agency, Dennis Green as director of Finance, Denise Lewis as director of the Personnel Department, Leon Atchison as director of Purchasing, and Michael Smith as director of Housing. His white appointees included Walter Stecher, director of the Budget Department; John Kanters, director of Transportation;

Creighton Lederer, director of Building Safety, and Phillip Tannian, a Gribbs holdover, as chief of police.[18]

The transition to this staff was a difficult one, raising all the old questions about the qualifications and competence of those new to Detroit's city government. Elliot Hall resigned after only one year, and the mayor appointed Nansi Rowe, a young black lawyer and mayoral liaison to the law department. This appointment drew fire from the legal community (for example, the Wolverine Bar Association, a black law group, opposed it) as well as the bureaucracy. There were claims that Rowe was incompetent and inexperienced. The mayor reacted to the association's attack by escorting Rowe to its annual dinner—his way of communicating that it is he who makes the appointments in his administration. Eventually, he replaced Rowe with Kermit Bailer, a more experienced lawyer. The mayor also had to fire William Lax, the city's airport chief, and, later, Chief Tannian as well. These moves were supplemented with transfers of some appointees and a personal defense of others.

Despite these distractions, the mayor worked desperately to articulate his agenda. His inner staff, which included Malcolm Dade and William Beckham (the deputy mayor), divided their administrative and political duties only to find themselves mired in a major recession, which was triggered, in part, by the oil embargo of 1974. The incoming mayor and his staff were aware of the spotlight on them and the need to appear as if they were "hitting the ground running." Their first task was to establish relationships with the economic elites and, secondly, to present their economic development case to the nation's new president, Gerald Ford.

Meanwhile, they were also fighting off the effects of the recession and preparing the public for tough choices that had to be made in the first fiscal crisis of the new administration. The new charter helped the administrative transition since it gave the mayor greater control, but economic development decisions had to be made with few internal leverage points. Just as the new administration members were adjusting to their offices, Henry Ford II was experiencing financing troubles with the Renaissance Center, then thought to be the anchor of the new Detroit. Uncertain times also provide opportunities to prove that an administration can govern. Under the new Young administration, Ren Cen financing was solved; layoffs and concessions were made to avoid a more serious fiscal crisis; the new city charter was implemented;

the new mayor met the economic elites; appointees who crossed the "edge of the pork chop" were fired; American Motors Corporation did not move its corporate headquarters to the suburbs; the mayor confronted the Detroit Police Officers' Association; President Ford was replaced by President Carter; and memories of the cautious and slow moving Gribbs administration were rapidly disappearing.

The city was treated to a new and faster pace. Coleman Young was clearly at the head of it but was admonished by his physician cousin, Claud Young, to slow down. Dr. Young claims that "Coleman became a model patient and even stopped smoking."[19] During this time Young maintained his political role, continuing to speak out for American cities. He quickly became the most visible black mayor in America, and his support of Jimmy Carter was a key to the Democratic victory in the 1976 presidential race. Yet, the mayor still had his critics.

The 1977 Primary: Coleman Young Is the Issue

By 1977 Mayor Young had a clear track record on which the electorate could evaluate him. After one term in office, he had abolished STRESS, appointed a black police chief, and launched an ambitious affirmative action plan. Throughout his first term he had ordered police layoffs and had faced recurrent budget problems. City residents had seen the mayor in action. Yet, by the time of the 1977 primary, Detroit had become a city with a population majority of blacks, and this change in demographics brought about a change in political issues. Unemployment threatened to cripple the city as it had in Newark and Gary, and fighting crime was replaced by economic revitalization as the most pressing political issue. Mel Ravitz decided not to run, but John Mogk chose to try again, and his campaign featured him as "Walking John," an epithet meant to suggest his acceptability and accessibility to all communities. Thomas Dailey, owner of a successful construction company, changed his residence from Southfield to Detroit in order to run for mayor. The most serious challenge facing Young in this election campaign, however, was councilman Ernest Brown, another black candidate.

Few serious policy issues were addressed in the primary. Dailey attacked the mayor's neighborhood restoration program.

All three candidates attacked Young on the issue of police morale. Brown and Mogk rode in squad cars to demonstrate their solidarity with the police. Brown took credit for formulating the Cavanagh administration's affirmative action policies. Clearly, one of the underlying issues in the 1977 primary had to do with the hiring of black men and women under affirmative action. The media had fostered the impression that new recruits were unqualified. Brown opposed separate promotion lists for whites and blacks in government and advocated a negotiated formula for promotion. Challenger Mogk favored relaxing the residency rules for policemen. Brown also attacked Coleman Young's lifestyle. He blasted the mayor as a street fighting man with "gutter" values, whose so-called swinger lifestyle, Caribbean vacations, and East Side vocabulary were bad examples to the children of Detroit. Mogk also attacked the imperial trappings of the mayor's lifestyle, his support for regional school boards, and his housing policies.

Coleman Young led the primary vote 164,626 to Brown's 63,210 (which was, ironically, only 404 votes short of Young's first primary total). While Young needed only to recruit those who had voted for Mel Ravitz and Ed Bell in the 1973 campaign, Brown needed more than a coalition of Dailey and Mogk voters, for these totals would merely equal Young's primary ballots. Brown would actually have to take votes away from Young as well as recruit new voters if he was to have any hope of winning.

The Young-Brown Runoff

The 1977 mayoral election was heralded as the first black-versus-black mayoral race in the city's history. In 1973 Young had only grassroots support; this time, he had the backing of the Detroit establishment. He was endorsed by Henry Ford II, Coretta Scott King, the UAW's Wayne County Community Action Program Council, the Metropolitan Board of the AFL-CIO, Michigan Teamsters Joint Council 43, the Tuskegee Airmen, the Urban Alliance, Detroit Civil Organization, and the Reverend Jesse Jackson. Now his campaign contributors represented the whole spectrum of power in the city. In turn, the *Detroit News* endorsed him for reelection.

Brown's campaign, on the other hand, never developed a base like Young's. Young had already obtained important and impressive endorsements to go along with his developing national reputation as an effective mayor. He had been selected vice chair of the National Democratic Committee in 1977 and had become recognized as a friend to Jimmy Carter, able to obtain favors from the president as well as provide them. Detroit Democrats recognized Mayor Young as a significant pipeline to Washington, and former aides to the mayor were now serving in the Carter administration.

The contest for mayor also involved questions of style. Brown offered a more traditional image, something paternalistic in the style of "Father Knows Best." The mayor took a pithier viewpoint and tagged Brown a "boy scout" and "white hope." To outdo Mayor Young, it was absolutely necessary for Brown to win most of the white votes as well as those of the disaffected black voters. Yet, he was never able to penetrate the monolithic support group that Young had constructed, and he was singularly unsuccessful at winning support in the mayor's original core group, the inner city districts.

Brown carried most of the absentee vote, as Nichols had in 1973, but he completely failed to make serious inroads into Young's inner city support. (While Brown easily won in white districts 5, 6, and 13, Young was competitive in 4, 7, and 19; see Table 4.) Overall, Brown lost the election by 70,000 votes. The turnout (47.4 percent) was lower, however, than in the Young-Nichols race (55.6 percent), and it was substantially below Young's prediction of a 65 percent turnout. The highest turnout in any district did not quite make 62 percent, in fact, and only occurred in one district. Despite the low turnout, the totals spelled a convincing defeat for Brown, and at the same time added credence to the mayor's emerging image of invincibility.

If the confrontation between Nichols and Young was the politics of race, with many voters selecting their candidate on the basis of his complexion, then the competition between Brown and Young had to do with politics of style. It is difficult to identify any specific issues from the 1977 campaign that had genuine significance in drawing a distinction between the two candidates. Both candidates wanted to revitalize the city, and both opposed crime and were willing to work hard for a safer city. Disagreements between Brown and Young emerged over relatively insignificant particulars about police department morale and the proper rate of economic change in the city. The choice this time was style, not substance. Coleman Young was resoundingly successful at convincing voters that his was a style that got results. Brown could not provide evidence to substantiate the notion that his style would produce more or faster results.

Table 4. 1977 Election Voting Statistics

District	Raw Vote Totals Young	Raw Vote Totals Brown	Percent Turnout	Winning Percentage	Ethnicity of District
3	7,758	1,519	47.4	83	white
4	4,839	4,928	46.5	59.4	white
5	2,341	14,867	49.6	86.4	white
6	1,746	17,316	59.5	90.8	white
7	5,863	6,466	49.7	52.4	black
8	13,754	817	56.7	94.3	black
9	9,212	2,239	49.7	80.4	black
10	6,170	1,648	51.2	78.9	black
11	4,439	1,762	36.4	71.5	black
12	10,525	965	48.9	91.6	black
13	12,319	5,098	57.1	70.7	white
14	12,938	3,777	53.5	77.4	white
15	22,103	2,299	61.2	90.5	black
16	7,738	8,996	46.6	53.7	white
17	7,895	9,576	47	54.8	white
18	1,941	14,061	52.6	87.8	white
19	8,327	6,968	47.5	54.4	white
20	16,429	1,394	55.3	92.1	white
21	13,514	3,439	55.4	79.7	mixed
22	13,949	779	54.3	94.7	black
23	11,964	824	53	93.5	black
24	4,933	1,590	44.6	75.6	black
25	1,603	8,396	52.5	83.9	white
26	9,023	1,964	57.1	82.1	mixed
Totals*	211,323	121,688			

*Absentee ballots not included.
Source: Detroit Board of Elections Commissioners.

The 1981 Primary: A Dearth of Candidates

During Coleman Young's second term as mayor of Detroit, the city's fiscal situation deteriorated while the nation's economy declined and local revenues fell short. Population losses were now beginning to affect the city's tax revenues, and Detroit was on the verge of its worst fiscal crisis since the Great Depression. The mayor's most visible response to the crisis was to establish a blue ribbon committee to review the city's financial situation. The so-called Secrest Committee found that the city had a forecasted deficit of $132.6 million and recommended that the city increase income taxes for both residents and nonresidents who worked in the city.

Many suburbanites who had fled the city to avoid the 2 percent income tax were furious. The proposal called for a one-percent increase in the nonresident rate, up to one-and-a-half percent. Although the increase was only half of the new rate for city residents, it stirred many of the old claims of mismanagement in city government. Some critics claimed that municipal unions had gotten excessive pay rates for membership and that the city was overextended in its expenditures. Now, they argued, the city was asking the residents to bail it out of its difficulties. The unions helped by making wage concessions for the 1982–83 fiscal year. The mayor won the campaign; residents voted to increase their taxes. If the 1977 election had not convinced the public of the mayor's invincibility, the vote on income taxes erased any remaining doubts, particularly in the minds of those who were interested in competing against Young for the job. Detroit's tax increase was an impressive victory given that it took place at a time when most voting on tax rates resulted in lower rather than higher rates.

Most Detroit politicians who harbored ambitions for the mayoralty decided to forgo the 1981 campaign, leaving it open as a race in which an unknown might hope to rise to visibility, perhaps even success. Patrick O'Hara, William Espy, and Perry Koslowski, a civil servant in the Detroit auditor general's office, were the mayor's opponents in the primary, but they were all but ignored by the media, which chose to concentrate on a current gambling proposal and on the feud between Mayor Young and city clerk James Bradley. (Young, a longtime student of election administration, had charged Bradley with poor management of elections and with being absent for critical elections.) The mayor emerged with a landslide victory.

The 1981 Election: Young versus Perry Who?

The real issue in the 1981 general election was whether a runoff was necessary. The mayor had won 71 percent of the vote in the primary against relative unknowns who were underfunded and could not generate issues of interest to the public. After the primary, the mayor said that he did not know his opponent, Koslowski—a remark that generated the media nickname, Perry Who. Not only did the mayor refuse to debate Koslowski, but he essentially ignored the mayoral campaign itself, concentrating his efforts instead on unseating Bradley and promoting a proposal for legalized gambling in the city.

Koslowski had little in the way of campaign funds or organization. He made his bid for the mayor's office from the presidency of a small white-collar union, the Senior Accountants, Auditors and Appraisers Association. With only 330 members, the association was hardly a power base from which to launch a campaign against a popular, incumbent mayor. Koslowski's campaign strategy was to present himself as a management and finance expert. He blamed the mayor for the financial problems of the city and vowed to slash the ranks of political appointees by 50 percent to eliminate the deficit. He also advocated going after tax delinquents. He said, "If I wasn't working for the city, I wouldn't be aware of mismanagement of city funds." And he attacked the mayor's lifestyle, saying, "If there was a white man who spent money like he did, people would attack left and right."[20] Koslowski opposed a current subway proposal, casino gambling, and the mayor's affirmative action program, saying, "The city program isn't an affirmative action program. It is a political payoff."[21] Koslowski hammered away at budget deficits, waste in government, and low productivity. He went after the anti-Young voters and anti-Young unions but was unable to make inroads in the mayor's favorable position with blacks and union workers. The election had in fact become a sideshow to the other issues on the ballot.

The mayor criticized city clerk Bradley for being out of town during the crucial income tax vote, alleged general mismanagement of the election commission, and opposed the election of a county executive for the city's home county, Wayne. During Young's tenure in Lansing, he chaired the Senate Election Committee and became a student of election administration, making him a tough critic of what he considered mismanagement. His feud with Bradley was partly personal and partly technical. And his own candidate, Shirley Robinson-Hall, a former Democratic National Committee member, conducted a lively campaign against Bradley on her own behalf.

When the returns were in, the mayor had won reelection by 63 percent of the vote but lost on his other objectives: Bradley's defeat, an elected executive for Wayne County, and casino gambling. On the subject of casino gambling, he was quoted as saying, "You win some, you lose some, and some you shoot craps or boxcars." Table 5 illustrates the dimensions of Young's reelection victory.

The 1985 Election: A Showcase for 1989?

By the 1985 primary Coleman Young had emerged as more formidable than ever. He had survived an attempt to link him to two major scandals. There was no evidence that the mayor was in-

Elections of Coleman Young

Table 5. **1981 Election Voting Statistics**

District	Raw Vote Totals Young	Raw Vote Totals Koslowski	Percent Turnout	Winning Percentage	Ethnicity of District
3	4,993	729	37.1	87.2	black
4	4,496	5,142	33.8	53.3	mixed
5	3,135	7,898	35.3	71.5	mixed
6	2,281	10,701	41.8	82.4	mixed
7	4,400	3,704	32.2	54.2	mixed
8	8,771	394	42.9	95.7	black
9	6,875	1,193	40	85.2	black
10	3,817	760	38.2	83.4	black
11	3,231	864	29.5	78.9	black
12	6,638	419	37.9	94	black
13	9,278	2,755	43.9	77.1	black
14	9,581	4,865	42.8	57.1	mixed
15	17,276	998	49.7	95.5	black
16	8,148	4,096	38.5	66.5	mixed
17	8,113	5,205	38.8	60.9	mixed
18	1,978	9,011	38	82	white
19	7,059	3,678	37.8	65.7	black
20	11,424	619	41.8	94.8	black
21	9,599	2,082	43.2	82.1	black
22	9,201	324	43.3	94.8	black
23	7,886	319	42.3	96.1	black
24	3,103	935	34.1	76.8	black
25	1,106	5,583	34	85.4	mixed
26	3,550	1,307	42	73	mixed
Totals*	155,939	73,581			

*Absentee ballots not included.
Source: Detroit Board of Elections Commissioners.

volved, but one of his appointees was convicted of bribery. The political picture was further confused when the mayor and his supporters became alienated from the state Democratic party organization. The party had accused the mayor of showing only lukewarm support of the group's nominee for governor. The two sides made up in time for the 1982 election, and the Democrats were able to win the governor's office. In the 1984 presidential primary, the mayor supported Walter Mondale, the eventual nominee, against Jesse Jackson, a black civil rights leader, and this move caused some consternation among young black Jackson supporters. Nevertheless, the mayor stood by his decision. After the election, Young returned to his downtown economic development plan, initiating a campaign to expand Cobo Hall and presiding over the completion of the Robert Millender Center. By then, too, he had amassed a large campaign fund for reelection. Political speculation started early as some journalists wondered if the mayor would run again. Young was sixty-seven years old, and a fourth mayoral term was unprecedented. The 1985 primary was marked by suspense early on, as Young waited until the last minute to file for candidacy. Was he really planning to call it quits? Even the veteran Erma Henderson, president of the city council, misread the delay and filed for the mayoral race. When the mayor filed his papers, she quickly withdrew.

The 1985 primary included a group of political amateurs and perennially minor candidates. An exception was the newcomer, Thomas Barrow, an accountant whose claim to fame was that he was a relative of the great boxing champion, Joe Louis. The Barrow campaign spent most of its time seeking name recognition for its candidate. Barrow's campaign signs were all over town. He sought every opportunity to make himself known to the voter. Nevertheless, Barrow came across as a young, inexperienced yet articulate individual who was staging for a future election.

In many ways the Barrow race was a remake of the 1977 Browne race. Although Barrow avoided Browne's name-calling, he made clever attempts to appear more thoughtful and reasoned in his general approach than the incumbent. In presenting himself through thoughtful and balanced rhetoric, Barrow fell into the same trap as Browne, and he became known as the white voter's candidate. In a *Detroit News* poll, Young received 82 percent of the nonwhite vote to Barrow's 10 percent. Barrow received 51 percent of the white vote to Young's 23 percent.[22] If Browne had been cast as the white hope of the 1977 election, then Barrow's campaign sought to make a sort of second coming. In a city with a highly politicized black electorate, any such characterization doubtless works against the white candidate. Although a candidate might have at least consolidated the anti-Young vote with this tactic, it would almost certainly doom any serious penetration of the hard core Young supporters. As Koslowski's campaign had demonstrated, the combination of the white vote and the anti–Coleman Young vote can yield approximately 35 percent of the total vote—not enough to win an election.

In the 1985 primary Young received 65 percent of the votes to Barrow's 28 percent. In order to defeat the mayor in the general election, Barrow had to hold his 28 percent, plus he had to increase the remaining anti-Young vote by 16 percent. Barrow's only hope was to split the pro-Young voters, a feat no opponent had done in twelve years. A logical strategy against such odds was to take the issue directly to the mayor and thereby create a debate.

Barrow adopted the perennial issues of crime, housing, and

Elections of Coleman Young 117

mass transit. His attack on the construction of a new mass transit program, the People Mover, proved to be a mistake since most of the anti–People Mover sentiment was located in the suburbs—not among Detroit voters. A *Detroit Free Press* poll conducted on primary day found that 68 percent of Detroit voters were in favor of the People Mover. Yet, Barrow made a debate out of its construction, and though he criticized the project, he provided no suggestions about how to solve the severe cost overrun problems. The mayor, on the other hand, concentrated his efforts on saving the project and never even joined the debate. Eventually, Young negotiated a city takeover of the Southeast Metropolitan Transportation Authority (SEMTA) People Mover project. Complicated negotiations involving the governor, the U.S. Department of Transportation's Urban Mass Transit Administration (UMTA), and the mayor of Detroit served to remind voters of the mayor's reputation as a great negotiator.

Young also coopted the crime issue. During the last days of the mayoral campaign, the city was shocked by a series of teenager shootings in the public schools. Young responded by promoting the idea of metal detectors and random searches of students, and he took on the local chapter of the American Civil Liberties Union (ACLU), which had decided to file a suit arguing that such searches were a violation of privacy. Young's reaction to these incidents provided yet another opportunity to show his constituency his seriousness concerning law and order.

Left without any clear issues, Barrow simply could not establish a base for his campaign. Since there were no real rallying points, he could not show in what ways he differed with the mayor on the issues. Barrow's problems were compounded by Young's decision not to debate his opponent, denying the young candidate so much as a platform. The young challenger's campaign began to drift, and it became clear that Barrow, like other general election opponents, would lose badly. He raised the opposition vote by only 4 percent (up to 39 percent). Barrow won in only four election districts (4, 5, 18, and 25). Barrow's opposition to locating a prison in a particular area helped him win his only inner city district (8), yet he was unable to replicate this feat elsewhere in the black districts. Although he did well in districts 7 and 17, the turnout in these districts was low. Table 6 shows the election results.

The general election became a referendum on the Young administration, and generally in such a contest, the incumbent has the advantage. As the contest for mayor continued in Detroit, community attention shifted to the more interesting campaign

Table 6. **1985 Election Voting Statistics**

District	Raw Vote Totals Young	Raw Vote Totals Barrow	Percent Turnout	Winning Percentage	Ethnicity of District
3	3,702	1,208	30.1	74.4	black
4	3,470	4,821	27.8	58.1	mixed
5	2,970	5,318	29.5	64.5	mixed
6	2,265	7,353	31.5	76.4	mixed
7	3,757	2,605	27.4	59	mixed
8	1,175	5,924	32.2	83.4	black
9	5,121	1,907	33.5	72.8	black
10	2,500	733	27.3	77.3	black
11	2,277	1,082	23.7	67.7	black
12	4,400	1,021	27.9	81.1	black
13	6,821	3,468	34.7	66.2	black
14	6,877	2,611	34.7	72.4	mixed
15	13,201	3,613	40.8	78.4	black
16	7,138	4,228	32.5	62.8	mixed
17	6,218	5,285	32.5	54	mixed
18	2,233	6,776	28.7	62.2	white
19	5,573	3,382	30	62.2	black
20	8,665	2,251	33.4	79.3	black
21	7,071	2,864	33	71.1	black
22	6,606	1,466	33	81.8	black
23	5,607	1,203	32.7	82.3	black
24	2,217	1,106	25.8	66.6	black
25	826	3,914	23.6	82.5	mixed
26	2,749	1,212	32.4	69.4	mixed
Totals*	113,439	75,351			

Absentee ballots not included.
Source: Detroit Board of Elections Commissioners.

for city council member where some colorful characters were challenging the incumbents. The mayor continued his feud with city clerk James Bradley. In 1981 Young had supported the candidacy of Shirley Robinson-Hall against Bradley, but Bradley had won. His new candidate, Morris Hood, a former state legislator who carried the endorsement of the local newspapers, the labor unions, and the activist community, was no match for the veteran Bradley. Bradley actually received 66 percent of the vote, a higher number of raw votes and a higher percentage than the mayor's 61 percent. At first glance it would appear that Bradley was more popular than Young, but in fact the city clerk's is a very low-profile office and its staff is among the most knowledgeable about city voting patterns. Bradley benefited from this and from the fact that he was the incumbent. His victory shows that Detroit voters, like voters in other areas, have a habit of returning to the incumbent.

Issues in Mayor Young's Election Campaigns

The classic work of voting behavior, *The American Voter* prepared by the University of Michigan's Survey Research Center, cites three tests for issue-oriented voters. First, the voter must be aware of the issues; second, the voter must indicate a preference; and third, the voter must perceive a difference between parties and candidates on the issues. In Coleman Young's first campaign, the main issues were crime management and economic rehabilitation. The crime prevention issue was somewhat clouded because of a public perception that fighting crime somehow involved racist sentiments. The use of "code words" such as *crime management* to indicate some other meaning occurred in many contexts and predisposed many black voters to interpret Nichols's tough anticrime rhetoric, for instance, as antiblack. They believed (with some justification) that STRESS was directly aimed at the black community. Young was able to say that he would fight crime but that he opposed using the rather hard-core STRESS program as a vehicle. The black community as a whole felt especially vulnerable about crime, for not only were they subject to a higher risk of being crime victims as economic conditions worsened, but they also faced a growing fear of being the innocent objects of police violence. By addressing the problems of the STRESS program directly, Coleman Young demonstrated that equal declines in crime rates could be accomplished by adding more blacks to the police force and instituting a set of programs that relies on visible uniformed police presence rather than explosive television-style raids. Young found that he could label Nichols a single-issue candidate, and once he managed to neutralize the crime issue, he was able to deny Nichols a fairly substantial bloc of voters, one that would have made the election far more competitive.

In Young's first reelection campaign, his challenger, Brown, managed to place the issue of role models on the agenda. It was clear that Ernest Brown wanted to enlist the voters' moral judgments in their ballot choice. He failed, however, to convince them that style was a legitimate factor that was of genuine concern to voters. Moreover, Brown's style simply did not compete with that of the mayor.

In Young's third election campaign, the city's fiscal management was the key issue, yet the mayor's successful bailout strategy had preempted it. Candidate Koslowski failed to elucidate meaningful differences between his proposals and those implemented by the mayor, and therefore was no real challenge.

Race nevertheless continued to be an issue for Coleman Young. Throughout three campaigns, despite any disclaimers, his electioneering had to be directed primarily toward white voters and their fears of black crime. Koslowski used race to differentiate himself from the mayor, unlike Nichols, who had visibly sought to disown racial identity. Brown had been the representative of an emerging black middle class, and as such, he inherited white votes. As a proxy of the establishment and clearly more assimilated into the mainstream than Young, he was a marginally more acceptable candidate to those white voters who feared the ethnic succession before them. Had Detroit been a city with a large white-collar middle class, Brown would have had a vastly improved chance of success. Detroit, however, with its blue-collar middle class, did not appear to find any flaw with the status quo or with the mayor's affluent lifestyle. Young's alienation from the black bourgeoisie, which had taken place before he ever ran for mayor, in time became an asset. If working-class blacks had any doubts about whether the mayor's office had changed Coleman Young, the Brown campaign erased them. By the third election, Koslowski's attempts to unite white voters were doomed due to the sizable emigration of whites from Detroit, which included many white conservatives. The whites who remained were primarily civil servants, the elderly, or simply committed city dwellers. Koslowski got some white votes because he was white, but he also lost some potential black votes because, essentially, he had no other qualities to recommend him—no organization and no history of involvement in community affairs or politics. The fact that Koslowski was against casino gambling did not persuade voters to support him, and it did not influence the outcome of the election.

It would appear that those who voted for Mayor Young, both black and white, were aware of the issues but did not dissociate support for the mayor from support for the issues he articulated. In 1973 he had won on the issues. In 1977 he already had a track record, one that persuaded voters that Young was a capable and effective incumbent. The complete separation of issues and candidates one sees in the 1981 election between the mayoral vote and the proposal votes supports the notion that issues have played a decreasing role in Young's election campaigns. In 1977 he successfully used the power of the incumbent to dictate the pace and tone of the race, in part by decoying Brown into a name-calling contest—an ideal forum for the combative Coleman Young. In 1981 he simply refused to take Koslowski's challenge seriously and thus rejected the possibility of a debate.

In the 1985 election the mayor faced an unknown who had no experience in politics. The real issue in the campaign was the overall economic strategy of the city. Young's opponent, however, Tom Barrow, was lured away with side issues such as the conditions of mass transit, abandoned housing, and the People Mover. Barrow mounted the People Mover cost overrun issue before the city had taken control of the project, and so, wisely, the mayor spent the latter part of the campaign wrestling the project away from SEMTA and making it a city responsibility. Barrow claimed that he would use monies obtained by the city for downtown development for other projects, which indicated his poor understanding of political administration; most federal money cannot be used for purposes other than those legislatively prescribed. Again, candidate Barrow, like his predecessors, failed to show how he would conduct city affairs differently and more effectively than the current mayor.

The 1985 election was significant in that it continued a trend of low turnout for city mayoral elections. Indeed, only 37.7 percent of the registered voters bothered to go to the polls—the lowest turnout since 1951. None of Young's mayoral elections have come close to the 70 percent turnout of the Austin-Gribbs race. Figure 2 shows voter turnout for mayoral elections since 1919.

The socioeconomic components of why people fail to vote have been the subject of various research endeavors. According to these studies, blacks tend to have a low rate of political participation. Nonvoting can signal satisfaction or alienation. Since the newspaper polls consistently find residents approving of the way the mayor handles his job, it is safe to assume that some nonvoters are satisfied with the mayor's performance. Many nonvoters support Coleman Young, so, if they were registered they could very well be persuaded to vote for Young. However, others are disinterested in city politics, and whether or not they represent a reservoir of votes that could be mobilized if needed remains to be seen.[23]

A significant point in luring nonvoters to vote has to do with the preparedness of the average black voter to accept the mayor's word on issues such as fiscal management of the city and economic redevelopment. Such an assurance failed, however, when Young tried to convince blacks to vote for casino gambling. Instead, they took the advice of the clergy and voted by their moral stand, which was consistent with traditional blue-collar ethics. Detroit's economic situation was simply not desperate enough for them to accept legalized gambling, which would enhance city revenues, as a necessity.

Percent of Total Turnout

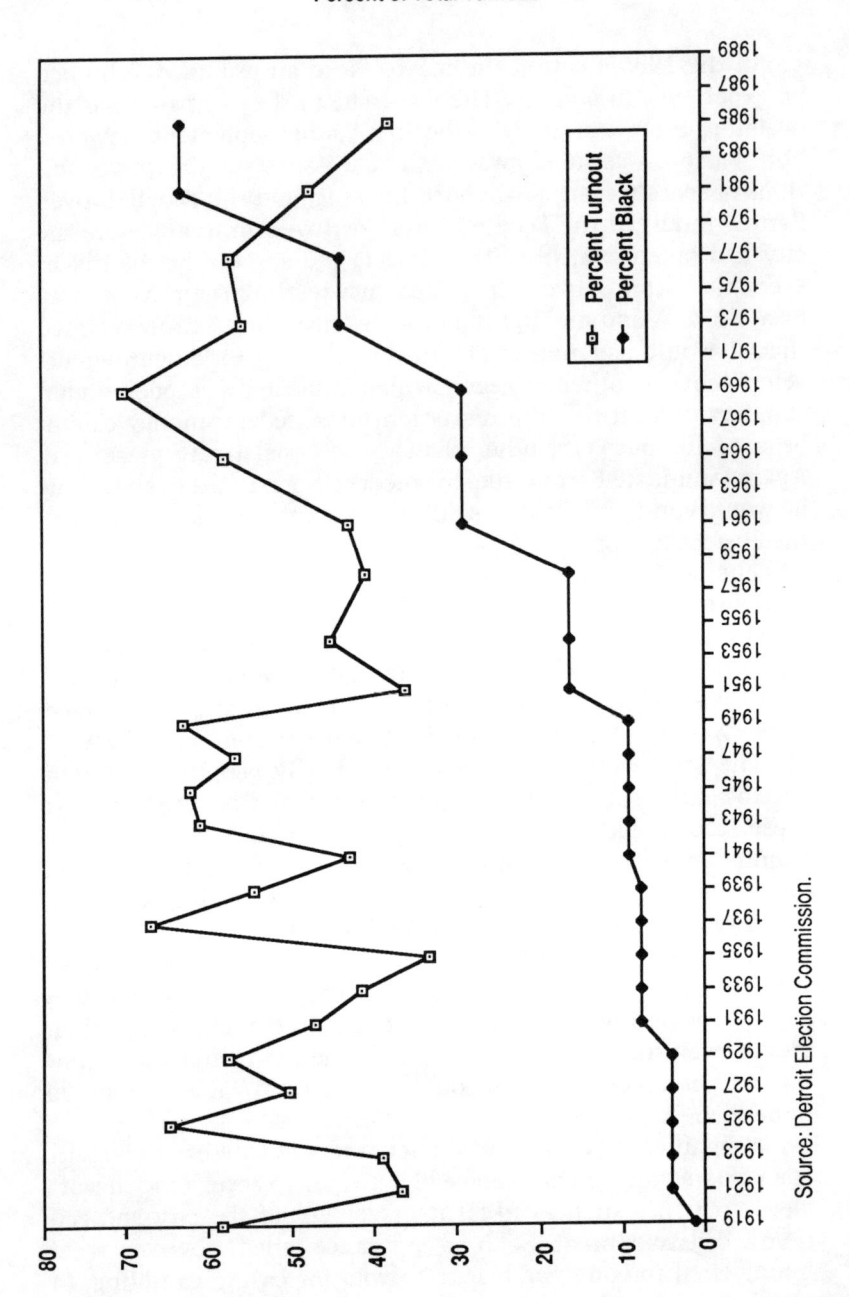

Figure 2. **Mayoral Election Turnout, 1919–1985**

Source: Detroit Election Commission.

On the whole Coleman Young has been successful at assessing what issues are most important to his constituency. He knows when to raise them and how to link them to given projects or decisions in order to obtain the support he deems essential. He is able to define clear differences between his office, the state, and federal governments, and uses these distinctions in political campaigns. His reelections are linked to the lack of a strong and well-financed opponent, as well as to the relative impotence of the Republican party in Detroit. Although issues have been debated along partisan lines in the city, Republicans in state government have tended to keep their views in Lansing and have stayed clear of day-to-day city operations and politics.

As a liberal-traditional Democrat, Young has espoused and practiced a pragmatic style of politics. He has chosen to deal with "bread and butter" issues rather than emotional ones. Aside from making the black politician's traditional appearances and speeches at churches during election campaigns, he has chosen to remain silent on issues that deal even indirectly with religion. On issues affecting equal rights and treatment for all citizens, he has been careful to be explicitly supportive of blacks but has avoided other more radical pronouncements. In fact, he has scorned other local and regional black politicians who appear to be excessively concerned with controversial issues that, in reality, they cannot directly affect. And Young has been extremely lucky. Beginning in 1980, the new and most pressing issue was President Reagan. Detroit voters reacted to their perceived loss of the Washington influence enjoyed by Mayor Young during the Carter administration by rallying for the mayor and reelecting him.

While Detroit voters are not inclined to think of mayoral elections in terms of issues, they are far from unsophisticated. They realize that, white or black, mayoral candidates have little power to actually alter the economic conditions of their daily lives. In the case of Coleman Young, however, they perceive an opportunity for a sort of vicarious participation in the affairs of the city. Such identification is simply not possible with a white mayor, and there are no other compensating benefits to be derived from such a candidate. Hence, an inner city voter might not fully understand the policy debates being argued in the campaign, but he or she is certainly capable of evaluating his or her own situation and making a choice based on experience. So far, Young has been able to produce a visible constituency at the polls. Yet, there is a possibility that inner city voters could become so complacent over time that they fail to go to the polls, and this is the popular mayor's greatest electoral challenge.

Turnout in Detroit Elections

Municipal elections in America are still not the great events that national elections are. Large cities such as Chicago, Philadelphia, New York, and Detroit receive national news coverage, but rarely do the outcomes of municipal elections affect the national scene. Therefore, it is understandable that voters do not view city elections with the same urgency they ascribe to national ones. Municipal elections are viewed as purely local events, turning on purely parochial issues. Detroit, like most large American cities, suffers from a relatively inattentive electorate. Under even the best conditions, a highly competitive mayoral race will rarely recruit a turnout of registered voters that amounts to as much as 75 percent. Viewed as a percentage of the total pool of potential voters, this is, of course, an even less impressive figure. Some commentators have attributed low turnouts to the nature of the American electorate in general. American voters are highly mobile and transient, and rarely do they harbor an abiding concern for political issues. A major election, such as the 1973 mayoral election when race was a supreme concern, will sway many individuals to register and vote. Yet, it is only when they feel threatened that they allow themselves to be mobilized. Once such a weighty election is over, few of these new voters will remain involved with politics. Indeed, some will never be roused from apathy to the polling booth again.

It is a myth that the increase in the percentage of black residents has paralleled a decline in voter turnout. Although blacks have moved from a minority of Detroit residents to a majority during the ten years under examination, voting turnouts remain comparable to those in past years. In 1969, for instance, whites simply outvoted blacks. The percentage of eligible residents registered to vote has varied in response to events, not ethnicity.

Conclusions

While Coleman Young has been able to enjoy the advantages of incumbency, he has also not been seriously challenged in either of his first two reelection campaigns. Certainly his incumbency accords him a competitive edge, and so far, any administrative missteps, scandals, and party factionalism that might have harmed him have failed to help his opponents. His rather uncompetitive opponents have simply selected the wrong issues and have ended up being ignored for the most part. Potentially competitive candidates have avoided confronting Young directly. Perhaps this serves as testimony to the personal qualities of the man, but it also reflects a wariness on the part of the organizational support he commands to abandon the mayor. Many potential candidates read the Brown defeat as a rejection of Brown's personal style, and certainly they have been aware that if one is to defeat Young, a comparable counterorganization must be assembled and effective means found for recruiting *all* anti-Young voters. And total media support is essential to any contender. The combination of forces needed to counter Young is formidable.

The election and reelections of Coleman Young do not necessarily mean that the electorate is in total agreement with either the man himself or his policies. Landslide defeats of Perry Koslowski and Thomas Barrow cannot be taken as a mandate but merely serve as an authorization for Young to continue. Many voters simply like Coleman Young, and, for this reason, a competitive candidate must find effective ways to neutralize the personality factor and force the voters to make choices based on political issues instead. While such a feat is certainly possible, it does not appear to be probable in the near future. Meanwhile, the mayor's steady and visible progress in the economic development arena may emerge as the legacy of his tenure.

5

Decade of Decision
Economic Growth and Change in Detroit

W. W. Rostow published *The Stages of Economic Growth* ten years before Coleman Young was elected mayor of Detroit. This book at first had a limited readership even among urban journalists and administrators since it was directed toward the development of the Third World. During the 1960s many nations that had just achieved their independence were looking for tangible ways to modernize. Rostow's work was more of a developmental approach to economic growth. By setting up a theoretical five-stage hierarchy of development, he attempted to outline the preconditions for growth and explain why some nations were economically ahead of others. Briefly, Rostow's five stages included the traditional society, transitional society, a takeoff stage, a drive toward maturity, and, finally, the age of high mass consumption. One could also read Rostow, particularly his first two stages, and ascertain a possible explanation of the way in which old American cities have developed (and could perhaps be redeveloped).

Rostow's traditional society shares the economic conditions of cities such as Newark, Gary, and Detroit. These cities, once giants of industrial America, were by the sixties being drained of both their populations and their employment opportunities. Many of the skilled trades workers and professionals had moved or were moving to the suburbs, leaving behind cities that had disproportionate numbers of poor, uneducated, and unskilled residents. Even more importantly, the remaining residents had little capital with which to refurbish their cities' infrastructures, nor did they tend to possess an entrepreneurial spirit. Accordingly, the once normal flow of commerce and manufacturing was reduced to a trickle, leaving little work other than in the service sector. The critical difference between Rostow's traditional society and modern urban societies such as Detroit is that one is agrarian and the other is a member of the secondary labor market.

The late sixties and early seventies saw the emergence of black political leadership in these declining industrial cities. The civil rights movement of the sixties and Lyndon Johnson's Great Society had politicized and mobilized black Americans. Rostow's second stage, called the transitional society, more closely resembles the urban problems that confronted the new urban leadership. Urban centers began to experience white flight, the migration of industrial jobs to the Sunbelt, and rising costs of city services as a noose closing slowly and strangling their future. The cities' foster children, the suburbs, now emerged as sharp competitors for industry and office space. Some Southfield office buildings were deliberately located just across the Eight Mile Road boundary to the Detroit city limits in order to take advantage of the Detroit city market while maintaining a Southfield address and low taxes. The manufactories of the new emerging high tech and information-based economy no longer needed to remain inside the downtown area. Work had become mobile, and people could stay in the suburbs. Implicit in these developments are the seeds of discontent as well as the preconditions for economic leadership that could be used to rally the political support needed to launch a recovery.

Detroit: Industrial City in Transition

As one of the nation's aging urban centers, to outsiders, Detroit appears to be worn out. Recently, the city's downtown has seen retail closings. Dayton-Hudson Company, a department store chain that was started on Woodward Avenue, no longer operates its downtown store. Ironically, the Detroit central business district (CBD) has become a victim of the industry it was created to serve—the automobile industry. Kent Robinson has concluded:

> The CBD and its inherent functions ... thrive on a location characterized by high-density development and close proximity of facilities. In other words the automobile industry operated most efficiently in a spread out landscape while the key attribute of a healthy CBD is its compactness. When the two are expressively incorporated ... economic survival of the CBD may be severely threatened.[1]

The construction of such outlying shopping centers as Northland (1954) and Fairlane (1976) in the span of 22 years had led traffic away from Detroit and caused familiar discount stores such as Woolworth to abandon their downtown locations. Two supermarket chains, Kroger and A & P, closed most, if not all, of their stores inside the Detroit city limits. Unemployment in the metro Detroit area continued to hover at 15 percent throughout the first Reagan term, finally abating in Reagan's second term when it dropped to 9.1 percent. Unemployment figures in the inner city climbed to twice that of the rest of the region, and the entire Midwest declined as an important American manufacturing center, which hit Detroit very hard. The Big Three automakers, once pacesetters for American industry, continued to find themselves challenged by Japanese imports, high labor costs, and an unpredictable national economy.

In recent years, the largest of the Big Three, General Motors, signed a joint automobile manufacturing agreement with its chief Japanese competitor, Toyota, to make small cars in California. One of the biggest prizes in automobile manufacturing plant development, GM's Saturn project, went to Tennessee. Indeed, other regions are challenging Michigan for its dominance in the car making business, yet Michigan remains in the competition as a new GM plant settled in Detroit. Moreover, the state has lured foreign automobile makers to Michigan. Ford and Chrysler have recently experienced great financial recoveries, but only Chrysler plans to build new facilities in Detroit. In the mid-eighties, another important Detroit company, Burroughs Corporation, merged with Sperry-Rand and created a new company called Unisys. In addition, they have indicated that they plan to expand their Detroit world headquarters building.

Detroit-based corporations have been targets for takeover battles. General Dynamics, a military weapons maker, has faced difficulties for years, including being the subject of a 1985 congressional investigation for overpayment on a navy contract. The company was reinstated after a brief hearing. American Natural Resources (ANR) succumbed to a takeover bid from Coastal Corporation of Houston, and the Stroh's Brewery Company now makes its beer in modern facilities outside of the state. Chrysler has taken over the ailing American Motors Corporation. Yet, there are hopeful signs of economic transformation for the city. In terms of its fiscal health, Detroit has cleared away the rubble of several years before and now is a city with interesting potential. Visually, the economic signs are mixed; some areas indicate progress; others remind an observer of the serious problems that still linger. It is difficult to truly gauge the city's long-term potential, yet a review of its human capital and financial resources provides a reasonable starting point for speculation.

Job Losses over the Decade

Job losses in recent years have brought employment in Detroit to its lowest level in thirty years. Most Detroiters watched the highly publicized closings of Hudson's downtown store, the Detroit operations of Stroh's Brewery, and the Vernor's bottling plant, but few were aware of the silent job losses that were occurring simultaneously throughout the city's economy. The loss of former jobs has affected the image and economic reputation of the city to be sure, but the real loss has been in the area of those labor-intensive industries (such as steel and automobile manufacturing) that now seem permanently lost to the city. The census reported a 21 percent loss in industrial operations during the five-year period from 1977 to 1982.[2]

Manufacturing is the key to any city's growth. If there is to be a big city, then there must be a product. For years Detroit has been synonymous with automobiles; it is called the Motor City. When Mayor Young first took office, there were 251,500 vehicle and auto equipment manufacturing jobs in the city. In 1983 there were 906,000 such jobs in the entire nation, but the automobile industry had been dealt a blow by the 1974 Arab oil embargo, which changed the face of the industry—and Detroit. For the first time American citizens realized the depth of their dependence on foreign oil. The subsequent discovery of fuel efficiency as a criterion to be used in automobile purchase decisions, and the immediate availability of fuel-efficient cars from Japan, would change the complexion of new automobile sales.

The security of the American autoworker, long considered among the highest paid and best organized and represented of American workers, was being threatened for the first time. There were layoffs (eventually followed by callbacks of some displaced workers); new, "real" growth had virtually ceased, and this trend served to halt, or at least seriously impede, the long-standing tide of immigration to the city of Detroit. In due time workers emigrated to the new industrial plants being developed in the Sunbelt. Indeed, California manufacturing grew by 17 percent during the period from 1977 to 1982.[3]

The availability of blue-collar jobs that paid a wage otherwise unavailable to the person who had neither higher education nor a skilled trade was for many years the magnet that attracted Detroit's population. Without this magnet, the city holds no lure for the unskilled laborer. Indeed, the paucity of blue-collar jobs becomes an insurmountable barrier to the underclass.

Although industry has doubled the number of jobs in Detroit, the real direction of industry is toward using fewer workers and more machines in the production of cars, and to conduct fewer operations in Detroit. Although the Japanese are willing to open plants in the Detroit area, the number of jobs will not allow generational replacement of workers; that is, children of automobile workers cannot expect to find jobs on the assembly line as they once could. General Motors, Ford, and Chrysler are very well aware of the changes affecting their employees, and they have attempted to soften the blow in various ways. They have allocated new manufacturing facilities to the area and are constructing new office space and new residential housing. The auto companies have joined the UAW in offering retraining for laid-off workers. Such actions are attempts to help the city make the transition to a service economy.

Although Detroit is not a leader in finance, real estate, or insurance, it has its share of white-collar service industries. In 1973 there were 75,000 white-collar service jobs in Detroit; by 1985 the number had grown to 95,000—a relatively modest rate of growth. Detroit does not have the population or a favorable tax environment to compete with New York or Chicago for white-collar service industries, yet if one considers its blue-collar service jobs, then Detroit is clearly competitive.

Government employment is another source for jobs that Detroit has yet to cultivate. In 1973 there were 231,000 government jobs in Detroit, and in 1985 the figure had dropped to 212,000. Employment in city government has also declined. In 1979 the city of Detroit employed some 25,000 persons; by 1985, this number had decreased to 19,000. Al Taubman, a leading shopping mall developer from Detroit, compares Detroit with Washington, D.C., another predominantly black city. He has observed that "in Washington, 720 jobs out of every 1,000 are white-collar jobs. The national average is 530 and [Metro] Detroit is below that because we don't have large financial institutions, large governmental institutions, or a large high tech industry."[4] As Taubman has pointed out, blue-collar workers might share the purchasing power of their white-collar cohorts, but they buy different things. Purchasing choices often dictate the location of retail outlets and malls. In other words, the lack of an income mix accelerated the decline of Detroit as a retail center.

Since the beginning of the Reagan administration, there has been a slowdown in the growth of government payrolls at all levels nationwide. Midwest regional offices of the federal government—most of them located in Chicago—have assumed greater and greater responsibility, and, with it, the personnel necessary to administer it. These jobs tend to attract college graduates, particularly liberal arts majors. With expansion in government virtually halted in Detroit, the city has a difficult time retaining these college-educated young people as residents. The city inevitably expends its resources in training its young people, who then take their expensively developed skills and go where the jobs are.

The Detroit area has an important retail trade industry. Oddly enough, since the 1960s, there has been an increase in trade jobs. In 1973 there were 323,000 jobs in retail trade in the Detroit area, and this number rose to 353,000 by 1983. Although parts of the downtown shopping area have been closed down, the city still holds its own in the retail trade industry. Retail sales increased 10.4 percent in 1983, following the lowest recorded increase in 1982 of 8 percent. Indeed, economist Wilbur Thompson, an expert on Detroit, argued as early as 1965 that the city needed a diversified economy like those of Chicago and Boston.[5] Others pushed for expansion as a way to save the city, suggesting that Detroit boost its convention trade, tourist dollars, and light commercial establishments. Indeed, there has been an increase in service jobs in Detroit. In 1973 there were 273,000 service jobs, and by 1985 the figure had grown to 418,000.

From Motor City to Service Hub

The transition from manufacturing to a service economy is never a smooth one. There is always a problem of matching jobs and workers and a disparity between wages in the manufacturing industry and those in the service industry. Detroit's solid industrial base makes it one of the leaders in hourly wages. In 1973 the hourly wage average in Detroit was $5.61, and by 1985 it had risen to $13.40—$3.98 more than the national average. This may explain why Unisys and Stroh's have situated their headquarters but not their production lines in Detroit.

Detroit residents are perhaps too wage-conscious to accept the transition to a service-dominated economy, whose wages are inevitably less. Having had manufacturing as the lifeblood of the city, Detroit has amassed a huge number of workers who expect high wages. Although Michigan continues to lose auto industry jobs, it still manufactures 37 percent of the nation's cars, and Detroit is still at the center of that industry. As the city enters the robotic revolution, there is no reason why it must lose its edge in heavy industry while it slowly diversifies.

As of this writing, there exists no detailed study of the emerging service economy of Detroit. Part of the reason for this lack has to do with the fact that there is no central collector and processor of such information. The U.S. census data remain the information base upon which most commentary depends. The census, taken every ten years, may not be sensitive enough for the fast moving service economy planners. If and when a new occupational group gains hegemony in this city, there will be no way to systematically track it. Urban planners, developers, and researchers must review the city work force against various growth opportunities available to the city if they are to have a hand in directing the city's economic future. Differentiation within the service sector is a particularly significant goal, since the data that exist show there is growth in service jobs in Detroit.

In *The Emergence of a Service Society*, economists H. Browning and J. Singlemann have divided industries into three types: extractive (such as mining) and transformative industries (such as construction and manufacturing) and distributive services.[6] Distributive services may be further subdivided into transportation/communications, wholesale and retail trade, producer services (finance, insurance, and real estate, for example), professional and business services, social services (health, education, and welfare), and personal services (domestic, lodging, repair, and entertainment). According to Browning and Singlemann, distributive services imply the simple delivery of goods to consumers. Producer services are related to property, while social services deal with collective goods. Personal services are supplied separately to the individual consumer on an as-needed basis.[7]

Thomas Stanbeck, an economist, has modified this typology to include a separate category for retail services and nonprofit services. In the analysis performed by Stanbeck and his coinvestigators, several cities revealed shifts from extractive and transformative industries to various service industries.[8] Neither the census data nor the 1984 *Economic Fact Book* shows the dramatic shift from extractive and transformative industries observed by Stanbeck and his colleagues in their national study. Nevertheless, a trend is evident. Detroit's share of government jobs is stable, but the number of service jobs has increased—a direct response to the decline of the automobile industry and the rise in government welfare programs. Despite the expansion of such programs,

Decade of Decision 133

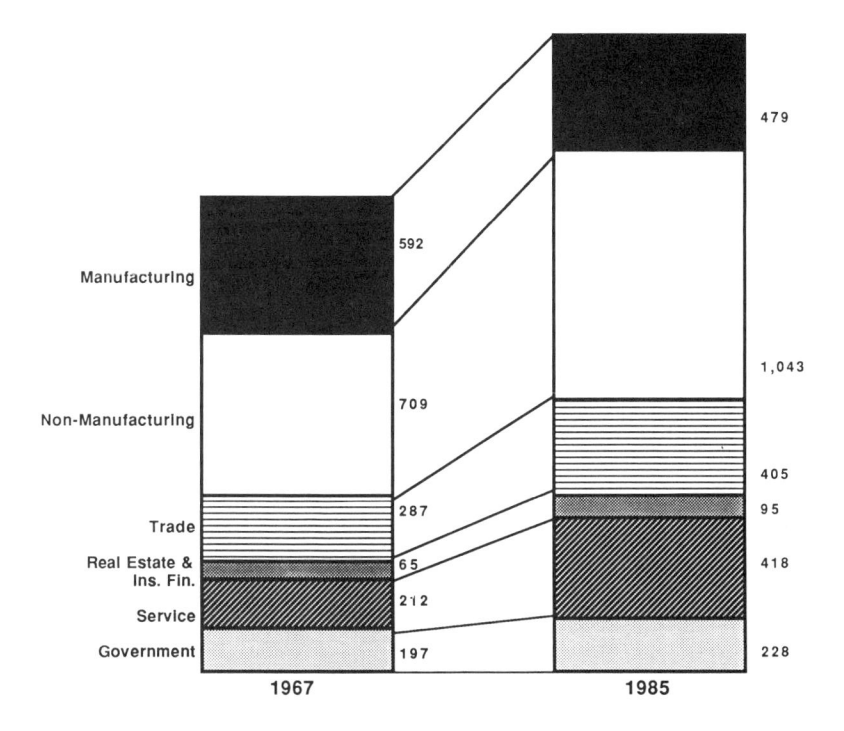

```
                        479
Manufacturing    592

                        1,043
Non-Manufacturing 709
                        405
Trade      287          95
Real Estate &  65       418
Ins. Fin.
Service    212
Government 197          228

           1967         1985
```

Source: Figure constructed from data in annual editions of Economic Fact Book for the Detroit Area.
* Jobs in thousands (latest available data)

Figure 3. **Job Shifts in Metropolitan Detroit, 1967–1985**

the rate of growth of government jobs slowed because of the recession of the late seventies and the growing taxpayer revolt over the cost of government.

The most dramatic shift in Detroit's economy has been in the area of producer services. Detroit has simply not been competitive in planning, management, financing, marketing, legal, or accounting services, in part because the city's economic elite have refused to recognize Detroit's potential as a center for such activities, and thus have not backed any moves toward more producer services for the city. Another impediment has been the lack of a suitable work force and the amenities to attract workers from other areas. Industries that recruit heavily among college-educated twenty- to forty-year-olds have not seriously considered Detroit or its suburbs as a viable location. Figure 3 shows the transition process now under way in Detroit, comparing 1967 and 1985 figures.

Clearly, there has been growth in nonmanufacturing and in

the service industries in Metro Detroit. Government has grown, but less dramatically than the service industries. The data tend, however, to distort Detroit's true condition. Most of the service industries are located outside of the city limit, although most of them consider themselves to be located in Detroit. Suburban hotels, for example, advertise themselves as located "near Detroit." The *Economic Fact Book*'s decision to lump data together for the entire metropolitan area was a deliberate one.

Some urban planners believe that Detroit could become an important center of regional government, although the view is not shared by many Detroit politicians, who believe that services are a threshold for urbanizing the suburban community. Development will be forced back into the inner city. Is Detroit in danger of becoming a white-collar town? The occupational profile of the city may be changing, but still Detroit lacks the income and educational mix to complete a transition to a service-oriented economy. To accomplish a true transition, the city would have to restructure its educational system and its labor market. Both the public school system and the universities would have to change their emphases. Presently, they are biased toward existing industries. The shift of the public schools to a more technical emphasis would only be undertaken if local firms would support the subsequent labor market. Firms not related to the automobile industry certainly have the wherewithal to compete for school graduates.

The economic future for Detroit proper may lie in the area of light manufacturing rather than in the "heavy metals" industry, which remains as the city's foundation. The question is how to move toward a new type of industry. Detroit has been virtually wed to the heavy metals industries, and now the association is getting old. Detroit is in a sense obligated to stay with its old industry until that industry dies, or else the city must nurse the worn-out structure until it returns to sound health. Meanwhile, city leaders have to face a set of serious questions. Should the city promote service jobs to fill the gap left by the dwindling manufacturing jobs? What incentives should the city offer to induce manufacturing to locate there? What are the long-range effects of tax abatements on the city's revenue system?

Wages in the Detroit labor markets, both primary and secondary, have benefited from the high wage settlements produced by the auto industry. The three automakers have bid wages up in times of expansion and employment, and other employers have had to match or approximate them in order to find and attract workers. A transition to a lower paying economy overall, what is now the secondary market, involves reorientation.

Work in a Transition Economy

Economic changes always contain disruptive elements. There are inevitable mismatches of worker skills and technology, worker attitudes and company commitment, and general uncertainties about the future. The concept of work is shaped by existing cultural definitions and work models. Work in Detroit is different from work in Miami, although both are presently involved in the convention business. In Detroit the best jobs are still in the auto industry. Accordingly, as they disappear, school graduates look for alternative yet comparable sources of income. The service industry has never been high paying, nor has it been free of the influence on its working environment created by the proximity of the auto industry. An attendant's job at Ford Hospital is not in the same wage arena as an auto assembly worker's, yet it reveals certain aspects of the general work atmosphere created across the world of work by the auto industry in the Detroit area. That wage is markedly different from a hospital attendant's in a region that has no extractive or transformative industry from which to make such a gain.

Economists have spent a good deal of time studying the effects of a transition economy on workers' expectations. How does one prepare to hold a job in which one will have a lower income and more modest aspirations than one's parents? What is the impact of downward mobility on the working class? Do its members adapt or drop out of the job market? Surprisingly, there are no studies of Detroit's economy that have addressed these problems directly. Instead, researchers have focused on the impact of economic change on auto manufacturers and labor relations. A case can nevertheless be made that whatever happens to Detroit's automobile industry will also change the expectations of workers in other, unaffiliated jobs as well.

The Other Detroit: The Underclass

Michael Harrington's *The Other America* chronicles the existence of entrenched poverty in an otherwise affluent United States twenty-five years ago. A similar study of Detroit will show that Detroit has always had its poor, and they have nearly all been on the city's East Side. As the city's black population increased in percentage, it also exhibited a lower mean income. The core of the city's underclass began to acquire new members rather than lose members to employment and social mobility—a trend that first appeared in the late sixties. Before 1960 the core did not show up in the unemployment figures, because people of the underclass were drifting into the nebulous official status of nonpersons. In the 1970s living off the street and by the help of relatives who were welfare recipients became a means of survival in an economy in which some people were no longer able to cope. Official statistics on unemployment show a steady rise, then a leveling off—a poor indicator of the growth and welfare of the underclass.

In the black community, the burden of poverty fell on black female heads of households. Such families place entire generations of individuals at risk. Since poverty increases the incidence of school dropouts, pregnancy among teenagers, crime, and so forth, an uneducated member of this group is left with few resources to compete in a transition economy and faces an even fiercer challenge than the worker who must adapt to a new occupational structure. Table 7 shows the drastic rise in social welfare levels from 1973 to 1986 in Detroit and Wayne County.

The figures indicate sharp increases in the number of Detroit residents who received benefits from the social welfare system. Coupled with the debilitating effect of this dependency on work attitudes and aspirations, such a labor force is not an attractive one. Increasingly, employers are looking for a more glamorous, better educated, and more mobile work force. Accordingly, a political elite planning for the future of Detroit must plan around the city's human liabilities and highlight its labor market's assets. Without an existing high tech population, it is difficult to induce high tech workers to move to the city. Overcoming barriers to economic growth requires more than simple resolution; it involves replacing the population.

Barriers to Economic Growth

The current economic development project in downtown Detroit provides only a staging position for the city. The economic and political leadership must decide how it plans to market the city. What are Detroit's comparable advantages over neighboring cities? According to Rostow, takeoff is only possible when there are buildups of capital, appropriate arrays of labor skills, and a

Table 7. **Detroit Welfare Recipients, 1973–1986**

Year	Program	Number of Cases	Number of Individuals	Percent of Population
1986	Wayne County (AFDC)	88,816	271,741	12.4
	Detroit (AFDC)	72,270	221,117	20.3
1973	Wayne County (AFDC)	82,417	282,150	10.5
	Detroit (AFDC)	65,933	225,720	14.9
1986	Wayne County (GA)	54,677	66,274	3.0
	Detroit (GA)	48,254	58,488	5.4
1973	Wayne County (GA)	29,179	33,127	1.2
	Detroit (GA)	26,261	29,814	1.9

Source: Michigan Department of Social Services, Publication of Statistics, 1986.

launching technology. Detroit currently lacks a magnet service industry that can serve as a starting point for the city's growth. It has overinvested in narrowly trained assembly workers (thus, has limited human capital) and in low-income housing, and it has underinvested in work force diversity.

Detroit's economic elite has failed to stir the imagination of the general population. Rostow foresaw the rise of a new class of entrepreneurs as a precondition to takeoff, but in Detroit's case, the city's black economic elite lacks sufficient capital to truly influence the direction of the city's economy. Also, it lacks a vehicle for aggregating capital. Robert Millender recognized this in 1977 when he suggested politics as an alternative; he observed, "I don't see blacks building a factory like Ford's or a major department store like J. L. Hudson's, but we do have the capacity to exercise power."[9] The city has, in effect, overinvested its talent in the public sector. The upper middle and middle classes gained socioeconomic prominence with the expansion of government in the sixties and seventies. Accordingly, most of the city's human capital has been invested in social welfare, education, and government—industries that are currently in a slump. There are no growth areas at the present time in Detroit, nor are there clear stages for the ascendance of a new elite.

The city also lacks the necessary buildup of capital to provide for the expansion of nonmanufacturing industries. With changes in the laws governing banking and financial investments, the city remains at the mercy of the marketplace for its resources. Financial resources exist in the metropolitan area, but the percentage invested in economic development projects in Detroit is small. No one can predict for certain which, if any, technology has the capacity to launch Detroit back into economic orbit. At present the city's economic decisions continue to be made by what might be called benevolent investors and the mayor.

Benevolent Investors and the Ideological Truce

The 1967 riot not only changed the political landscape of Detroit, but it also served to waken business communities to acknowledge the extent of alienation among black Detroiters. Blacks were burning their own communities. Local authorities were unable to put down the rebellion, and federal troops had to be brought in. The nation saw Detroit as a city out of control. The business community reacted quickly to what they regarded as threatening anarchy. First, it seemed clear to the so-called economic elite that they had been misled by black leaders into believing that black elected and labor officials could quell any race rebellion. The collapse of black superintendency was an important lesson for the business community, reminding it in the harshest of ways that cooperation with grassroots leaders is essential.

The newly organized New Detroit Committee became a vehicle for communication between various city groups. J. R. Hudson, head of Hudson's department store, served as the first chairman, and former councilman William Patrick served as the first president. The committee included so-called militants such as Frank Ditto (a self-styled community leader), corporate executives, church leaders, and politicians. New Detroit was designed to be a forum for venting dissatisfactions, complaints, and ideological arguments. The old black leadership (labor leaders, for example) was dissatisfied, however, with equal treatment accorded their rivals, the grassroots or militant black leadership. The older group saw the new group as interlopers and talkers who lacked organization—a conflict that was played out in the dispute over a grant to Reverend Cleave's organization. To the surprise of whites, the new black leadership opposed the grant.[10] This and other confrontational incidents, which reflected the need of the older, more traditional leadership to discredit the new group, created conflict within the committee. Conversely, black militants needing to prove that they were not selling out by participating in the meetings sought to appeal to their supporters by defiant rhetoric ("telling white folks off"). Lack of a leadership consensus and a true agenda led white members and corporation sponsors to rethink the mission of New Detroit and their mode of relating to black leadership. The depoliticizing of the New Detroit program included corporate heads assigning subordinates to attend meetings for them, downplaying personalities, professionalizing the staff, and transforming the organization into a service/lobbying group.

Ideological truces are important in the conduct of economic affairs. A truce is defined as a cessation of hostilities, a willingness to negotiate peace and plan for the future. In the original New Detroit Committee, action got bogged down in a war of words and turfs, and to move forward, Detroit needed to have a truce between the largely white business community and elected black leaders. Moreover, the economic conditions that led to the riot continued to haunt the city. A decision was made to create other vehicles for economic development and change besides New Detroit. Henry Ford II's contribution was to build the Renaissance Center as an anchor for the redevelopment of the downtown area. Financier Max Fisher contributed by establishing the Detroit Renaissance, an organization of business leaders, to facilitate planning for redevelopment.

In recounting the events that led to the creation of the Detroit Renaissance, Fisher asserted, "There was a downward trend. Everyone knew something had to be done." He recalled how the newly elected mayor, Coleman Young, had impressed the new group, saying, "He seldom missed a meeting. He was very involved. He used [Detroit Renaissance] as a forum for his dreams for the meetings and decisions." The fact that Young attended the group's meetings and avoided using them for ideological catharsis, coupled with his ability to follow through on ideas, convinced business leaders that the mayor was a man with whom they could work. They discovered that Coleman Young had one agenda: the redevelopment of Detroit. He was not interested in reaching a higher office or grandstanding at their expense. This was evident when the mayor and members of the Move Detroit Forward Committee, which included many Detroit Renaissance members, made their famous trip to Washington in 1975. According to Fisher, the group discovered Young "was able to talk to people" (meaning really that he was prepared to negotiate with a Republican president), and he was not afraid to say, "'I need your help on these things.' And he did not mind putting pressure on [people from whom he asked favors.]."[11] In other words Coleman Young was prepared to announce an ideological truce and solicit the local economic elite's assistance in rebuilding the city.

The political left believes that alliances such as that between the mayor and business community always facilitate the agenda of the businessman at the expense of the masses. Indeed, a recurring theme in political science literature is whether a mayor, particularly a black mayor, can act as a countervailing force against a well-organized and determined business elite. This argument builds on the notion that white ethnic mayors are mere puppets and therefore black mayors can expect to be treated even less deferentially by the economic elite. Given their entrenched interest, this elite can easily control the urban redevelopment agenda. For political scientists and journalists who buy into the argument, Young's decision to reconcile with the elite group confirms his acquiescence to a so-called corporate strategy for downtown redevelopment. Such an interpretation is appealing, but it is only partially correct.

The choice for Coleman Young was not whether he should work with the business community or not but how. He could have taken Cleveland's mayor Dennis Kucinich's tactics of confronting the business community. Although Young comes from a populist tradition, he made a rational, albeit risky, decision to facilitate the business community reinvestment in the city. Young's decision, however, was not so simple. For Coleman Young, a man with no personal ties to the business community or for that matter to downtown development, the early part of his first administration was not only a time for personal and political actualization but also a time for the business community to observe his operational style. And during this period, they delayed investment decisions. Young was the one in the hot seat because he hoped to get reelected, and, to do so, he must show evidence of economic change. He had to establish his ambitions, style, and amenability early.

Equally important to Young's willingness to abide by the ideological truce was the personal impression Young left on the elite. In economic discourse, norms of affinity are not absolute requirements, but they help soften the interaction between unequals. In cases of black/white interactions, racial anxiety can be eased by simple cordiality. In the early period of the Coleman Young administration, in other words, it was important that members of the business community liked Coleman Young. This does not mean that they would invite him into their homes or into the social elite, but rather they needed to be able to trust him. Today they remain effusive in praising him for his efforts to revitalize the city. They were willing to recognize his intelligence and his ability to understand their economic limits. For example, Peter Stroh recalled an incident in which he informed the mayor of the company's decision to close the outdated Detroit Stroh's Brewery and lay off its workers. According to Stroh, Young's response was, "Now you know how I felt when I laid off 600 policemen." Young's understanding of the marketplace (in this case, Stroh's needed to expand and move to survive) has served to enhance

Young's relationship with investors reacting to competition. His ability to communicate is equally as important as anything the mayor can do organizationally and politically for the business community.

Mayoral Leadership and Economic Growth

The combining of mayoral politics with economic growth policy is something like making salad dressing. One takes vinegar, oil, water, and some herbs and spices. If the mixture is well shaken, it makes a good dressing. Left in the bottle, undisturbed, however, the herbs and spices will settle to the bottom, and the oil, vinegar, and water will separate. Over the years, the mayor has been like a bottle shaker, constantly trying to make things happen. In 1980, for example, the city sued the U.S. census for undercounting city residents. It asked the court to invalidate the census and adjust the figures, and its leaders were alert enough to know that if Congress, in its wisdom, linked many of its grant-in-aid programs to census data, then population was certainly an asset, or what Charles Reich has called "new property."[12] Indeed, the city won in district court but was overruled in appeals court. It was a bold act, nevertheless, and it put the powerful Census Bureau on notice that Detroit was not going to be "robbed of its federal funds"—a major source of capital for the city and, hence, job-related. Most politicians make a promise to create new jobs, but voters often expect Detroit's mayor to present new ideas, bringing in new industry and erecting new downtown buildings to bring more traffic to the downtown area. Translating promises into realities requires absolute control over the elements of economic growth and development, and certainly Mayor Young has never had control over all the elements. His real contribution has been in his ability to negotiate with economic game players. If he has concocted "salads," then they are the direct result of his steady willingness to shake things up.

Competing for jobs has meant presenting Detroit's work force in its best light. Selling industry and commercial complex developers on locating in Detroit has meant obtaining approval for tax abatements, zoning changes, and certain amenities. Creating retail traffic has been an even more difficult task, as downtown stores have fallen farther and farther behind suburban malls in floor traffic as people increasingly prefer driving directly to a shopping center and parking free while they spend their dollars in these modern replacements for city centers. Inducing people to shop at downtown retail stores would by now require a public image of downtown police visibility and protection, correct analysis of the desirable kinds of shops, and the creation of magnet events, any organized public activity intended to draw people into the downtown area.

For black politicians, the politics of economic growth amounts to finding ways to enlist white entrepreneurs' investments and means to reassure them that their properties will be protected. This is a process like clearing the underbrush—the tangles and thickets of mutual misunderstanding and neglect on both sides. In this endeavor the mayor must be a point man. He must set the pace of negotiations and be available as final arbiter in intrastaff disputes as well as those between his staff and the developers and investors. As Millender observed, "This system is based on a decision maker. There is no question Coleman Young is a decision maker who can affect the welfare of blacks and others in the community."[13] Unfortunately, Detroit faces a disadvantage in these situations, for it has less leverage than the outsiders it hopes to win. The city is now almost a beggar, even though its representatives still make their bids and presentations in three-piece suits. Robert Woods has called this practice "municipal mercantilism." Detroit must compete with other cities who also desire commercial and industrial development. The most entrepreneurial city, the one that makes the best offers, usually wins the economic prize.

The process of municipal mercantilism also exposes the city's vulnerable areas and weak suits. Detroit's shortcomings are highly visible, and the city has had to make its presentations to developers fully exposed. Aside from being old, the city's salary and benefits structure is not consistent with the national marketplace. The mayor cannot advocate lower wages and personnel reductions for the private sector, nor can he endorse plant modernization, which is necessary to keep a facility current. He can really only enter growth politics when jobs are threatened or in matters of where to locate. But the mayor can be proactive in creating ideas in the minds of developers; if he convinces them that they can make money, he can emerge as a key player.

A critical part of any development scheme has to include the federal government as senior partner. With its Urban Development Areas grants (UDAG), project grants, and block grants, the federal government has mandated itself a place at the negotiation table. Administering grants can be a very partisan operation. A highly visible Democratic mayor, for instance, will invariably encounter some problems during a Republican administration. This is particularly true if that mayor is Coleman Young, who has been especially critical of the Reagan administration. To offset partisan interference, Young has cultivated a pool of local tutelary Republican officeholders and fund-raisers. His skill in working cooperatively with Republicans was developed while he served as Senate leader but was honed during the Milliken administration. Young and Milliken were known as the "odd couple" because of their rather unlikely admiration for each other.[14] They were total opposites, one a moderate from a rural community and the other a radical from the city. The Young/Milliken nexus helped to formulate the state equity plan, which returned tax monies to the city to pay for services and facilities used by state residents. Most importantly for Detroit, Milliken served as a bridge to the Ford and Reagan administrations. He was included in the group that met with President Ford during the first Young administration. In addition, Young has never hesitated to consult with Republican officeholders and fund-raisers when it looks like they could help the city, and he makes an appeal to their civic pride and their egos. Because they know that the mayor is a prominent Democrat nationally, Republicans expect a quid pro quo is possible even when their party is out of power. Partisanship should not be allowed to inhibit economic development, and keeping it out of day-to-day growth operations is a trademark of Young's executive office.

Mayoral Decision Making and Action Clusters

In economic development decision making, a mayor of Detroit is invariably constrained by the city's reputation as a heavy metal city. He is equally constrained by the information about what, if anything, there exists to be developed. Young claims that the "secret of economic development is land. If you want to control economic development, then you must control the land. You can dictate what goes on it." Accordingly, at the core of the mayor's economic development strategy is first acquiring the land and then negotiating its use. There are several city-owned vacant parcels of land dispersed around desirable building sites (for example, the riverfront). Competing investors either suggest their own uses for the land or the mayor tries to plant ideas in their minds. If a suggestion meets the mayor's criteria for feasibility, then it becomes a project, or "job."

Young attributes the success of his recent economic project development to his appointees: "We still get money from Washington despite Reagan. Everyone said because I called Reagan old pruneface I would not get any money. We get UDAG grants because our staff put together the best proposals." Young also attributes his projects' success to selecting the right project managers. He says, "I like Turner Construction Company. They are best adapted to my way of working. It has become standard operation to hire a construction manager. I turned the People Mover over to Turner."[15] Decision making within the mayor's office is not always easy to understand, and who did what in arriving at a particular decision is difficult to ascertain from interviews. Members of the mayor's staff are always cautious about revealing their role in a decision. Remaining an insider requires keeping one's advice to the mayor confidential. Part of the mayor's method—some call it his charm—has to do with keeping outsiders guessing. No one is ever really sure of anything he plans to do until he is prepared to "go public." The maneuvering, negotiating, and concession making take place on the inside, sometimes with the mayor at the center of the interaction, and other times before and after matters reach his desk. Power relationships in that circle change, as in any small group. Ascertaining who did what in some given situation does not provide reliable guidance for assuming similar roles in some future situation, no matter how similar it appears. Accordingly, the core of the mayor's decision-making methods seems to involve a system of loose action clusters. In *Future Shock* Alvin Toffler predicted that such task forces would be the norm for future organizations and that permanent power arrays would become obsolete. Executives would find temporary task forces to be a better means of securing quick and effective action than by some static and longstanding organization. He wrote,

> The high rate of turnover is most dramatically symbolized by the rapid rise of what executives call "project" or "task force" management. Here, teams are assembled to solve specific short term problems. Then, exactly like the mobile playgrounds, they are disassembled and their human components reassigned. Sometimes these teams are thrown together to serve only for a few days. Sometimes they are intended to last a few years, but unlike the functional departments or divisions of a traditional bureaucratic organization, which are presumed to be permanent, the project or task force team is temporary by design.[16]

Toffler called the rise of such groups the "new ad-hocracy." The teams do not necessarily replace traditional departments, but they recruit the best and brightest and assign them to lead projects. The mayor utilizes these teams or action clusters as the situation arises. Emmett Moten says that "the mayor thinks through the job and a team is put together."[17] Young often farms out executive staff members to departments for months or years and then suddenly brings them back to City Hall to work directly for him. Some assistants are loaned to local corporations, while others are assigned to department heads as staff. Everyone in those organizations is aware that the individuals work for the mayor. Mayor Young has found that bureaucrats, even in situations in which they agree with him, are incapable of responding rapidly to changing conditions. He prefers a dynamic, action-oriented (also optimistic) group. Toffler has compared such groups to modularism in architecture, an attempt "to lend durability to the whole structure by shortening the life span of its components." Hence, the term "throwaway organization" seems appropriate for Young's approach. The people who work best with the mayor are those who resist "going native" (that is, integrating fully with the bureaucracy) or those who work for him, not for the city (they work for the city *through* him).

The composition of an action cluster is determined by the situation being monitored or facilitated. Economic development projects have been particularly well suited for action clusters. The mayor remains in ultimate control, but members of the action clusters manage day-to-day negotiations with developers. Action cluster members are required to mount a project and see it through to completion. Accordingly, they must know how to direct a project that encounters unanticipated problems just as well as the rare smooth case.

To an astute observer, the composition of an action cluster often indicates the degree of the mayor's interest or involvement. Some people are regulars on a staff, such as Emmett Moten, director of Economic and Community Development. Others are temporarily assigned, either from the mayor's staff, such as Ron Hewitt, who is now planning director, or are borrowed from other departments. The remaining members may come from the booster community. This is a collection of groups, usually led by whites, who are professional liaisons with the corporate elite. In this category are such personalities as Bob McCabe (president of the Renaissance Center) and Robert Spencer, of the Economic Growth Corporation. Although these people do not work directly for the mayor, they are constantly in touch with his permanent staff.

At the opposite end of the action cluster is the decision not to go forward, in which a project is assigned to the "back burner." The development of the Monroe Street side of the Kern block and the renovation of the Book Cadillac Hotel were assigned to back burner status, which happens when a project is somehow infeasible at present, or else in financial difficulties. Such assignments are not permanent, if money or developers can be found. The Cobo Center expansion project was revived when evidence mounted that the city would get more hotel space by its completion and could accommodate more conventions if "setup time" could be reduced.

Assessing the political environment and seeking funding for a project are major duties of the action clusters. In performing this role, they must be mindful of the mayor's preferences, minority interest, media attention span, and the impact on the careers of other political actors. At the center of the mobilization drive is the mayor, and his support is critical to a project's success. Hence, part of the developers' task is to convince the mayor of the opportunities being offered by a particular plan or project. City leaders are adept at assessing whether a particular entrepreneur or group has the means to pull a project together. Ethnicity is one of many significant factors, and minorities are encouraged to submit projects, bids, and plans. In many cases, the city will "go the extra mile" to get a minority project off the ground, because any successful minority project provides important leverage with the black middle class, which is frequently critical of city decisions, and particularly so of its apparent reliance on white developers. In any case, a smooth scenario will follow from the decision-making model presented in Figure 4.

A major decision to advance a project, adopt an existing economic effort, or generate interest in an idea ultimately depends on its feasibility. Feasibility is a broad concept, which embraces more than merely whether or not the money can be found. The city must consider the competence of investors and what they expect from the mayor. A successful project enhances everyone's prestige. The construction of the Robert Millender Center is a clear example. It was constructed across the street from the Renaissance Center as a parking structure, hotel, and apartment complex. The new structure has given the city a new underpass and has added a new dimension to the city skyline. A given project must also meet a test of its potential to assist the city in gaining a competitive advantage in the service economy. Creating jobs always sounds good, but how many jobs? And how long should they last? Do the jobs created match an available labor supply? Can the investors use a minority angle to enhance the project and

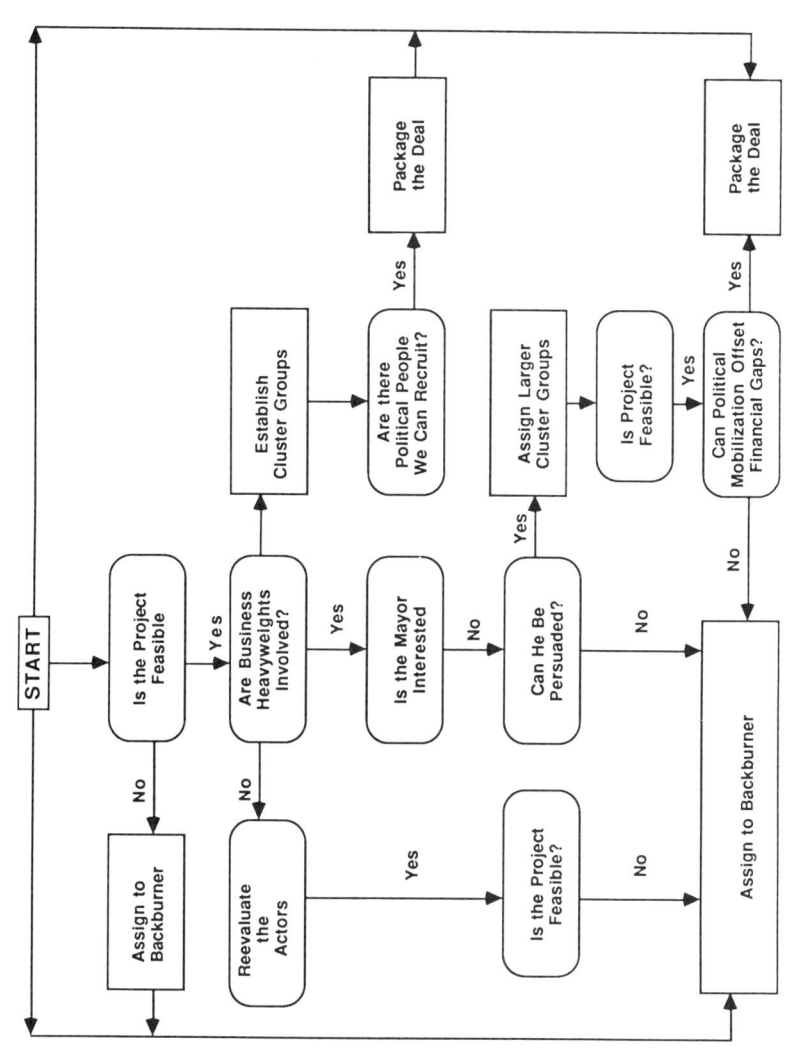

Figure 4. **A Model of Economic Decision Making in the Mayor's Office**

increase the city's political clout in matters of ethnicity and equality? A prudent investor must be able to convince the mayor's "man" of the financial viability of the project. Those that hold promise for making Detroit bigger, grander, and more economically productive will inevitably triumph over "nickel and dime" projects.

This model suggests that economic growth politics are dynamic; it calls for maximum flexibility at every stage of a project. It also provides enough slack for mayoral maneuvering, either in support of the project or to allocate blame for its downfall or shortcomings. By rationing his input, the mayor maximizes the weight accorded a given project and the actors involved. The participants in his action clusters are people chosen for their preference for working out details without daily reports to the mayor, reserving their contact for obtaining his help at critical points. The realities of economic development demand mayoral attention for the following reasons: (1) Detroit's economic system favors established economic groups over newly formed ones, and raising capital has historically been difficult for small minority firms. (2) Officially sponsored projects allow the city a needed planning and financing role. It is important that development is consistent with city planning. (3) Even under the best of conditions (a surprise-free scenario), most projects, plans, and developments meet resistance and some inevitable impasses.

When and if the mayor intervenes in a project, it is always to protect the interests of the city, as he sees them. He is aware that the blue-collar version of the future for Detroit is the service economy. This explains why he consistently vetoed ordinances by the council that would ban gambling, a possible magnet for the city's growing convention business.

In order for Detroit to keep its place as one of the nation's economic centers, it has been necessary to move quickly in order to develop a competitive edge. Two elements of revitalization are worker readiness and human capital accumulation. Mayor Young inherited an industrial city which in 1973 was beginning to show signs of serious job losses and de-mobility. De-mobility occurs when a person from a family background of stable class structure is not able to find a job that compares in status or security with that of his/her parents. Such job losses and the types of jobs that have been developed to replace them have added to the woes of city government. Detroit's economic development decisions must be understood within the context of the city's job losses. A decision to promote project A over B is in fact a decision to pursue certain types of jobs—that is, it affects what jobs will be made available and who will get those jobs. The mayor seems intent on returning the city to an era of good jobs, but to accomplish this feat, the so-called progrowth coalition and the poor must wait out the Reagan administration. There is much at stake in the consequences of the 1988 presidential election.

Summary: Private Power and Economic Transition

While a good deal has been written about the financial giants of the Motor City, no one is prepared to gainsay the influence of men like Charles Fisher III, Peter Stroh, Al Taubman, and Max Fisher. Yet the issue remains: what is the relationship of this economic elite to the black political decision makers? Catherine Ewen has chronicled the great families of Detroit and has analyzed the ways in which its capitalists have consolidated power through entrepreneurship and marriage. She concludes that the political elites have been supplicants to economic power.[18] Floyd Hunter reached a similar conclusion in his sociological study of Atlanta.[19] Clarence Stone, a political scientist, has also found that the economic elite hold an advantage over other groups in a system that is biased in their favor.[20] More recently, another political scientist, Todd Swanstrom, found the same forces at work in Cleveland. In all but Stone's analysis, blacks were portrayed as essentially powerless; black politicians and professionals were seen as decision facilitators and implementers. According to the authors, decisions are always made in a manner that promotes the interests of the economic elite, and blacks do not share financially in such projects. They are merely employees who get paid for services rendered.

The pluralists posit an interest group conflict theory of economic decision making, and they claim that blacks potentially have a role to play to the extent they are able to aggregate their interests economically and politically. There is no evidence that blacks are developing an indigenous capitalist class capable of outbidding whites or assuming the initiative in economic development. The drag on the city's ability to take off, to return to Rostow's typology, is its dependency on whites for investment. There simply were no black groups prepared to take over the empty Hudson downtown store when Hudson's abandoned it or build a rival to the Omni Hotel in the Millender Center. Finding the capital to build large downtown buildings is beyond the reach of most small businessmen. Hence, the mayor has been obliged to deal with white investors.

The lack of an effective political or economic countervailing force—either one indigenous to Detroit or nationwide—to the business or economic elite promotes the concentration of power in the hands of a few, who also enjoy an advantage because there is no effective party, union, or reform opposition group to seriously challenge them. There are remonstrators, of course, but they are either not organized or they lack the leverage to veto decisions. Accordingly, the mayor and investors decide and build with little resistance. Investors are obliged to negotiate only with the mayor's office, and the whole process seems to work, because this mayor is amenable to change and economic growth. Mayor Young does not have to "sell" economic projects to the general community; they trust his judgment. On the rare occasion when some salesmanship is necessary, the mayor has proven himself capable of the task.

Coleman Young's success rests in large part in his relationship to local Republican businessmen and politicians, who generally like him and want to do business with him. They trust that he will deliver on his promises. Young has reconciled himself to the fact that whites control the economic lifeblood of the city, and he is not prepared to cut any essential arteries or refuse proffered transfusions. His relationships with Republican William Milliken and Democrat Jimmy Carter proved to be an asset to the city's development. His relationship to the late Henry Ford II, Max Fisher, the late Max Pincus, and others has helped facilitate the economic development process. The Democratic mayor has no problem dealing with Republicans, corporate whiz kids, developers, or presidential candidates as long they desire to help the city and treat him and the city with respect.

Times are changing, and, as the economy shifts to the service sectors, old names will play a less visible role in public affairs and new names and new money will gain hegemony. The captains of the emerging service industries will not possess the degree of power their predecessors held, because they lack the clout of organized labor. One of the most effective forces in the organization of transformative industries has been the labor movement. Distributive industries are biased instead toward white-collar workers who are not generally led by their unions—or not so amenably—as their blue-collar counterparts. Although blue-collar workers will likely continue to outnumber white-collar workers in the new economy, advantages such as job mobility and high wages lie with the educated, professional class.

Under the new economy, the poor will lose job mobility. The prediction of downward mobility in wage scales is consistent with the situation of black workers in cities where the service industry, as an economic base, is more highly developed. This prediction assumes that blacks will continue to be underrepresented in the high tech and white-collar jobs. To prevent this misallocation from occurring will demand greater coordination between local universities, industry, and the political establishment than is presently the case.

Economists Stephen Cohen and John Zysman disagree with the prediction that the economy will become dominated by service. According to these experts, manufacturing will always be fundamental. They believe that the so-called postindustrial society is a myth and that, at best, the service economy will coexist with manufacturing. America cannot afford to reduce its manufacturing sector, they argue: "services are not a substitute, or successor, for manufacturing; they are a complement."[21] If Cohen and Zysman are correct, then Detroit, even more than other cities, needs to keep this economic tandem.

The issue is whether the economy can be transformed in a just and equitable manner. The city would gain little advantage if its underclass did not profit from economic change. Although Mayor Young seems to be committed to improving the lot of the underclass, there are forces in a service economy that are simply not amenable to political control. The poor have consistently supported Young, believing that his proposed changes will eventually improve their life chances. In making himself the center of the transformation process, the mayor has also made himself the target of all those who are afraid to take risks or who do not wish to see changes made. In focusing on the problems inherent in specific projects, critics often miss the larger accomplishment, which is the profound economic transformation that Detroit is undergoing—one in which the city's economic elite scramble to retain some influence over matters such as downtown construction projects. Such projects are important in development efforts because they indicate progress. Yet, the transition they represent was in full swing even before many of the projects were off the drawing board.

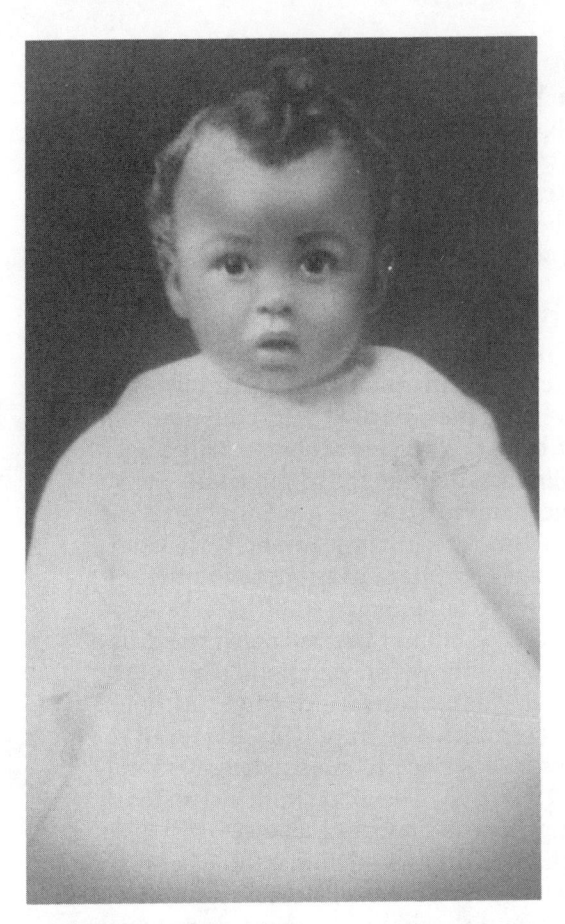

Coleman Young as an infant. (Photo courtesy of the city of Detroit.)

Class Picture at St. Mary's. Coleman Young is third from the right. (Photo courtesy of the city of Detroit.)

Coleman Young's mother, Ida Reese Young. (Photo courtesy of Bernice Grier.)

Coleman Young's father, William Coleman Young. (Photo courtesy of Bernice Grier.)

Coleman Young as a soldier in World War II. (Photo courtesy of Bernice Grier.)

Coleman Young and Paul Robeson. Robeson is at the center, Coleman Young seated at the left. (Photo courtesy of Sid Rosen, photographed by Isadore Berger, FRPS and FPSA.)

Coleman Young testifying before the U.S. House Un-American Activities Committee. Seated at Young's right is his lawyer, George Crockett. (Photo courtesy of the *Detroit News*.)

Coleman Young, insurance salesman, selling a policy to Gus Scholle, president, Michigan AFL-CIO. (Photo courtesy of Robert Vanderbeek.)

State senator Coleman Young at a news conference with Ken Cockrel. (Photo courtesy of the *Detroit News*.)

Governor Milliken signing the No Fault Insurance Bill. Senator Young was one of the sponsors of the bill. (Photo courtesy of Robert Vanderbeek.)

Young politicians: Robert Kennedy is flanked by state senator Coleman Young and Basil Brown. Others in the group include Murray Jackson, Eileen Richards, Freddie Burton, Joel Ferguson, and Willie Baxter. (Photo courtesy of Murray Jackson.)

Portrait of state senator Coleman Young. (Photo courtesy of the city of Detroit.)

Former UAW president Leonard Woodcock, Governor William Milliken, Coleman Young, Henry Ford II, and secretary of state Richard Austin. (Photo courtesy of the city of Detroit.)

Coleman Young with Richard Hatcher, mayor of Gary, Indiana, Maynard Jackson, mayor of Atlanta, and Robert Blackwell, mayor of Highland Park, Michigan. (Photo courtesy of the city of Detroit.)

Coleman Young at a black mayors' forum. The group includes Andrew Young of Atlanta, the late Harold Washington of Chicago, Johnny Ford of Tuskegee, Alabama, and Richard Hatcher of Gary, Indiana. (Photo courtesy of the *Detroit News*.)

David Rockefeller, Coleman Young, and Henry Ford II. (Photo courtesy of the city of Detroit.)

Coleman Young and Dr. Benjamin Hooks, president of the NAACP. (Photo courtesy of the *Detroit News*.)

Coleman Young in the Oval Office with President Jimmy Carter. (Photo courtesy of the city of Detroit.)

Coleman Young with novelist James Baldwin, Dr. Thomas Bonner, president of Wayne State University, and businessman O'Neil D. Swanson. (Photo courtesy of the city of Detroit.)

Rev. Martin Luther King, Sr., Henry Ford II, Mrs. Coretta Scott King, Coleman Young, and Dr. Robert Green. (Photo courtesy of the city of Detroit.)

Roger Smith, chairman of General Motors Corporation, presents a check to the city before the construction of the General Motors plant at Central Industrial Park. (Photo courtesy of the *Detroit News*.)

Coleman Young sharing a laugh with Lee Iacocca, chairman of Chrysler Corporation. (Photo courtesy of the *Detroit News*.)

Coleman Young explains the urban crisis to Eric Sevareid of CBS News at the Republican National Convention in 1980. (Photo courtesy of the city of Detroit.)

Coleman Young presents the key to the city to vice president Hubert Humphrey. (Photo courtesy of the city of Detroit.)

Speaker Jim Wright, Coleman Young, congressman George Crockett and his wife Dr. Harriet Crockett, and Dr. Arthur Johnson. (Photo courtesy of the city of Detroit.)

Muhammad Ali and Coleman Young frightened by trick-or-treaters at Manoogian Mansion. (Photo courtesy of the city of Detroit.)

Ms. Bernice Carter, Coleman Young's personal secretary, keeps tabs on the mayor's national and local schedule. (Photo courtesy of the city of Detroit.)

Coleman Young, Unisys chairman Michael Blumenthal, and federal judge Damon Keith. (Photo courtesy of the city of Detroit.)

Coleman Young, a visible figure in the Democratic party, campaigning in Texas for local Democrats. (Photo courtesy of the city of Detroit.)

Coleman Young enjoys a brew with members of his constituency. (Photo courtesy of the *Detroit News*.)

Coleman Young and Detroit children during his second campaign. (Photo courtesy of the city of Detroit.)

Coleman Young. (Photo courtesy of the city of Detroit.)

6

The Nurturing of Economic Development Projects in Detroit
Money, People, and Commitment

The power of both municipal agencies and the mayor over the shape and direction of economic development in Detroit has grown remarkably in recent years. With the suburbs erecting office buildings and attracting light industry, Detroit has had to become more aggressive in protecting its economic foundation from siphoning by surrounding communities. The economic engine of the city has become increasingly driven by politics. Although private corporate money still selects most items on the city's project agenda, the process of creating the agenda runs two ways—between the political leadership and outside developers. The Young administration's ascendance in the economic realm has meant a more proactive involvement in who builds what, when, and where. Until Young was mayor, the city had not anticipated the impact of shifts in population patterns, changes in shopping and entertainment choices, and in alternative uses of the downtown area. Staying ahead of these changes has been the single greatest preoccupation of the Young administration.

Under the tutelage of Young, Detroit has slowly been undergoing a metamorphosis of major significance. Detroiters are correct when they say that "Detroit is not what it used to be." No modern American city is. All cities change, some faster than others, and as cities go, Detroit is proceeding at a moderate pace. Its pace is affected by forces inside and outside the city. Cities after all live in a political environment of multiple veto points, which obviate any attempt at rational planning and economic project selections.

The federal and state governments continue to play a crucial role in every major project the city undertakes. This is particularly true for the city's use of the Urban Development Action Grants fund and Michigan pension funds. Vetoing a project can be accomplished by nonaction or weak support at critical moments in its development. In the development of downtown Detroit there has never been a shortage of ideas about what needs to be done, but ways to fund the plans have often baffled the city's political elite. In order to get initial funding Detroit has had to be inventive and aggressive, since the normal route, through its tax base, has been rapidly deteriorating.

Competition from the suburbs and other cities has forced Detroit to articulate and assert its new vision and to move aggressively in order to avoid losing its competitive edge in the struggle for resources, jobs, and people. During the first ten years of the Young administration, many development plans were conceptualized but not finalized. They were attacked from many directions and for a variety of reasons, yet buildings and other projects have been completed to alter the city's skyline.

Each development project has constituted a political test for the mayor and his staff. The questions are always the same: Can a predominantly black staff oversee a multimillion-dollar project from ground breaking to completion? Can cost overruns be handled in an orderly and peaceful fashion? Can the staff handle local reporters' needs for newsworthy information? Many of these questions contain racial overtones, but the more complicated issue is more directly race-related: How can a city with a population that is increasingly black and poor support these projects? How the media and local officials address critical issues in project management related to economic development is significant in gauging the mayor's role in redevelopment and that of other key players.

Case studies of three major projects that the Young administration has backed—the Joe Louis Arena, the Central Industrial Park (CIP), and the Detroit People Mover—will provide some insight into the efforts of the mayor and his staff to meet the challenges for economic redevelopment of the city. Each of these projects has different aims and has required very different strategies to implement. As examples of redevelopment efforts, they give us some perspective on the ability and effectiveness of the mayor's staff and of their own relative impact on the entire economic development effort.

The Joe Louis Arena, the most ambitious and costly effort at the time, was built primarily to house sporting events. As a for the city's major sports franchises, it counters the trend in professional sports toward suburban locations. Sporting events bring people to the downtown and are generally a major source of traffic for downtown businesses. The Central Industrial Park project, arguably the more controversial of the projects, is primarily home for a new General Motors assembly plant. This project was aimed at the retention of jobs and the city's image as the center of the American automobile industry. It will not directly contribute to the city's industrial tax base, however, until after the mayor is out of office. GM won so many tax breaks to build the park in Detroit that the city treasury will not receive any tax revenues from the GM plant until after the year 2000.

The financing and politics of these two projects differ significantly. Joe Louis Arena was designed to capture the sports dollars of hockey and basketball fans, and it competes with the suburbs for such events. On the other hand, although the city has invested millions in land acquisitions for the Central Industrial Park project, the capital cost of the plant will be borne by General Motors. Nevertheless, the politics and economics surrounding these projects tell us much about the nature of Detroit's transformation and its leaders.

Building the Joe Louis Arena

Within the last two decades, big league sports franchises have become more demanding of their host cities. Many of them have sought to follow their primarily white fans to the suburbs unless municipalities agree to share in the cost of renovating and maintaining their facilities. Because the franchises are closely identified with Detroit, they have been successful in extracting concessions from their hometowns. Among the most common demands they make are for tax breaks and new facilities and parking. The combination of neighborhood crime, inadequate parking, and aging facilities has led all the Detroit teams except the Tigers baseball team to seek new homes. A few years before, there had been another attempt to promote a new riverfront stadium, and after it failed, team owners began to act on their threats to go to the suburbs. The Detroit Lions football team was the first to move to the newly erected Pontiac Silverdome, which took them almost forty miles away from their previous home. Although a new facility with greater seating capacity and ample parking were the reasons management gave for the move, black inner city residents were dubious, and many of them claimed that it was to appease the white fans.

After the Lions moved, both the Pistons basketball team and the Red Wings hockey team also threatened to leave. Faced with the loss of three of Detroit's four major sports franchises, Mayor Young was forced to take action. The Pistons complained about a lack of seating in the 13,000-seat Cobo Arena; the Red Wings were unhappy with the size and age of Olympia, their home on Grand River Avenue near downtown. There had been serious crime incidents connected with the games near both arenas, including two murders near Olympia.

Faced with the dismal prospect of a downtown area with very little entertainment to offer, the city began to formulate a plan for a new riverfront stadium in the fall of 1976 under Mayor Young's leadership. Availability of federal construction money from a $2 billion public works bill signed by President Carter—the mayor's ally and supporter—encouraged the city to apply for a $5 million grant to begin construction in October of 1976. An additional incentive at this time was competition from a suburban plan to construct another stadium in Pontiac Township near the Silverdome.[1]

The Young administration's plan was announced on October 20, 1976. At that time it called for a total of $15 to $20 million to be spent to erect an arena just west of Cobo Hall, the city's other major arena, in the central business district.[2] Despite the fact that both the Pistons and the Red Wings rejected the contracts, the city forged ahead. Young made it clear that the city was not going to wait to secure a major tenant before proceeding with its plan.

The city's determination to proceed was based on a very real need to submit the project proposal to the federal government. A funding program such as the one it sought help from invariably has more applications than funds, and late submissions have a disadvantage. In Detroit's case, within a week "initial bonding authority, architectural expenses, and the transfer of capital budget funds" for the arena were approved by the common council.[3] The estimated cost for the project had already risen by $5 to $10 million, according to planning department director Anthony T. Revito.[4] The city was forced to act quickly, because it had to be able to show that construction could begin within ninety days of the grant approval.

While planning and negotiations were going forward on the arena, the city was also engaged in discussions for the purchase, renovation, and lease-back of Tiger Stadium. Tigers owner John

Fetzer at this time predicted, "There will never again be a stadium built by private enterprise."[5] Mayor Young apparently concurred in this belief, because his administration was energetically pursuing plans to put a new arena on the riverfront, assuming that the Tigers would remain in the city.

The Search for Funding

One of the first acts of the Economic Development Commission (EDC) of the Department of Commerce in the new year of 1977 was the approval of Detroit's $5 million grant application, as part of $14 million in grants for southeastern Michigan, and this triggered a frenzied attempt to secure financing for the project.[6] The first in a series of setbacks occurred just over a month later, when the Michigan Municipal Finance Commission (MMFC) "refused to approve the city's request to borrow [by selling general obligation bonds] $1.5 million to start engineering studies for the riverfront stadium." A commission spokesman said they would wait "until the city submitted feasibility studies showing the stadium would be self-supporting." The commission was concerned that Detroit taxpayers, who already paid the highest city taxes in the state, might be saddled with a financial white elephant.[7] This is exactly what had been said about Cobo Arena when it was built. Considering that Cobo was being subsidized at between $1.5 and $2 million a year, it was highly unlikely that the new arena would be able to meet the commission's requirements. City officials justified the subsidy by pointing to the millions of dollars it generated in convention business.[8]

The mayor's executive aide, William Cilluffo, said that the loan had only been "tabled, not shelved."[9] The city continued to pursue permission to sell bonds to support the project, and a week after the original rejection, the commission "reluctantly approved" a $1.5 million loan to begin preliminary work and construction by 1 April, before the ninety day deadline expired. MMFC had no choice but to approve the arena construction project, because the Young administration had given ample public notice of its intent to borrow the money, and because the city appeared to be able to repay the loan. One member of the commission, attorney general Frank Kelley, urged the city to reconsider the project, while admitting that "Detroit is a home rule city" and "it is a question for the city to resolve."[10]

Further tension between the city and the MMFC arose due to what one commission member claimed was the "general uncooperativeness" of city officials in "supplying information necessary for the commission to make the ruling."[11] This tension was representative of the pervasive anti-Detroit attitude among public officials outside of the city. House Republican floor leader Bill Bryant, the only Republican lawmaker representing Detroit, warned that the legislature might take a dim view toward continuing the project. He said that building the arena at the taxpayers' expense "would jeopardize" aid to Detroit in the next fiscal year. "If we are going to use state tax dollars to aid Detroit," said Bryant, "then we must insist that Detroit not embark on projects that are wasteful of tax dollars." The fact that Bryant represented one of the few remaining white sections of Detroit, a community bordering the suburbs, also illustrates the rift within the city between a dwindling white population (many of whom were forced to live in the city in order to keep their city jobs) and the mayor. Mayor Young countered his opposition by saying that, despite the fact that the stadium would not be self-supporting, "the city subsidies required to operate it flow back into city coffers after sports fans start spending pre-game and post-game money downtown."[12] At this time, financing plans envisioned funds culled from two sources, a $5 million Economic Development Agency (EDA) grant and $17.8 million in four proposed bond issues over two years. If the city had any financial problems with the project any future bond issues would require commission approval.

Norris's Shot on Goal

During the maneuvering for funds, Red Wings owner Bruce A. Norris announced, in a seven-page letter to Mayor Young, that he would not be moving his team to the proposed riverfront arena. He said, "If we are to move our operations, they should be moved to the suburbs."[13] Norris's letter was candid about the characteristics of hockey fans. It asserted that hockey fans and patrons are overwhelmingly suburban, thus a new home for the Red Wings should take their desires into consideration. Nothing gets city fathers' anger up as quickly as an announced departure of a sports franchise.

City officials stated that they were taken by surprise by Norris's announcement, which is unlikely, since there had been rumors of such a move. Deputy Mayor William Beckham said he "thought we were still in negotiations." Young hinted that the widely circulated letter sent by Norris might just be a maneuver to negotiate a "better deal"; he said, "It sounds like we may still be negotiating."[14] Otherwise, he reasoned, why were Norris's written complaints so detailed? The letter listed a number of complaints about the then-proposed agreement between the city and Norris's organization. For one thing, he thought the proposed $2.2 million rent (to be used to pay off the bonds) was too high. He also felt that planned parking was inadequate.

Negotiating cost in public served to solicit public support for the team's owners. The *Detroit News* reported, "The hockey club was known to be bargaining for complete control of the new arena and its concessions, guarantees against competition at Cobo Hall, and freedom from existing labor agreements between the city and union workers who would be employed there."[15] Why not stage a power play for the whole game?

Young, acting as goalie for the city, responded to Norris's threat by asserting that the city was going to go through with its building plans without any assurances from the Red Wings. "Clearly, we would like the new arena to house Detroit's professional sports teams," he said. "However, it's not an essential ingredient to success. Professional teams represent only a small portion of the income at an arena."[16] Young made a good defense play while mounting an offensive. He argued for the riverfront site instead of Pontiac because "the fans in . . . Wyandotte, and Dearborn, and Westland, and many downriver communities, as well as the fans from South Oakland and South Macomb counties will be able to reach the new downtown arena in much less time at much less cost than an arena north of Pontiac."[17] Hence, the mayor now appeared to have hockey fans' interests in mind. The shot was blocked temporarily, but Norris was going to try again.

The Role of the City Council

During the encounter between Norris and Young the common council had been studying alternate proposals, including the possibility of expanding the 13,000-seat Cobo Arena. The council's role grew out of its power to reject the project. Some council members were reluctant to approve the project following Norris's letter, which enabled the council to call for further review. Councilwoman Maryann Mahaffey, known as an advocate of social welfare issues, said she had not made up her mind, but that she was generally against using public money to build something that will be turned over for private profit. She commented, "I want to see some hard economic data. I want to know how much they expect in economic spinoff. I would want to know first that there was a definite cost-benefit to the city."[18]

Despite opposition by homeowners' associations, the Detroit Police Officers' Association (DPOA), officials of Olympia Stadium, and several members of council, on March 9, 1977, the common council voted 5-4 to approve initial construction contracts in order to meet the 1 April deadline. Their action followed a report from researcher Jay Brant which said that although the revenues would be less than the mayor projected, and costs would be greater, the arena would still generate more revenues than it would cost to run, but not enough to make the mortgage payment.[19]

The Young administration maintained its optimism even though suburban developers announced they were going to go ahead with their plans. The mayor and his aides expressed the opinion that chances of a suburban arena would decrease once "a shovel is in the ground." Their theory was that private investors would be afraid to compete with a publicly financed arena. Malcolm Dade, a mayoral aide, brushed off charges by council president Carl Levin that this was the most unpopular project he had witnessed in his seven years as a public official by saying, "there is certainly mixed opinion," and "We have found an equal amount of people favorable to the project as against."[20]

Putting Judges in the Game

The next challenge for the project occurred when a suit was brought in Wayne County Circuit Court to halt the initial $1.5 million bond sale. An attempt by Governor Milliken to get the Michigan Supreme Court to take jurisdiction, following Mayor Young's request, was rebuffed. In March 1977, Judge Peter B. Spivak ruled against the city in a suit that was brought by a suburban resident who owned property in Detroit. Judge Spivak found three faults with the city's notice of the project. First, the notice used the word *stadium* rather than *arena*. Second, the city failed to give notice of the project's "contemplated cost"; it only said that the $1.5 million was to be used for the "development of a riverfront stadium." Third, the city had not obtained approval of its notice from the MMFC, as called for in a landmark Michigan Supreme Court ruling five years earlier, which involved an attempt to build a domed stadium on the river.[21]

City officials were fearful that the delay might wind up costing them the entire $5 million federal grant. The EDA grant was contingent upon the work beginning by April 6 and the city providing the first $1.5 million in development funds. One journalist reported, "City officials declined to say whether [the money] could be raised from another source," such as the development of other city expenditures.[22] The EDA was also somewhat vague as to the effects of a delay, but its chief counsel, Thomas Harvey, said he believed that a "temporary delay that was not voluntary" would not necessarily result in cancellation.[23] The city then made a second attempt to hasten the progress of the suit to the state supreme court, and the EDA gave the city a forty-five-day extension. City planner Anthony Devito said it came because the EDA recognized the city's efforts at compliance.[24]

Meanwhile, the Pistons had begun to consider the planned new stadium. Herb Tyner, administrative chief executive and owner of a share of the team, said, "We have no commitment to Detroit and no definite commitment to Pontiac. . . . I want to make it clear that we have made no commitment to stay in Detroit even if the riverfront arena is built."[25]

The Red Wings organization had been very busy since that long letter from Bruce Norris to the mayor, and Norris now announced that he had a tentative agreement with officials of Pontiac Township and an investment group, and that they planned to erect a $15 million arena, to be called Olympia II. Ironically, the financing was to come from tax exempt bonds issued by the newly created Pontiac Township Economic Development Group.[26] Would Norris's second try work?

The Young Team Returns Aggressively

In late April Detroit sued the proposed Olympia II arena. Mayor Young said, "They are talking about taking jobs from Detroit where unemployment is already high and using state support to do it." When asked if the city's suit was in retaliation for the earlier suit to block Detroit's arena, he said, "No. It's just in our own self-interest."[27] City attorney Bruce Miller said, "The law was not designed for municipalities to engage in economic cannibalism."[28]

Earlier that month Wayne County elder statesman Alfred Pelham convinced the Michigan National Bank of Detroit, where he sat on the board of directors as an advisory member, not to approve a loan for the proposed Pontiac arena. Pelham, also a member of the mayor's Committee on Economic Growth, told the bank's officials that making a loan so injurious to the interests of Detroit could jeopardize the bank's more extensive dealings with the city. When asked directly, Pelham stated that he had not discussed the matter with the mayor but that he felt he should direct their attention to a possible consequence.[29]

A month later the Michigan Supreme Court reversed the circuit court ruling, which had blocked the first bond sale and construction start-up. The decision stated that "Judge John Spivak had erred on all three counts" in making his ruling. The high court found no significant difference between the terms *stadium* and *arena* and held that the city was "not required to provide the projected cost of the project," nor was it required to provide notice to the Michigan Municipal Finance Commission.[30]

Following its own good news, the city could better tolerate rejection of its suit against Olympia II. With construction of Detroit's arena going forward, the mayor and other city officials felt it would be difficult for a suburban arena to compete with their publicly funded project. At the same time, they were aware of the extent of their own commitment to ensuring the continued viability of downtown.

Game Ends in 1-1 Tie

Early in August Mayor Young and Bruce Norris held a joint press conference to announce their agreement that the Red Wings would play at the new riverfront stadium. The *Detroit News*, which had opposed the downtown location of the arena and argued instead for it to be built at the state fairgrounds, declared that the arena "is one of Young's prime achievements in revitalizing the downtown area. That he got the Red Wings to sign up is considered a big victory for him."[31] The Olympia II project was lightly dismissed. Norris said the suburban stadium would not be built, and Young described Norris as "a longtime supporter of downtown Detroit." Norris commented to the mayor, "People must wonder how did it happen so fast. But I understand you do things like that."[32] Young proved once again to be a tough defender and one willing to take a risk.

The terms accepted by Red Wings owner Olympia Corporation and the city called for the corporation to lease the new arena, as well as Cobo Hall, and to book events for both arenas. Rent on the new arena was announced as $450,000 per year.[33] The agreement was hailed as a "totally new concept." It called for the city to receive a surcharge on each ticket sold for events held at the arena. Along with parking revenues collected from the structure to be built across the street, this surcharge was to be the source of funds used to pay off the revenue bonds the city was offering for sale. The payoff rate was estimated to be $2.2 million per year. Revenues to be allocated from parking were estimated at $3.5 million annually. Additional revenue of up to $252,000 each year was anticipated from property taxes on the two arenas. Mayor Young predicted that the new arena, combined with Cobo Arena, would draw more than two million fans per year—compared with Pittsburgh's downtown stadium's one million fans a year, which are estimated to generate $20 million annually for that city.[34]

Did the Goalie Have Assistance?

The story of Olympia Corporation's reversal revolves around a dinner conversation between Fisher Theater owner Joey Nederlander and Max Pincus, who was then president of a chain of clothing stores. The two economic leaders concluded that they should arrange a "last-ditch" negotiating effort between the mayor's team and the Red Wings management. Nederlander called Red Wings official Lincoln Cavalieri and persuaded him to call the city. Mayoral aide Cilluffo later told how he had received a call one morning that indicated the possibility of an agreement. He in turn passed the information on to the mayor and went out. That afternoon he was called out of a meeting to the mayor's office and arrived to find Young in conference with Cavalieri.[35]

The last-minute negotiations that produced the Red Wings contract continued until 3:30 A.M. on the day the announcement was made. After the fact, some council members expressed their doubts as to whether the Red Wings had ever, in fact, intended to leave. The actual contract came under fire in that election year from councilman Ernest Brown, who was running against the mayor.[36]

The arena project was dogged by delays from start to finish. The next problem to arise had to do with a parcel of land owned by Penn Central Railroad, which was then in bankruptcy proceedings. This was the land intended for the parking structure. While the city waited for the court to approve the land sale, it was forced to transfer $8 million from the Public Lighting Commission budget in order to have operating cash. Mayor Young incurred considerable criticism for this move, but his spokesman assured the press that the money would be repaid as soon as the $34 million bond issue was sold.[37]

Financing problems marched in lockstep with the delays throughout the project. Nevertheless, the Young administration team managed to maintain its momentum and fought its way through. As the price tag on the arena rose, the MMFC again withheld approval on a bond issue. In fairness, they had a reason to be cautious, haunted as they were by the spectacle of the Pontiac Silverdome, which produced an enduring $800,000 annual deficit. They were also concerned because the city was offering *all* of its future municipal parking revenues as security rather than merely those from the structure under construction.[38]

In June of 1979 a strike by Teamsters workers failed to stop progress on the building. Mayor Young was reported to have had personal discussions with Teamsters vice president Bobby Holmes, who then worked out details that would permit work to continue. Young announced, "We are pouring concrete at Joe Louis today. We got a special arrangement with labor and management which allowed us to get a cement mixer for the site."[39]

While construction proceeded, the bond issue still faltered, due to the economy's poor condition. Then, in September the MMFC granted approval for bond sales, despite a contrary recommendation from its staff. The city then faced the hurdle of Moody's grading, which is the standard by which the interest rate of a given bond issue is determined. A Moody's executive, Frieda Ackheimer, expressed doubts as to whether "the project—particularly the parking garage—would generate enough money to repay the bonds." The state of the economy and the record high gasoline prices then in effect (which have never since been equalled) caused the rating service to question many aspects of the project. The city decided to forgo a rating rather than risk being rejected.[40]

In November city officials decided to attempt a different financing method. Section 108 of the U.S. Housing and Community Development Act of 1974 "allows cities to borrow an amount triple their annual grant."[41] A letter from the Young administration to the city council announced its intention to seek a $38 million loan from the federal government for the purpose of purchasing Joe Louis Arena. It explained that the act permitted cities to borrow money against future block grants pledged by the federal government. The letter did not include an explanation of why the city wished to purchase the arena from its constituent agency, the building authority, nor did it include information on repayment of the loan.[42] The reason, of course, was that economic conditions were steadily strangling the money supply for construction, and Mayor Young's team was resorting to ingenious stratagems indeed to maintain progress on the arena. They had already used a $6.8 million surplus from hospitalization fringe benefits, a $5.7 million surplus from state urban grants revenue, and $15 million in new parking revenue bonds.[43]

Most immediate reaction to the city's latest effort was negative, and those who advocated more expenditures in the neighborhoods and less downtown were increasingly strident in their objections. The Association of Community Organizations for Reform Now (ACORN) was most vehement in its objection to using block grant funds as collateral. In response, William Cilluffo compared the action to "taking a second mortgage on your home."[44] While he admitted that there was a potential risk, he pointed out that the arena was only three weeks from opening and that to discontinue construction at this point would cost the city more in penalties from construction contracts than the cost of completion. Further, cancellation of contractual commitments for the use of the arena and the parking structure would be extremely expensive. Emmett Moten also conceded the risk but only if "the economy goes to pot. . . . If that goes, we all go."[45]

Even before a new loan had been approved by HUD, the arena was open for its first event. Although there were some last-minute criticisms of its design and possible safety flaws, things went reasonably well. The council approved the mayor's loan request 7-1. Ken Cockrel, the lone dissenter, proclaimed himself unsatisfied. The council, however, had imposed riders on their approval, which required that in the event of a default, neighborhood programs would receive priority over the downtown for any remaining funds and that a request be submitted to HUD for an extension from six years to twenty on the loan period. Such an extension was intended to circumvent the need for a 70 percent repayment, which would have been done in five years under the original plan.[46]

Loan approval by HUD did not actually occur until three months after the arena opened.[47] Despite reservations, the council acquiesced under the mayor's pressure and approved his plans.[48] They had extracted further potentially damning statements from various members of city government, particularly city auditor Marie Farrell-Donaldson,[49] but finally approved the package four months after the arena opened.

Central Industrial Park: Ethnicity versus Economics

Building the CIP

Detroit—the Motor City—has looked to the automobile industry as a major source of jobs for most of this century. Coleman Young inherited a city of decaying economic fortunes, including outdated plants and a dwindling labor force. For decades on end Detroit had enjoyed the fruits of its leading industry's success, but the Detroit in place when Young came to office was no longer the growing, dynamic metropolis it once was. In the eyes of most people, it was simply moribund—beyond help. The massive growth and high wage rates of a highly expansionist industry had served to exacerbate the decline of "the core-dominated city," which is manifest throughout the heavily industrial northeastern quadrant of the country.[50] Core decline is itself an outgrowth of the automobile age and its support of suburban economic growth. Lower land costs in outlying areas, combined with worker mobility resulting from mass ownership of private transportation, made it not only more economical for employers to locate outside the city but also more feasible. As a result of their increased mobility, employees were now able to come to work wherever it might be and were thus freed from core city location constraints.

The factors that have rendered Detroit unattractive to manufacturers include its high taxes, high crime rates, and high wages and benefits, plus there are the overall disadvantages of manufacturing in Michigan—high workers' compensation costs, increased energy requirements of a cold climate, and a growing body of environmental protection laws. Corporate decision makers facing such a discouraging list are unlikely to choose Detroit, and in fact many have moved to more amenable climates for weather, labor, and law.

Detroit grew as the auto industry expanded, and as it did, its reserve work force, the poor, increased. Managing this population involves expensive welfare and public safety services, and the city has been forced to increase taxes to meet these costs. The correspondingly higher taxes, crime, and congestion have acted to prohibit new industry from entering the city.

Other costs—so-called intangibles such as racial conflict, including the riots of 1943 and 1967—have also made suburban locations more attractive. Insurance policies, which the public assumes cover all possible losses to manufacturers, carry exclusions for civil disorder, thus exposing a business to incalculable risks. All in all, the trend toward suburban location and relocation has been unbroken by Detroit manufacturing concerns. The Young administration has made the halting and reversal of this trend a primary goal. Developing techniques for redeveloping a tax base and job sources is essential to the future of Detroit, as it is for all large cities and their populations.

Mayor Young took action in 1980 for the specific purpose of seeking resolution to the problem of locating industry in Detroit. He approached the Big Three automakers with the request that "if they had any plans to build or expand new plants, that the City of Detroit be given the first opportunity" as a site.[51] In testifying before the circuit court, his response to questions regarding his reasons for seeking new manufacturing was, "Well, I think the most serious problem facing our city today is deterioration of its economic base, and specifically the great escalation in unemployment—in other words, the loss of jobs—and I consider that the primary need of the city at this moment is to provide more jobs for its population."[52]

In response to the mayor's offer, General Motors announced on June 23, 1980, its plan to merge two Cadillac plants in Detroit and place them on a new site—within the city if possible. Emmett Moten, director of the Community and Economic Development Department (CEDD), and one of the mayor's closest advisors, said, "Between eight and ten sites were 'under consideration.' ... We're really at square one. We have not discussed financing of the project. It's not a very easy thing to do. You have to consider a number of things, such as rail and truck traffic." A GM spokesperson said, "We aren't going to speculate what will happen if we can't find a suitable site in Detroit."[53]

The project immediately took on an aura of urgency. It was important to both the city and GM that a suitable site be found. According to reports published the next day, GM preferred to stay in Detroit in order to retain its trained work force, and Mayor Young—under state law—could prevent GM from receiving tax concessions elsewhere in Michigan.[54] Despite the fact that GM had not given the city a deadline, it had recently relocated a downtown St. Louis assembly plant after having told St. Louis officials it would renovate that plant. GM decided that it needed a new plant, and city officials could not find a site within the city limits that the automaker found suitable. The plant was relocated to Wentzville, Missouri, forty miles outside of St. Louis.[55]

Several sites were proposed for the new Detroit plant, yet, from the start, the prime candidate was located at I-94 and Mt. Elliott on the city's East Side. Because it was immediately adjacent to one freeway and close to another, had nearby rail lines, and large amounts of cleared land already, it was most attractive. None of the other sites had the potential to provide the four hundred acres which GM had said was required.[56]

Director Moten soon emerged as the city's key spokesperson on the project, emphasizing the competitive nature of the situation by pointing out, "GM doesn't put all its eggs in one basket ... urban centers are very hard-pressed to compete for these plants." He compared Detroit's landing a new auto plant with saving one's own life and stressed that the city could not stand to lose even one more plant. Other city officials reinforced his expectation that Detroit would have competition for the site and suggested that other offers would probably include such enticements as free land, sewers, and roads—not to mention tax breaks.[57]

One of the questions asked most at the time was why GM would choose to locate a new plant inside the city of Detroit when the trend was toward the suburbs and the Sunbelt. GM's president, Pete Estes, responded that a primary reason for staying in Detroit was that the company felt it had a "social responsibility" to help maintain the city's tax base and refrain from adding to its already drastic unemployment rate. He specifically referred to Detroit councilman Kenneth Cockrel's charge that the corporation was playing games, insisting that GM did indeed have a serious commitment to the concept of a new Detroit plant, although it was not making guarantees. He said, "[M]aybe we won't do anything if we can't stay in Detroit. We're that serious about it."[58] He explained that it was always possible to renovate an existing facility but that the cost of renovation was equal to the cost of developing a new operation on a completely vacant site.[59]

GM should, indeed, have been feeling benevolent toward the city at that time. In the preceding year, Detroit had magnanimously permitted the corporation to shift Cadillac engine production from the Detroit plant to the nearby suburb of Livonia. It was alleged, however, that the city's reason for doing so was to avoid provoking GM into moving those operations to another state.[60]

By the first week in July, the city of Hamtramck (a suburb that is bounded on three sides by Detroit) had joined Detroit in urging General Motors to locate its new plant on a 500-acre site then occupied by the abandoned Dodge Main assembly plant. The proposal anticipated the relocation of about 150 businesses and 1,500 residents; a hospital and several churches were also located within the tract. Corporate officials were pleased with the site and announced that they thought they could establish their plant there.[61]

First estimates of the total cost were set at $750 million, and GM projected opening production for the 1984 model year. It was expected that funding would be supplied primarily by federal urban renewal grants.[62] GM forecast a payroll of 3,000 workers, which represented a drastic cutback from the 10,000 workers then employed by the two existing plants combined. A net loss of 7,000 jobs was painful to contemplate, but less so than the loss of the entire 10,000. Detroit and Hamtramck agreed that Detroit would oversee property acquisitions and relocations.[63]

CED director Moten became the city's most extensively quoted official early in the project, "taking the heat" from many directions throughout. The mayor's team put together a very thorough plan to acquire and clear the land with maximum speed and efficiency. They decided that it was better to spend more money "up front" to get willing cooperation from residents and businesses than to force their relocation through condemnation proceedings and thus displease the electorate.

Even careful plans were not enough, however, to prevent opposition. Some residents genuinely wished to stay where they were, and they were aided in their protest by others, some with political experience, who saw this project as an opportunity to bring the mayor's political juggernaut to a crashing halt. They helped residents to organize.

U.S. representative Lucien Nedzi (a Democrat from Hamtramck) became an advocate for the residents who wished to remain. He asked, "How do you duplicate those properties elsewhere at the compensation that will be afforded them?" A typical example of the dilemma was the plight of one longtime resident: Julia Landeck, a seventy-seven year old woman who had lived in the same house since 1928, along with her two brothers, said, "We have a big home—four bedrooms upstairs. We'll never get one like this again. Where do you go when you're up in age? What do you do? Start all over again?"[64] The city offered homeowners the market value plus $15,000 and a $4,000 moving allowance to renters, and this compensation served to quell many residents' objections.

Land clearance was scheduled for early spring 1981. First, though, it was necessary to create a joint economic district, which would be the product of the Economic Development Councils of Hamtramck and Detroit. A significant feature of this plan was the absolute requirement for close cooperation rather than the rivalry that often characterizes relations between neighbor cities. Hamtramck city planner Bill Onapa said, "We're not going to let municipal self-interest blow this deal."[65]

The likelihood of court challenges to the project was realistically planned for. Land clearance and the relocation of businesses and people would have to be held by the courts to be a "public necessity," which invokes the right of eminent domain. Other land uses in the project area that were expected to cause some difficulty for project planners were Catholic churches that would have to be demolished. The parishes themselves would disappear once homes were removed, since the parishioners, mostly elderly, were few in number and would be dispersed among other parishes once they were relocated. There was also a Jewish cemetery situated in the affected area that would have to be moved.

In mid-July, the Detroit Economic Growth Corporation (DEGC), a private agency, approved a $3 million loan to help with project start-up costs. DEGC was created as a nonprofit foundation for the purpose of revitalizing the Detroit economy by a consortium of fourteen major Detroit corporations, including the Big Three automakers and the J. L. Hudson Company. Its loan came from a $4.5 million revolving credit line extended by seven Detroit banks. DEGC vice president James Schafer claimed that this redevelopment scheme was "the biggest thing in history to happen to any U.S. urban area."[66] Emmett Moten shared his view, asserting that Detroit was pioneering efforts in urban revitalization that had not been attempted by any other American cities.[67]

By late July, the Poletown Neighborhood Council threatened a lawsuit if the city did not respond to its demands for proof that the proposed auto assembly plant would be the best possible use for the site, as well as fourteen other issues. The group was led by Tom Olechowski, who said, "We're talking about a working-class neighborhood that's about to be obliterated by a factory that won't be employing any residents of the community.... We can't be anything but serious about it."[68] The city announced the following week that the East Side Housing and Community Coalition would be assisting residents to relocate. Emmett Moten also announced that "a recent survey conducted by the DEGC revealed that, of 500 homeowners, less than 10 percent were opposed to General Motors' plans."[69]

On July 31 the mayor revealed the city's initial financing plan. He said that the city "will lease the plant to General Motors and the lease payments will take care of the loan payments. That's the strategy we're looking at now." He also said that he felt this was the simplest and most direct plan, although it was by no means the only one. The Young administration let it be known that their proposed scheme was merely one possibility among a number of alternatives, yet the creativity and initiative that the mayor's people were exercising was opposed at every turn, and one federal grants expert was quoted as saying the plan was "fantastic—[it's] really fantasy-like. There's no way to assemble federal financing to that extent. They were talking about borrowing $150 million for site acquisition. That is more do-able, but it's still very tough."[70] Young responded by saying, "The federal government has more money than anybody else, and I think we can get it."[71]

The build-and-lease plan depended on being able to obtain funding from President Carter's $50 million auto industry recovery package, plus grants from a variety of federal agencies and other sources. The city also proposed to sell $500 million in industrial revenue bonds. Emmett Moten believed that the bonds would sell easily, but the size and apparent audacity of the plan awed federal officials, who said that a project of these dimensions had never previously been attempted. A final decision between two alternatives had yet to be made. Considering the sheer size of the project, and the number and variety of opponents its promoters had to face, having a contingency plan was a minimum precaution.

The opposition was beginning to increase in volume and in numbers, too. Public meetings of residents gave hostile receptions to city representatives, because residents saw Poletown as one of the last "real neighborhoods" in Detroit. The prospect of moving to new neighborhoods and living among strangers was threatening. That many of them were retirees made them even more resistant, while at the same time it elicited public sympathy. The common council was also developing resistance to the GM project, though it never reached the point of intransigence that was evident in the neighborhood councils.

Now the Young administration began to press the council for approval on its federal loan applications. The fact that haste was essential offered administration officials a lever, which they used with great skill to obtain the things they wanted from the council. The most vocal of the objectors to this tactic was councilman Cockrel, though he was by no means the only one. The council resented being pressured, and the media and neighborhood citizen groups enthusiastically encouraged them toward open rebellion—but in vain. The council unanimously approved an application, which it was unable even to see because it would adjourn on August 6 and the application had to be submitted to the Department of Housing and Urban Development in advance of the federal government's fiscal year end, September 30.[72] And the final decision had yet to be made on whether the city would become GM's landlord or merely its purchasing agent for the plant site, although the latter seemed increasingly more likely. Through it all, CED director Moten endured the pressure of being the mayor's point man and recipient of the accusations, vilification, and recrimination that the council, the media, and the neighborhood organizations heaped on him. In downplaying his role, Moten asserted that he was "no different from our department heads," implementing those goals the mayor had set out in his State of the City addresses.[73]

By the end of September, land acquisition and demolition costs had risen from the original $126 million to $200 million. The city was still waiting for a letter of intent from General Motors so it could prepare its environmental impact statement. At a meeting of the EDC, Moten defended the higher costs on the basis that the originals had been appraisals, not estimates. He also announced a $1,000 relocation bonus to anyone agreeing to move within ninety days of receiving a purchase offer from the city. The intent of this additional incentive was to reduce the threat of court delays once the official development plan was adopted.

In early October, Moten updated the council on the plan. GM now was requesting a 12 year/50 percent tax abatement, which was the maximum legal amount under Michigan law. He also informed them that the industrial revenue bond plan exceeded federal limits for the amount that could be sold and thus had been dropped. Moten reportedly told them that the delay in getting a letter of intent from GM stemmed from city officials' fears that the city would be unable to perform its part. The stunning revelation that Hamtramck would be contributing nothing toward the project was explained by its mayor, who reported, "We simply have nothing to contribute."[74] Detroit, meanwhile, was planning to start issuing purchase offers as soon as the program was accepted by the common council and reviewed by the Citizens' District Council.

A Section 108 loan for $60 million was approved on October 8, along with a waiver of the normally required environmental impact statement, and this gave the city authority to begin disbursing money immediately. Normal procedures require that the environmental impact study be completed and accepted prior to using the funds, but an exception was granted for the purpose of helping the city to meet GM's 1 May deadline for property acquisition.

Two days later the long-awaited written offer was received from General Motors. The corporation proposed to pay $6.8 million for the land ($18,000 per acre) provided it was granted the maximum allowable tax concession—twelve years or $120 million. The expected total cost of the plant at this time was $700 million, which included $200 million for site acquisition and $500 million for construction. Mayor Young announced that the letter was encouraging and that he anticipated the council's approval of the plan the following week.[75]

The Citizens' District Council announced its own list of demands, however, before the common council had an opportunity to pass the matter on. One of the items to which they attached great importance was a request for a guarantee that displaced residents would not face higher taxes in their new homes. Later, the CDC retreated from its original list of such demands to another, more practical one.

Before October had passed, the common council was disputing both the necessity and the size of the proposed abatement. Administration officials who testified before it were claiming that the project would yield an additional $9.625 million per year in local property taxes, which included levies by the city, Wayne County, and the Detroit Public Schools, even after allowing the maximum 12 year/50 percent tax abatement. Meanwhile, GM officials had conceded that they wanted tax abatement of a different kind.

The common council now debated whether or not it should make its tax abatement subject to a guarantee of long-term employment of at least six thousand workers by GM. It did not take long for GM to let the council know that such a stipulation would be unacceptable. A Moten aide testifying before the council late in October was forced to admit that the 6,150 jobs promised on the federal application were evidence of "psychological grantsmanship."

Although practically every member of the common council had had either questions or objections to one or another feature of the project, its only committed opponent on the council was Ken Cockrel. At this juncture Cockrel made an accusation that was clearly directed at Young's administration through the aide then testifying: "You talk about 'new' jobs, and keep pumping up the 'big lie,' while anyone questioning the administration's credibility is considered stupid. It's beginning to sound like a shell game."[76]

That was not the end to discoveries of various discrepancies between reality and the Young administration's representations regarding the Central Industrial Park project. Linda Barnes, a senior aide to Governor Milliken, refuted Moten's testimony that the state had promised a $25.8 million contribution toward repayment of the $60 million Section 108 loan. The state had its own budget crunch and would be unable to help Detroit, and she said that the city already knew this.[77] Nonetheless, before the month was out, the common council had approved diversion of some $60.5 million which had already been allocated to neighborhood projects for acquisition and clearance of land. It also authorized $51.5 million for future block grants to repay $130 million in federal loans, which the city had requested. Moten assured the council that the diversion would not affect previously approved projects.[78]

On the day before the council was scheduled to vote, the growing opposition was fueled by a syndicated columnist who alleged that the tax abatement was not a necessary inducement to GM, citing the Baltimore and St. Louis development projects as evidence. Baltimore had been able to retain a plant, along with its expansion, without granting a tax abatement. St. Louis, on the other hand, had been unable to retain a plant replacement, despite its offer of a 99 percent tax abatement.[79] On that same day GM board chairman Thomas Murphy announced that other locations had requested that they be considered for the plant slated for the Central Industrial Park project.

The confusion continued. Detroit city officials claimed that GM demanded tax abatement as a nonnegotiable condition. GM officials claimed that tax abatement was a minor issue—that the company recognized the damage to its image that would result from moving its operation away from Detroit.

On the appointed day, the Detroit Common Council approved the plan submitted by the Young administration. Councilman Cockrel accused GM and the mayor of bringing "murderous pressure" to bear on the council to obtain their approval, without even disclosing how and where the city would obtain the $200 million estimated needed for site preparation. The council was advised by a GM spokesman that the company wanted a more substantial tax concession from the city than what was normally given to industries building or expanding in the city. Another GM employee stated that the automaker wanted a "rehabilitation" tax abatement. This particular plan provided for freezing the corporation's tax bill for twelve years at the level then assessed on the two West Side factories that the new plant would replace, which was reportedly between $4 and $6 million per year.

On that same day the Poletown Neighborhood Council (PNC) challenged the new "quick take" state law (P.A. 198), which the city used to acquire title to the properties. This law makes it possible for the governmental authority that is preempting the land to gain title to it and begin clearing, with the purchase price to be determined by the courts, and thus avoid hindering progress on large projects due to court delays. The law was new—it had just been enacted the previous year—and this was the first occasion that a governmental body had had to employ it. The suit also charged that the project would violate the Elliott-Larsen Act. This state law provided for the preservation of stable, integrated neighborhoods. It further alleged that the state law which authorized the formation of the Detroit Economic Growth Corporation (DEGC) was in violation of a 1976 opinion by the Michigan attorney general. It also alleged that there was a conflict of interest because the DEGC board of directors included Coleman Young and (then) councilman Nicholas Hood.

In short, the Poletown Neighborhood Council had fired a "scatter shot" in hopes that some of their mixed bag of charges would stick. The PNC attorney also inaugurated a media crusade against the project, stating that the city and GM had overestimated the number of jobs that the project would save and questioning the funding sources the city proposed to use for the project.

The question the lawsuit would answer had to do with the primary purpose of the project. If it was adjudged to be primarily public, then it qualified as eminent domain and faced a particular set of laws. There was no question as to whether or not there would be both public and private benefits. What would determine the city's authority was what the court decided was the more significant benefit to be derived.

Many city officials and experts were called as witnesses in circuit court. The PNC attorney was able to find many public employees who had some questions about various aspects of the GM project, and he skillfully played on every unanswered question and every unfinished detail of the plans.

The possibility of using a Tax Increment Financing (TIF) district was brought to light during the trial, as a CEDC staff member was asked to define how the city might fill a shortfall of some $72.9 million in project financing. The only area of the city then using such a plan was the downtown area. That plan allocates all tax increases from tax base expansion to pay for improvements in the district. Since the city administration had been suggesting that the tax base increase would benefit the city, the plan immediately became the basis for additional allegations of duplicitous dealings.

The trial took about six weeks, and the court voted in favor of the city; it had already begun to take resistant homeowners to trial. Now, the mayor and EDC chief Moten both expressed some concern about financing. The city of Hamtramck was ineligible for federal funds because there was a housing bias suit against it, so it was up to Detroit to carry the financial responsibility.

Ralph Nader versus Coleman Young

Early in 1981 Ralph Nader, the famous consumer rights crusader, came to town ready to fight for the PNC. Nader was perhaps bold to assume that he could invade the hometown of the automobile and challenge its mayor with impunity, but instead, he provided a target of opportunity for Coleman Young, who ended up calling him a "carpetbagger." Nader responded by calling for a public town meeting, and Young replied, "He arrogantly proposes to set up a meeting. What the hell does he think elected officials do in this city?"[80] The exchange was fast and furious, but the hometown champion easily defeated the intruder.

Meantime, a new administration had taken the reins in Washington. The Reagan administration lost no time in setting its agenda, which included little in the way of benefits for rustbelt cities. It became apparent quite early to Young that he would need the help of his friends in the Republican party. Michigan Governor William Milliken supported Detroit's request for the $30 million UDAG grant. Early in February, he lobbied President Reagan for the money and professed that he was "hopeful and to some degree optimistic" that approval would be granted; on the following day, he announced that approval. The *Detroit News* hailed the governor's new role "as conduit for federal funds to Detroit."[81]

The next obstacle was a Michigan Supreme Court restraining order that halted progress on the project on February 20, 1981. The PNC had requested it "to assure Poletown residents that they will have a neighborhood to return to, should the Supreme Court block the project permanently." The court promised a fast ruling.[82]

During this hiatus the mayor again blasted Nader, who was now threatening to file a federal suit to stop the city from turning over the first bloc of property to GM. Young averred, "This man [Nader] has a phobia. Whenever you mention General Motors Corporation, he foams at the mouth." In his response, Nader claimed that GM had "totally intimidated the city government."[83]

On March 14 the Michigan Supreme Court kept its promise and returned a prompt verdict, ruling in favor of the city and GM.[84] Mayor Young called it "a far-reaching vindication" and went on to condemn the various steps toward appeal that Nader was contemplating publicly. Young said, "Nader doesn't live here. He comes in, he sues, he leaves."[85]

The following week, GM announced that it would accept the 12 year/50 percent tax abatement that the city had proposed, and credited its decision to a "persuasive State of the City talk" by Mayor Young. Under threat from GM to reconsider the project,[86] and Emmett Moten's warning that rejection would effectively be a default of the city's agreement with GM,[87] on 15 April the common council approved the GM tax abatement.[88]

The revelation, two weeks later, that a TIF district would indeed be used for financing was unable to slow the project's momentum. Ground breaking occurred as scheduled, on May 2, 1981, and the mayor was unworried by remaining lawsuits, saying that they were "of a nuisance character."[89]

The originally projected mid-1983 opening of the CIP was postponed by GM to 1984 that same year. The abrupt and unexpected turnaround in the auto market took away the company's urgent need. Some were skeptical of the quick evaporation of GM's need for the new facility. The fact that no one had been able to predict the economic recovery, or its gradually increasing momentum, must be considered in an appraisal of this massive project. That it was accomplished at all, given the kind of massive opposition it engendered and its own landmark size, also sheds light on the ability and dedication of Young and his administration. Certainly the construction jobs that were created by the project had their own impact on the feeble Detroit economy.

The People Mover Project: A Mayoral Takeover

Projects that can shape a city's future very often spring up unnoticed, but in January, 1982, when the Southeastern Michigan Transportation Authority announced that it planned to begin construction of an automatic rail system to be called later the Detroit People Mover, people knew that with it Detroit would never be the same. Putting a ring around the city's downtown business district would change the skyline and advance a new futuristic image of the city. More importantly, the construction for the People Mover would further the economic transformation of the city from an industrial base to a service center with convention business as an anchor industry.

The transformation of the economic function of downtown Detroit started with the shift by retail shoppers to shopping malls in the surrounding suburbs and away from the city. But this conversion was accelerated by chain stores' decisions to close their downtown facilities and invest in more modern quarters in shopping malls; retailers claimed there was simply not enough traffic to support downtown facilities. In this respect, Detroit is similar to other older American cities.

The building of the Renaissance Center, the cylinder-shaped icon of New Detroit that contains offices, shops, and a hotel, did not reverse the rush by consumers to the suburbs. The construction of the Ren Cen and its linkage to the new Millender Center and the City-County Building by elevated walkways marked yet another milestone in the downtown redevelopment plan. The key to a city's commercial redevelopment is not direct competition with suburban shopping malls but the provision of a different array of goods and services. To attract a buying traffic, magnet entities such as the People Mover are sometimes needed.

Part of city redevelopment strategy entails creating a "building reputation." Investors are made to believe that they are getting in on a building boom. Since the sight of construction cranes, for example, is so important to this type of development pitch, it is essential that all construction in progress proceed without delay; any termination or slowdown in building projects could have serious implications for Detroit's development pitch.

General Dimensions of the Project

The People Mover, formerly called the Central Automated Transit System, is an automated elevated transit system designed to carry passengers on a 2.9-mile track at 12.6 mph. The cars are powered by electricity with the capacity to seat thirty-four persons. The guideway, which includes a single lane, is elevated throughout the route and has station stops at Greektown, a cluster of Greek restaurants; Bricktown, a cluster of restaurants and bars; the Millender Center, home of the Omni Hotel and an apartment/parking complex; Joe Louis Arena; Cobo Hall; the Renaissance Center; and the Cadillac Center, a complex of office buildings. There are also stops planned at Fort Street, Michigan Avenue, Times Square (Grand River Avenue), Woodward Avenue/Grand Circus Park, and the so-called Financial District (near the Pontchartrain Hotel).

The system was built by the Urban Transit Development Corporation (UTDC-USA), a subsidiary of UTDC Limited of Toronto, Canada. SEMTA negotiated an open-ended contract that called for twenty percent of the contract dollars to go to minority and female-owned firms. The project management team included several local companies, including minority-owned enterprises. The firms ranged from inspection services to construction operations.

The construction of the project created over two thousand new jobs.

The critical question for planners was, Who would ride on the system? During the initial planning stages, it was estimated that 71,000 people a day would ride the system, but during each crisis of the construction, the estimates changed. Near the end of the construction, the estimates had been downgraded to 15,000. Despite such low ridership estimates, initial enthusiasm for the project continued. The mayor and others of its backers envisioned that it would alleviate automobile traffic and facilitate street crossing by pedestrians. They also hoped the new system would trigger the revitalization of the Grand Circus Park area, a largely neglected area, and assist it in becoming an important tourist attraction.

A Project with Too Many Foremen

The construction of the People Mover was a classic case study of interorganizational conflicts. The federal agency charged with public transit, the Urban Mass Transportation Agency (UMTA) of the U.S. Department of Transportation, was the primary funding agency. UMTA emerged in the seventies as the promoter of People Movers for various cities. With a budget of $200 million, the agency solicited cities to apply for a demonstration grant. Detroit, not at first a finalist, was awarded a grant after the city of St. Paul, Minnesota, declined the project. UMTA decided that Detroit indeed could have a People Mover but that funding must come from a $600 million transportation commitment (which included plans for a subway) made to Mayor Young by the Ford administration. The project was originally budgeted at $137.5 million with UMTA paying for 80 percent of the cost.

The second major player in the People Mover project was SEMTA, the largest transit authority in the state. SEMTA negotiated the construction contracts. Created in 1967 by the state legislature, the agency's primary mission has been to provide bus service for the increasingly developed suburban cities of Southfield, Birmingham, Troy, and Mt. Clemens. These cities' separate governments regard their bus service needs in rather narrow terms and are not interested in SEMTA's project for Detroit or, for that matter, SEMTA's efforts to coordinate intracity services. The SEMTA board, made up of representatives from the tricounty area, nevertheless were convinced that the People Mover project would change attitudes about mass transit and serve to enhance the agency's image as the regional coordinator of transportation services.

The third participant in the program was the Michigan Department of Transportation (M-DOT) and Highways' Bureau of Urban and Public Transportation. Having agreed to pay 20 percent of the construction costs, the state had a long-term interest in completing the project. The bureau's role in the construction process was primarily that of inspector. Although the bureau assigned a liaison person to SEMTA, it followed a long-standing policy of not interfering with the day-to-day operations of local authorities.

Each of the agencies—UMTA, SEMTA, and M-DOT—viewed the People Mover differently and was determined to maintain its standard operating procedures throughout the construction process. SEMTA initially saw the project as separate from its primary mission, and it was not formally integrated into SEMTA's operations until Albert Martin took over as the agency's administrator. During his tenure, SEMTA emerged as the construction manager, inspector, accountant, and spokesagency for the People Mover project.[90]

The Crisis of the People Mover

In the summer of 1985 the Detroit People Mover faced a series of crises occasioned by cost overruns and construction controversies. Originally budgeted at $137.5 million, estimates climbed as high as $210 million in cost overruns. The Michigan State Senate joined UMTA, who earlier had demanded that a cost ceiling be set, and the newspapers began publishing charges, countercharges, and assessing blame.

During the first week in June, SEMTA signed a revised contract with UTDC. The remedial action was not enough, however, as Ralph Stanley, the UMTA administrator, insisted upon a formal commitment to cover any future cost overruns. Mayor Young and Governor James Blanchard refused to accept responsibility for overruns. Again, charges and countercharges were made among the participants. Nevertheless, the parties resumed negotiations in August.

It became clear during this crisis that SEMTA was an inappropriate agency to serve as construction manager. As the project became more controversial, UMTA sought to present the People Mover as simply a case of mismanagement by inexperienced administrators, and SEMTA board chairman Tom Turner was quite anxious to get rid of the project. SEMTA was wary of adverse publicity. Meanwhile, cracks began to appear in some of the system's guideway beams, and this created yet another crisis of cost overrun. Again, the governor and Stanley declared publicly that they would not cover the cost overruns. Blanchard stated that he could "reassure the People of Michigan that there will be no blank check on any overruns—indeed, no check at all from the state."[91] Under the circumstances, the mayor was faced with at least five decision options.

Young might have allowed the project to continue to drift and lay the blame for any failures on its other participants, or he could fault the Reagan administration for its insensitivity to the transit needs of cities. Governor Blanchard could have been compared unfavorably with former Republican governor Milliken, who had supported Detroit's public projects. There was little doubt among politicians that the mayor had the rhetorical skills to make a case for negligence on the part of his partners. There was also no doubt that he would win points with his constituency if he charged the Reagan administration with breaking a commitment made by presidents Ford and Carter. Also, the mayor was not above charging both the state and federal administration with racism. Choosing to abandon the project as a policy option was not pursued, however, because it yielded little good to the city and would allow the mayor's critics a chance to cite the terminated People Mover as an example of a flawed economic growth policy.

The second possible policy option involved increasing partisan pressure on the Reagan administration. Some members of the Michigan Congressional Delegation—particularly the Democrats—would have relished a rhetoric battle with UMTA. Again, using the potential People Mover collapse as an example of Republicans' insensitivity to cities had its appeal, but this option was also rejected. It violated the norm of nonpartisanship and thus could have alienated local Republicans.

The third option involved reorganizing SEMTA and allowing elected officials direct control of the project. The struggle over the structure and governance of regional transportation policy predates SEMTA. The mayor and the other partners in the agency disagreed over representation. Suburban counties wanted equal representation with Detroit, but suburban riders would account for only 10 percent of the ridership in the new consolidated regional system. The entire issue of the structure of SEMTA got caught up in the controversy over the People Mover's construction. Mayor Young proposed a realignment of SEMTA in April 1985. The so-called Big Four, which included the mayor, William

liam Lucas (Wayne County executive), Daniel Murphy (Oakland County executive), and Walter Franchuk (chairman of the Macomb County Board of Commissioners), met and agreed on a plan to abolish the existing SEMTA structure. A bill was introduced and passed in the Michigan Senate then stalled in the House. This option, too, was abandoned as cost overrun problems began to occupy the attention of all the parties.

The fourth option was to have the state assume cost overruns. This option was repeatedly rejected by Governor Blanchard, who was gearing up for reelection, and the state legislature. It proved to be a weak option, because no one could produce any fixed or estimated figures for the final cost overruns.

A fifth option called for the city to take over the project and assume the entire cost of overruns. This meant that the management of the remaining construction on the project and its operation would be turned over to the city. SEMTA would remain in the project only as a conduit for federal and state funds. The federal government agreed to increase its share to $200 million, and the city agreed to create an entity to oversee the People Mover's construction and operation. The events leading up to the city's successful takeover illustrate how Mayor Young operates in periods of uncertainty.

The Politics of Takeover

An environment of fiscal crisis and management failures tends to bring out the best and worst in political actors. The summer of 1985 was one of wild accusations, threats, and vendettas, and it is during such times that the mayor operates at his best. He takes every opportunity to maximize the city's interest and assumes the other actors will also act in their own interests. He apparently saw SEMTA as an agency overwhelmed by its attempt to build the People Mover. His initiative attack on SEMTA started with an accusation that SEMTA had not performed its conduit function because the city's Department of Transportation (D-DOT) had not received all the monies to which it was entitled. The mayor asserted, "I can tell you that SEMTA has repeatedly refused or failed to pass on the DOT monies due. And that is the source of the problem of DOT." Albert Martin, SEMTA's general manager, denied the charges. Later, in the heat of controversy over the People Mover's cost overruns and cracked beams, Young announced to the press, "SEMTA is broke. They don't have enough money to perform their function. For a long time now, I have been saying to you that SEMTA is a disaster, that there was no way of managing anything, no controls. It is pretty obvious to me that we cannot wait indefinitely [for change]."[92] It was the mayor who led the so-called Big Four efforts to reorganize SEMTA.

The mayor's interaction with UMTA administrator Stanley also provides insights into the politics surrounding the takeover. Even during the heat of the 1985 summer, the mayor kept his lines of communication open to Stanley's office, and Stanley's stake in the process was very transparent. As a new political appointee, Stanley sought to demonstrate that the Reagan administration would punish local governments that mismanage federal funds. Throughout the summer, he raised questions about SEMTA management and their cost overruns but declared that his agency would not cover them. Indeed, he hinted that the project would never be finished. Stanley's high profile made him a target for all the participants. During opening ceremonies for the People Mover, the mayor recounted his encounters with Stanley, and described Stanley as a "man with fire in his eyes," who had come to Detroit to stop construction on the project. The mayor arranged for a meeting with Stanley to be held in Max Fisher's office. Fisher, an important Republican fund-raiser, persuaded Stanley to allow the project to continue and transfer it to the city of Detroit. Young, in turn, promised to bring the project in under a new $200 million budget.

On August 30, 1985, Albert Martin formally proposed the transfer of the People Mover to SEMTA's board, and a month later the board voted to permit the transfer. The city's impending takeover in turn unleashed a host of critics. The governor, who had earlier expressed doubts, was persuaded to go along with the agreement, but two state legislators filed a suit to stop the transfer and another asked the state attorney general to review the deal. UMTA extended its deadline until 1 October. The actual transfer was made on 3 October. Ralph Stanley tried to salvage something of the situation for UMTA:

> I hope that there's been a lesson learned—that there isn't an endless pot of money in Washington. . . . If I were to give one simple bit of advice to the city on urban transportation, it would be to measure a project not by how much money you can spend, but what you've brought.[93]

Despite the People Mover's construction problems, the takeover provided Mayor Young with certain advantages. First, the project had become identified with the mayor's downtown strategy and, thus, his administration identified with it. To the mayor, the takeover was an example of pareto optimality. The city would

Nurturing Economic Development 199

be better off because of it—that is, in complete control—without making the other actors worse off. Second, SEMTA, the weaker of the participants, could return to its main function—bus service—and end the charges of mismanagement against it. SEMTA board chairman Tom Turner expressed it succinctly when he said, "Thank God this is over."[94] Third, a takeover avoided continuous, unwanted, and unwelcome confrontations with the Reagan administration, and fourth, perhaps most important of all, the takeover gave Mayor Young control of a decision that could affect his overall downtown economic development strategy. It allowed him a chance to consolidate all communications and information related to the project and provided him with an opportunity to fold the project into his overall construction strategy. In other words, the city's takeover of the People Mover project allowed him to select a maximizing strategy in order to reap maximum political benefits.

In retrospect, the politics of the People Mover takeover was exactly analogous to a game. The objective was to win but not run up the score on one's weak opponent. Being political, the players expected to play again, and they did not want to humiliate the losers. There was still a subway to build, the present structure of SEMTA to protect, and contractual obligations to construction companies to honor. In addition each player had different personal stakes in the game. Mayor Young was in the middle of a reelection campaign. His opponent, Thomas Barrow, had attacked Young over the People Mover spending. Although Barrow posed no real threat to the mayor's reelection, the mayor needed to reassure the public that the system's problems were being managed.

Albert Martin, the first black director of SEMTA, attempted to protect his and the agency's management reputation. UMTA administrator Stanley attempted to present a fiscal watchdog image to win points with his conservative/Republican constituency. With his eyes on Michigan voters and a reelection campaign in the following year, Governor Blanchard sought to disassociate himself from the project. The People Mover was an example of the axiom that it does not matter who wins or loses but rather how one plays the game. Norton Long, a political scientist, observes:

> These games provide players with a set of goals that give them a sense of success or failure. They provide the determinate roles and calculable strategies and tactics. In addition, they provide the players with an elite and general public that is, in varying degrees, able to tell the score . . . man is both a game-playing and game-creating animal, that his capacity to create and play games and take deadly seriously is of the essence, and that it is through games or activities

that he gains a satisfactory sense of significance and a meaningful role.

The People Mover's Beams

One of the most widely held and rarely articulated issues during the People Mover construction was, in fact, whether blacks were ready to manage and govern. Simply put, the question was whether or not blacks were competent enough to manage a multimillion-dollar corporation—the city of Detroit. Somehow the question had not been answered sufficiently, and it needed to be put forth again, yet no one seemed to be prepared to raise the real issue. Silence was broken in a local newspaper interview, when U.S. District Court Judge John Feilkens, a man with some liberal credentials, asserted that blacks needed time "to learn how to run the city government." He added that black people "talk about a problem and don't know how to solve it." Although his remarks were not aimed at the managers of the People Mover specifically, black administrators across the city reacted bitterly to Feilkens's comments. Albert Martin, one of the administrators interviewed, asserted, "We don't need time. What we need is an objective evaluation of . . . the actions that are taken."[95] Although other administrators joined Martin in his criticisms, the concern over black competence still remains in the minds of some whites. It may not be racist to criticize the performance of a black administrator in a given situation, but it is racist to try to generalize the evaluation to all blacks. Mayor Young and his appointees have been targets of racist criticism, which is itself often directed at projects built in Detroit. Indeed, Mayor Young found it necessary to admonish white outstaters regarding their attitudes toward the People Mover, saying,

> Unfortunately, there are a lot of people in our state who don't want to see anything positive done for the city of Detroit. Detroit is looked upon as a black city. To a lot of people, when you say Coleman Young, you are talking about black folks. That is a code around these parts. The People Mover is not any more Detroit versus the rest of the state than the Zilwaukee Bridge is Saginaw versus the rest of the state.[96]

Another tangled mass of underbrush had to do with the linkage of the People Mover with transit subsidies to the poor. John Mollenkoft, a political scientist, has argued that Reagan's urban policies or nonpolicies are aimed at defunding the progrowth coalitions that dominate city politics. These coalitions, composed of business leaders and elected Democratic politicians, have used large city construction projects to stay in power. In other words, policies that espouse helping the poor are vital to maintaining the progrowth coalition.

Colin Buchanan, an urban transportation specialist, argues instead that UMTA is the captive of the heavy construction and transportation lobbies, which have a stake in selling local agencies on systems that Buchanan claims have the "smell of a space-age boondoggle."[97] Projects such as the People Mover are promoted to advance the interests of new technology and not to facilitate the movement of people.

Perhaps a more interesting argument is one made by conservatives. In an article in *The Public Interest*, Tony Snow attacked Congress's attempt to modify transportation behavior with transit funds. He claimed that Congress has been attempting to turn cities into "miniature Manhattans, teeming with gleaming skyscrapers linked by futuristic rail systems." Fancy rail systems will not reverse the decade-long flight by residents and businesses to the suburbs. Snow observed:

> Mass Transit subsidies represent a high tech form of welfare spending. Transit, say politicians eager to pressure federal funding programs, provides the best hope for moving American poor around the cities. If you try to cut out mass transit money, you effectively condemn the helpless to a life on the street.... This is hogwash. While poor Americans make slightly greater use of mass transit than the population generally, the difference isn't significant. In fact, poor Americans go to extraordinary lengths to avoid using mass transit.[98]

Despite the 1980 census data showing the decline of workers commuting to work in Detroit—from 7.9 percent in 1970 to 3.7 percent in 1980—Young decided to pursue the People Mover system. He also disregarded telephone surveys that showed that of the 42 percent of those who used public transit in the tricounty area, only 39 percent were likely to ride on the system. Young ignored the statistics because the city he envisioned as a setting for the People Mover would accommodate a new transportation system in the making.

Conclusions

The Joe Louis Arena, Central Industrial Park, and the Detroit People Mover serve as examples of situations in which the mayor has overcome odds, utilized creative financing, and skillfully matched deadlines to obtain some desired end. In each project, opponents have been reactors and not proactors. In the case of the Joe Louis Arena, whites who most ardently criticized the project did not live in the city, thus their criticisms did not amount to much. After losing the Pistons to a suburban location, black support for Joe Louis was only lukewarm. The mayor knew, however, that once the project was started, jobs would be generated and construction downtown would once again attract the attention of potential investors. City hotel owners would locate downtown only if there was a convention facility and clientele to serve. Having the hockey and baseball teams downtown has kept suburbanites interested in the city. Red Wings hockey team owner Mike Ilitch would later pay the mayor back for his foresight; he actually made a radio commercial supporting the mayor's reelection campaign in 1985. Ilitch also agreed to renovate an old abandoned movie house into a downtown office building for his growing pizza business.

The Central Industrial Park, also known as the Poletown project, was a different matter entirely. It involved one of the nation's largest corporations, General Motors, which asked for tax abatements to locate in Detroit as it had before in other cities. It is true that the plant could have been located anywhere, but the mayor fought to have a plant inside the city limits. Some called the mayor's concessions to the corporation's demand for tax abatement corporate blackmail, but there were no other options; GM could have built the plant elsewhere, which might have been inconvenient for the company but not impossible. Apparently, it was the corporation's claims of "social responsibility" that bothered critics of the new plant.

The common council was more active in the creation of the CIP. Media coverage, which focused on the appearance of Ralph Nader, showed the supporters of the Poletown Neighborhood Council (including GM heir, Stewart Mott, who donated $1,000) trying unsuccessfully to present the city as taking away people's homes when there were other sites available. For the media it was a human relations story. The residents became heroes in a drama that many did not truly understand.

The real issue regarding Poletown was not neighborhood displacement or tax abatement but how the city would respond to competition for jobs from other cities. Locating the plant in rural Michigan could not solve Detroit's job problem, and the city needs jobs to keep residents.

In each of the three projects, the mayor stood fast against pressure from opposition groups. Young's encounters with Norris and Nader were like classic theater confrontations staged around basic brick and mortar enterprises. Mayor Young took the heat and the risk, and the city was the winner. Bryan Jones, a political scientist, had a similar conclusion:

> Mayor Young was critical to the success of the Central Industrial Park project in three ways. First, and most importantly, his firm and deep popular support assured that opponents of the project would be an isolated minority and allowed Young almost unlimited room for maneuvering. It allowed him to act as the sole spokesman for the city's interest, a role that he performed with considerable skill. Young's uncanny ability to project an image of sweet reason on some occasions and that of a vicious stump speaker on others became a prime asset when it was backed up with the solid electoral support that he enjoyed. A vitriolic attack on consumer activist Ralph Nader, who intervened on behalf of opponents of the project, during which Young characterized Nader as a "carpetbagger," was leveled with no harmful effects to Young's local political support but with considerable to Nader's.[99]

The People Mover problems pointed out some of the difficulties of implementing new programs or projects with multiple participants and perspectives. Mayor Young ended the so-called complexity of joint action by taking over the system.[100] A takeover was the most rational course of action given Young's goal of maintaining the appearance and substance of his economic development policies. The mayor acted at a strategic moment when an incredible amount of uncertainty had been introduced into the decision-making matrix. The other participants, UMTA and SEMTA, lost control and could not tolerate uncertainty.

In retrospect, all of the predictions of economic doom, or of a failure to entice people downtown, have proven false. Naming the Joe Louis Arena in honor of a great boxing champion was indicative of the mayor's fight for the project. Less than a year after it opened, the arena hosted the 1980 Republican National Convention and was part of the Detroit Renaissance, an event that was showcased on national television. One of the mayor's most daring gambles paid off, and hindsight demonstrates that the arena has become a significant component of the city's continued viability, and that the city's loss of two of its four major league sports teams has not spelled economic disaster. When the roof of the Pontiac Silverdome collapsed from snow during the winter of 1984–85, the city was able to extend a dowager's graciousness to the temporarily homeless Pistons. The city's triumph was short-lived, however, and the Pistons moved back to Pontiac. The peripatetic Pistons have recently moved to a new arena in Auburn Hills, close to Pontiac. On July 31, 1987, the People Mover opened, and suburbanites came both to view and ride a new wonder of Detroit.

7

Affirmative Action and Collective Bargaining under Fiscal Adversity
The Case of Detroit

A critical epoch in urban history and municipal employment has been distinguished by the confluence of three important new phenomena—the ascendancy of black politicians to the mayoralty, the rise of police unionism, and the development of affirmative action recruiting. When Young took office, blacks, long denied equal opportunities in general and access to the Detroit police departments, inherited control of the police bureaucracy, although it remains predominantly white. After the 1973 election there were several questions regarding the department's role in the future of the city. Black politicians quickly discovered that leaders of police departments viewed themselves as a political community, indeed the last bastion of white influence in city politics. As such, they were prepared to take on the newly empowered politicians in the courts, in the media, and in collective bargaining. Under the banner of law and order, the police union leaders sought to test the mettle of Coleman Young.

The Detroit Police Department, once the instrument of the old political machines, has since been transformed into an autonomous bureaucracy. Building on collective bargaining and movements toward greater professionalism, the Detroit Police Officers Association and the Lieutenants and Sergeants Association (LSA) evolved into powerful interest groups in city politics. DPOA and LSA are among the most cohesive of municipal unions because of their special paramilitary status and their strong fraternal history. A modern union takes on several roles. Politically, it endorses candidates and also contributes money to their campaigns.

Representatively, it can call for strikes and other job actions. And, organizationally, it serves as an administrative structure for aggrieved officers. Although the police unions are relatively unsuccessful in taking on city mayors, their stature seems to grow with each new challenge. To the union's leadership, Coleman Young seems particularly vulnerable to political broadsiding.

During his terms in the state Senate, Young had campaigned for more blacks on the police force. As a mayoral candidate, he had promised to open up the department with a massive affirmative action program. To many police officers, affirmative action was simply another reform scheme designed to weaken the solidarity and professionalism of the force. Others saw it as an effort to recruit officers who were not mentally and physically qualified. Still others saw it as yet another encroachment by politicians into day-to-day affairs of the department. But few saw it as perhaps the most important change in the sociology of police departments since World War II.

The Detroit Police Department, like most entrenched municipal bureaucracies, traditionally functions with considerable autonomy. Allowed to function separately from the regular civil service system, it has its own recruitment, selection, and dismissal procedures. James Q. Wilson makes a similar observation:

> The patrolman is neither a bureaucrat nor a professional but a member of a *craft*. As with most crafts, his has no body of generalized, written knowledge nor a set of detailed prescriptions as to how to behave—it has, in short, neither theory nor rules. Learning in the craft is by apprenticeship, but on the job and not in the academy. The principal group from which the apprentice wins (or fails to win) respect are his colleagues on the job, not fellow members of a discipline or attentive supervisors. And the members of the craft, conscious of having a special skill or task, think of themselves as set apart from society, possessors of an art that can be learned only by experience, and in need of restrictions on entry into their occupation. But unlike other members of a craft—carpenters, for example, or newspapermen—the police work in an apprehensive or hostile environment producing a service the value of which is not easily judged.[1]

As long as there were no scandals or civil disturbances, the internal personnel activities of the department had been largely ignored by local politicians. Affirmative action changed all that, however, since it exposed the recruitment process to public scrutiny. Accordingly, affirmative action and white officers' response to it created a serious community relations problem for the police department. The resistance of white officers was viewed as evidence of racism, and the department's credibility with blacks was low just at a time when it needed community support to recruit black policemen. Sociologists Joseph Fink and Lloyd Sealy believe that good community relations are critical to good law enforcement. They assert:

> If police do not solve the dilemma of community relations, they cannot survive as an institution. And they cannot solve the dilemma without first decisively breaking with the view that their primary task is law enforcement. In some circumstances, in some communities, at certain times, it may be. In other circumstances, in other communities, and most of the time, it assuredly is not.[2]

In Detroit the relationship between the police department and the black citizenry had not been good before the 1967 riots. Throughout the sixties the police and blacks were at loggerheads, or were what Hans Toch has called "warring minorities."[3] Both groups believed that they were victims of persecution, prejudice, and misunderstanding. The riots reinforced the antiblack reputation of the Detroit Police Department, tarnished the leadership of Mayor Jerome Cavanagh, and temporarily disabled the liberal white coalition in politics.

The department and local politicians recognized their community relations problem and began working to improve the image of the city's police force. Part of their strategy was the recruitment of more black policemen as a way of easing racial tension. Black police officers were actively and aggressively recruited throughout the latter part of the Cavanagh and the Gribbs mayoral era. After the riots Mayor Cavanagh set up a Special Task Force of Recruiting and Hiring, which recommended changes in examinations, hiring hours, recruitment center locations, and background investigations staff. Senator Coleman Young served on the task force. In its zeal to be tough on crime, the Gribbs interregnum between Cavanagh and Young created the STRESS unit. Then, the 1973 election of the first black mayor coincided with accelerated white flight and increased black pressure for more progress in the recruitment of officers.

Mayor Coleman Young came to office promising to share political power with whites on a 50/50 basis, despite the fact that whites were losing their city population base. His power-sharing pledge was not an act of political magnanimity, but rather demonstrated his genuine belief that blacks and whites could live together in cities with black mayors. Of course, it was also an obligatory posture for a newly elected black mayor who hopes to facilitate racial cooperation. One of Young's first obligations was to implement his pledge to add more black officers to the police department. Although Jerome Cavanagh had a national reputation as a reform mayor, under his administration, the leadership of the police department remained almost lily-white. When Cavanagh left office in 1970, blacks composed 11 percent of the force, considerably below their 44 percent share of the population. Roman Gribbs maintained this recruitment pace and managed to double the percentage of black policemen during his tenure as mayor. After the 1972 passage of the Equal Employment Opportunity Act (EEOA), new federal regulations were applied to recipients of federal funds. During the Gribbs administration, the recruitment of minority officers was low key but fairly effective. Indeed, Detroit was cited as a model for other cities.[4] According to Michael J. Falvo, the recruitment process became controversial with the institution of quotas. White officers, already threatened by an increasing black population, saw themselves as victims of reverse discrimination.

By 1975, affirmative action programs were in their heyday. Gerald Ford, a conservative, was in the White House, and the nation was committed to using affirmative action to integrate its predominantly white institutions and organizations. Minorities and women were recruited and promoted at record rates. Municipalities suddenly opened up new opportunities for blacks. Police and fire departments, on the other hand, remained most resistant to change. The question for Detroit was: How amenable would the city's police department be to the mayor's insistence on maintaining a fixed percentage of blacks in the department?

Removing STRESS

Aside from insisting on more black police officers, Young promised to reform, reorganize, and restrict the police. The latter effort took the form of a pledge to eliminate STRESS, which had been initiated in 1971 and used decoys and questionable surveillance methods to fight crime. During a thirty-month period in the early 1970s, there were an estimated four hundred warrantless police raids and twenty-two related deaths (mostly of blacks). Detroit's had the highest number of civilian killings per capita of any American police force.[5] Yet, this particular anticrime program revealed an antiblack bias, and in 1972 the so-called Rochester Street Massacre, a shootout between police and blacks in which one black deputy sheriff was killed and two others wounded, Detroit police confirmed the force's reputation as "trigger happy cops." Consequently, STRESS further undermined the credibility of the police force within the black community.

The mayoral campaign of 1973 focused on street crime and featured debates on the best ways to reduce crime. Police unions and their candidate, John Nichols, a former policeman, saw the election as a struggle between professional control and community control. Could crime be reduced without the use of STRESS? What were some alternatives to STRESS? Coleman Young's victory over John Nichols was in part a repudiation of the STRESS program and its methods by the black community. As Georgakas and Surkin have observed, "In Detroit, a vote for Nichols meant a vote for STRESS."[6] Young also won votes for advocating an aggressive affirmative action program.

The new mayor's affirmative action policy had several objectives. Designed as a recruitment device, as well as a way of changing the attitudes of white policemen, the policy was a mechanism to exert more control over a largely autonomous bureaucracy. In other words, the new mayor wanted to build a different kind of police force to replace the one he had inherited.

The New Mayor

"The saying over at 1300 Beaubien [police headquarters] for years has been, 'Mayors come and go but the department goes on,'" said Young. "They've got the built-in, self-perpetuating bureaucracy over there and there's only so far that any mayor can get in to change that damn thing within his term of office. Well, I'm going to try to get a bit further in than any previous mayors have." It was clear from the time of Young's first campaign that he would be a no-nonsense executive who would keep the department on a short leash. Young, who had served on Cavanagh's Special Task Force on Recruiting and Hiring, considered himself well informed on police activities, and he endorsed many of the recommendations of Touche-Ross, a management consultant organization hired by his predecessor Mayor Gribbs to reorganize the police department. Three months after his inauguration, he announced the disbanding of STRESS. Four months later he announced the formation of fifty-five mini-stations to be located around the city. Both of these proved to be critical moves for the mayor.

During the campaign many questions were raised regarding the mayor's commitment to law and order. In speeches Young sought to dispel any notion that he was soft on criminals. In his inauguration address, he invited criminals to leave town; his administration would be for law and order. Equally crucial to his stand on crime was Mayor Young's early handling of the Obie Wynn incident. Wynn, a black teenager, was shot and killed by a white bar owner. Some blacks reacted by looting the bar and setting the carpet on fire. The incident threatened to escalate into a full-scale disturbance, but the mayor arrived on the scene only to be jeered when he tried to calm tempers. Nevertheless, he reacted angrily to the crowds and denounced the participants, calling them "hoodlums and ripoff artists," who were "taking advantage of the situation." The mayor's tough posture helped create his reputation as a law-and-order man, a reputation that was often downplayed by the press. The mayor's reputation, combined with his affirmative action initiatives, created drama between the police and the mayor during the period from 1974 to 1984.

The aftermath of the riots of 1967 and the administration of Roman Gribbs had done little to improve the racial climate of the city. When Coleman Young became mayor, racial polarization and white flight had acquired independent momentum. Blacks continued to view the white-dominated police force as an occupying army. Despite residency requirements, many white police commuted to work, and small confrontations between white police officers and black residents had become commonplace. Heedless of the feelings and needs of minority citizens, a few white officers developed reputations as ruffians in uniform, and some blacks were alarmed by the mere presence of the police.

To assuage these fears, Young implemented aggressive recruitment and equally aggressive enforcement of a residency rule that required city employees to live within the city limits. He also instituted a parity requirement that mandated the promotion of a black officer each time a white officer was promoted. The new recruitment campaign had scouts cruising the city's black neighborhoods, signing up potential applicants, and encouraging word-of-mouth advertisement. The Chrysler Corporation contributed two vans to assist in the police department's Outreach programs. Police recruiting offices opened in inner city areas, including a notable one on West Grand Boulevard near 14th Street. The idea was to encourage inner city youths to consider police work as a career, and to demonstrate its serious intent, the department was coming to them asking for their help. These tactics had the effect of legitimating the new administration's commitment to affirmative action and increasing the number of black applicants. The percentage of black applicants to the police force rose from fifty-four percent in 1973 to eighty-one percent in 1975.

The next step was to facilitate the selection process. The barrier for many blacks trying to join the police force was the entrance examination. Blacks had charged that the examination was culturally biased and not job-related. In 1971 the U.S. Supreme Court ruling in *Griggs v. Duke Power Company* agreed with blacks that the test had adverse impact on minorities and required that all employment tests be job-related. The court case changed the whole field of personnel testing, and as a result of this ruling, a subsequent North Carolina case placed all personnel examinations under scrutiny. Prior to 1974 Detroit used examinations for all civil service positions and a rule of one in hiring. In the police department, which had its own separate testing system, a four-hour general knowledge entrance examination was replaced by a more streamlined test that was clearly related to the job. But when Young took office, he ordered the test changed again after he concluded that it still contained biases against minorities. The department changed its promotional exams as well.[7] The percentages of blacks and whites who now pass the tests are virtually identical—a crucial test for lack of bias in the eyes of the courts.

While the upgrading of recruitment and selection processes was accomplished without excessive conflict, enforcement of the residency rules and the more controversial policy of parallel promotions continued to meet bitter opposition from the white-dominated police unions. On July 4, 1974, a new city charter went into effect. The new charter gave the mayor more control over mayoral agencies. The police chief's job became a departmental post, subordinate to a five-member board of civilian commissioners, and under this new structure, the mayor could impose more direction for the police.

Remaining consistent with his electoral mandate, Coleman Young moved to consolidate support for a major reorganization and reorientation of the department. Like many other newly elected big city black mayors, Young also sought to assuage white fears—in this case, of a black takeover of the police department—and he did this by retaining the incumbent white police chief, Phillip Tannian. In addition, Young installed a respected white labor leader, Douglas Fraser (then head of the Chrysler department at UAW world headquarters) as chairman of the board of police commissioners.[8] According to newspaper accounts, Young had decided to retain Tannian for two reasons: first, Tannian was white, and, second, he was malleable.[9] Through Tannian, the new mayor was able to facilitate the reorganization of the police department—a process that offered opportunities to review headquarters staff, implement transfers to break up unit cliques, create mini-stations, and return some desk-bound police officers to the streets. All of these moves were designed to reorient the department to the new political realities of the city.

Getting Blacks into Blue

One of the first acts of the new board of the police commission, appointed by Coleman Young, was adoption of a formal affirmative action program, which gave the mayor added leverage in instituting the most aggressive affirmative action program of any police department in the nation. The new administration's goal was to change the composition of the force from 18 percent black in 1973 to 50 percent minority officers by 1977. Table 8 shows the breakdown by race, sex, and rank of the department prior to the new mayor's policy.

The racial and gender disparities were obvious. Blacks and women were underrepresented in every rank. To achieve a 50/50 split, blacks would have to replace half of the current force, assuming, that is, that white recruitment would level off, that attrition would continue, and that blacks would be recruited aggressively. Although a move to recruit black officers was consistent with population changes, the local media did not read it as a "catch-up" tactic, and instead viewed it as an attempt to make the police department an ethnic enclave in reverse. In a study of the New York City Police Department, writer-policeman Stephen Leinen summarized the value of having black officers on the force.

> For a number of younger black officers entering the department . . . being a part of the larger black experience heightened their sense of identity with the community and led to a rejection of many traditional police values. These younger men openly expressed interest in the affairs and problems of the black community, an attachment foreign to all but a handful of white officers. Because they grew up in the ghetto themselves, they had a better understanding of its culture. Consequently, when assigned to patrol, they were less apprehensive than white cops in their dealings with black people and more likely to attempt to mediate problems without resorting to provocative behavior, unnecessary force, or arrest. Also, because these younger officers felt less threatened in contact situations with other blacks, they tended to integrate themselves into, rather than isolate themselves from, the community. In short, for many blacks living in the ghetto, the added presence of the young black cop in the street represented a significant break with traditional methods of patrolling these areas and a move toward fulfilling the real meaning of the "service" model of policing.[10]

Table 8. **Breakdown of Police Personnel by Race, Sex, and Rank, 1974**

Rank	White M	White F	Black M	Black F	Other M	Other F	Total
Superintendent	1						1
Chief of Patrol	1						1
Deputy Chief	3		3				6
Commander	11		4				15
Inspector	52	2	6				60
Lieutenant	207	6	11	3			227
Sergeant	1069	15	89	5			1178
Officer	2943	96	836	56	3		3934
Totals	4287	119	949	64	3		5422

Source: Detroit Police Department.

An inevitable parallel to race discrimination is gender discrimination, and Mayor Young was equally committed to the elimination of both. The mayor's efforts to recruit more women were assisted by a ruling from U.S. District Court Judge Ralph Freeman, who mandated that one woman must be hired for each man to bring the department up to acceptable equal opportunity standards.[11] White policemen reacted bitterly, and directed much of their frustration at Chief Phillip Tannian and his staff. Feeling threatened, apparently, by the new affirmative action policy in their department, white officers insisted that their union leadership do something to protect them. Union leaders in turn began searching for ways to take some significant action to indicate their anger at department policy. They staged an epidemic of "blue flu," for example, over statements made by the department leadership. Thirty-nine white officers of the Tactical Mobile Service called in sick after their black lieutenant was quoted in the *Michigan Chronicle* as having said he intended to change the image of the unit through affirmative action.[12] White officers' reactions reflected the uncertainty of their role in the future of the department; they sought reassurance from the new administration.

The Naming of a Black Police Chief

In the quest for a new image for the Detroit Police Department, it became obvious that the city's mayor needed "his own man" in charge of department affairs. The appointment of a black police chief carried considerable symbolic appeal and also political risk. The idea of getting control over the department and making it more community-oriented and less antagonistic toward blacks would not be complete without a black chief.

In 1975 Mayor Young appointed Frank Blount, a black man, to the newly created post of deputy chief of police. This move was seen by many as the first step in replacing Chief Tannian, and, indeed, Blount assumed considerable administrative power over department activities. In a white-dominated bureaucracy, Blount's appointment was inevitably viewed as an ethnic takeover. The dual administrative arrangement with Blount and Tannian did not work well; it divided the department ethnically, rendering Tannian's position as chief untenable. The anticipated replacement of Tannian was delayed because of allegations charging that Blount was involved in illegal activities.[13]

On 21 August Blount was put on indefinite sick leave by Chief Tannian.[14] On 22 August the justice department confirmed that Blount was the target of an investigation into narcotics payoffs involving other ranking police officials. A month later Blount was put on "educational leave" and was replaced by another black officer, William Hart. Chief Tannian was relieved of his duties on 28 September, and Hart was named the first black police chief in the history of the department.[15]

The ascendancy of Chief Hart, a highly educated man with a Ph.D. in psychology who had been a police officer since 1952, had different meanings for each of the partisans in the affirmative action struggle. To blacks it meant that one of their own had finally achieved a significant position of leadership, and they could now expect the mayor's new policy of affirmative action to be faithfully implemented. To the white police officers and their unions, Hart's appointment was yet another indication of the drastic political changes taking place in the police department. Many white officers felt the need to rely more on union leadership as a defense against the new administration.

With Hart as the new department head, a definitive affirmative action policy statement was promulgated by the department, which read:

> The Detroit Police Department fully recognizes its responsibility under the United States Constitution and the Bill of Rights, as well as numerous federal statutes and court decisions from all parts of the nation, to guarantee to all employees equal opportunity under the law. The department has a responsibility to pursue an aggressive affirmative action program, in order to insure that no member of the department shall be denied fair and even-handed treatment on the basis of race, color, creed, sex or national origin. A department which more accurately reflects the pluralistic characteristics of our city will be the best equipped to carry out the primary responsibility of the department—effective, fair, equal, and profes-

sional law enforcement. Furthermore, a truly representative department will encourage more citizen participation in, and support of, the law enforcement process.[16]

On the surface, the statement seemed reasonable enough. Proof of the department's commitment would be reflected in recruitment and promotion policies. In the case of promotions, blacks had been traditionally discriminated against and this caused considerable morale problems for black officers. Any change in the department would necessitate a move toward more blacks in leadership positions such as commanders, inspectors, and captains.

Black Officers and the DPOA

The Detroit Police Officers Association, which represents most of the officers in the department, declined to participate in bargaining over a compromise of affirmative hiring while maintaining layoffs by seniority.[17] As expected, the union was protecting senior white officers and abandoning the newly hired minority officers. Black DPOA members reacted angrily, and approximately forty-five officers picketed DPOA headquarters, claiming that they did not have fair representation within the DPOA. Aside from not protecting them from layoffs, they asserted, the unions locked them out of leadership positions. While more than a fifth of DPOA members were black, there were no blacks on the union's executive board or on any of its important committees.[18]

Mayor Young reacted to the DPOA's unwillingness to negotiate on seniority by threatening to lay off 550 white policemen (since the injunction barred layoffs of minorities) unless an agreement could be reached.[19] District Judge Freeman replaced his temporary order with a ruling that barred the city from laying off 275 police officers, predominantly blacks and women whose jobs were federally funded. This ruling, which some white officers regarded as antiseniority and an example of reverse discrimination, prompted a protest rally by about a thousand white policemen that ended in violence and the beating of a black officer. If ever there was a low point in black/white police officer relations, the year 1975 was it.

The actions of the white officers further alienated the mayor and the black community. Aside from further exacerbating black officers' sense of separation from their white counterparts and thus dividing the department into warring camps, these incidents, city politicians and leaders worried, would damage the city's image and the collective bargaining process. The search for compromises took on an emergency tone, and the stage was finally set for negotiation. As a result, the city and the two police unions (DPOA and LSA) reached an agreement in which concessions replaced layoffs.[20] In the wake of this tentative agreement, however, while both sides were praising the role played by Judge Keith in arranging the compromise, the DPOA rank and file rejected the agreement.[21] DPOA president Ron Sexton stated bluntly, "They simply don't trust the administration to keep their word."[22] After Judge Keith announced in open court that he would not allow the city to renege on a ratified economic agreement, the DPOA's membership accepted a slightly revised version.[23] Though conflict between the administration and police unions was temporarily resolved, other issues came in quickly to fill the void.

Struggle over Residency

Many white officers want to live in the suburbs and believe it is their right to do so. The city has resisted allowing nonresidents to become policemen because its council believes officers should live where they work. The argument is that Detroit would receive less police coverage if some of its force were to live outside the city. Police are required to be armed at all times and are technically on duty at all times, yet what good does it do to have an officer living in Livonia or Warren who would have to commute to an emergency? The struggle over residency requirements resembles that of most large urban centers, with white policemen generally demanding the right to live in the suburbs, and Detroit is certainly not unique; many cities require police officers and other civil servants to live inside the city. Because police force salaries are now ample to accord officers greater social mobility, many want better schools and protection for their families and therefore choose to live in the suburbs.

Levinson's study of residency requirements asserts that the Detroit police have been fighting for the right to live outside the city since the 1960s. Under the old police commissioner system, the commissioner could grant a waiver of the residency requirement on a person-by-person basis. In 1968 the city council passed extremely rigid residency ordinances. The DPOA took the city to court over the matter, and the court ruled that residency was a bargainable issue—the union could regain the residency clause at the bargaining table. The department's layoff policy raised the issue again, since the threat of a layoff was directed at individuals who were holding their jobs illegally.

The logic of a residency law is simply that a city is not obligated to hire people who are not residents. Called by some legal scholars the "public coffer theory," it assumes that people who live in an area have a stake in the welfare of their community. Opponents of residency laws, primarily police unions and associations, believe such restrictions are unconstitutional and, in some cases, discriminate unfairly against whites. According to these critics, whites should be allowed to live outside the city and still work for the city. Residency laws are frequently litigated and are found constitutional.[24] Nevertheless, white Detroit police and firefighters have continued to press for exceptions for the uniformed services, and Coleman Young has stood foursquare against waiving the residency requirements.

In the fall of 1975 the DPOA announced that it would appeal an arbitration ruling made to the Wayne County Circuit Court that upheld the residency requirement.[25] Despite the appeal, police chief Tannian announced that trial board hearings would begin within thirty days; according to Tannian, the city had "200 documented cases that will go before the trial board.... There are many more to come."[26] The effort by Chief Tannian and his successors to enforce the residency requirement continues to be a leverage point for the central police staff, which has apparently regarded the residency issue as a tool for demonstrating to politicians their vigilance in such matters and their choice of prerogatives in the enforcement of department discipline.

In 1976 the U.S. Supreme Court upheld the authority of the Philadelphia Civil Service Commission to impose and enforce residency requirements.[27] The court found that such requirements do not violate civil or protected rights to travel. Many states have preempted local governments on this issue, but Michigan has left the matter to local authorities. The city of Detroit has enforced the requirement, albeit selectively, although it continues to be a topic of collective bargaining and arbitration hearings. The union leadership has strongly advocated changes in the requirements but is usually prepared to trade off the issue for other concessions.

Layoffs as Fiscal First-Aid

Tensions within the department continued to mount in 1975 and in fact took on a new dimension as the city announced that the fiscal crisis demanded layoffs of police officers.[28] Mayor Young had announced a 1 May date for laying off 825 policemen. Cutbacks would begin with the firing of those officers found violating the residency laws.[29] An accompanying reduction-in-force schedule called for the demotion of 260 sergeants to the rank of patrolman and thirty-five lieutenants to sergeant. If federal funding were made available in thirty-one days, however, 255 laid-off officers would be reinstated.[30] It became obvious to all parties that the layoffs, if implemented according to seniority, would impede, if not eliminate, the progress made recently by black and female officers.

The threat of layoffs prompted a group of women and black officers to file suits in federal court charging that layoffs by seniority would destroy affirmative action programs. Judges Damon Keith and Ralph Freeman, the U.S. district judges hearing the cases, asked plaintiff groups to meet with union and city officials to negotiate a compromise that would preserve some of the gains achieved through affirmative action. The judges also granted temporary injunctions barring the layoffs. In 1974 the city and the union had reached an agreement avoiding layoffs; in 1975 the fiscal and political environments were quite different. The willingness of the DPOA to sacrifice new officers in layoffs exacerbated a long-standing conflict between black officers and the union.

Continuing Fiscal Crisis

Budget deficits, which had been serious during the early part of the Young administration, became more critical during 1976. Early in March Mayor Young warned that the city might be forced to lay off up to 1,600 police officers after 1 July, as the city's deficit approached $100 million. The Guardians, an association of black officers, appealed unsuccessfully to all officers to make additional concessions in order to avoid layoffs.[31] Battle lines were drawn, but then a new player entered the arena.

U.S. labor secretary William Usery issued a regulation limiting the number of laid-off city employees who could be rehired by Comprehensive Employment Training Act of 1973 (CETA) funds. The rule led to a legal battle between the city and the labor department, which began during layoffs in April. The dispute continued as layoffs scheduled for July took place.

The city was faced with a choice—proceed with its layoffs, defy the labor department, risk loss of CETA funds, or try to achieve cost reduction through other means. It decided not to challenge the federal government, and Deputy Mayor William Beckham announced that the city would not defy the new regulation. This capitulation was further evidence of an open secret—that is, the dependency by Detroit on outside funds to cover city housekeeping costs. Originally intended to supply jobs for chronically unemployed persons, CETA funds were being used, with the knowledge of federal officials, to supplement the budget. Cities like Detroit, faced with a financial crunch, had consistently utilized CETA funds to supplement the revenue side of the budget. Indeed, the inventive use of CETA funds had become an art form among city administrations. One tactic was to lay off employees just long enough so that they were considered unemployed (usually fifteen days) and then rehire them with CETA funds. CETA, as originally designed, would only have allowed the hiring of new personnel for public agencies. However, union contracts prohibit the hiring of new personnel while former employees remain on layoff, in order to protect the rehiring rights of laid-off personnel. In April federal officials had allowed Detroit to continue its unusual payroll practices pending further negotiations.[32] The agreement was later extended to cover July layoffs as well.

The July layoffs were themselves further complicated by a 1 July ruling by U.S. District Judge Ralph Freeman stating that seniority could be waived for 347 women officers because of past discrimination on account of gender. Ironically, similar protection sought by some black male officers was denied in a ruling by Judge Keith.[33] Total layoffs numbered 973 officers, and this added to the city's problem of preserving the earlier gains made by minorities while reducing the department to a size that could be supported by an austerity budget.

Promotional Practices and Discrimination

In the period from 1977 to 1978, promotional practices became the dominant issue. In 1973 black males represented only 4.1 percent of Detroit's police sergeants and 3.9 percent of the lieutenants. By 1979 the percentage of black male sergeants had grown to 15.6 and to 20.6 percent for lieutenants. As blacks and females increased in percentage of the force, the overall number of such positions declined—from 1,153 to 876 sergeants and 226 to 189 lieutenants. In many ways, promotion became the most controversial of the several issues facing the police department because it involved veteran white officers and their chances for advancement. Promoting is considered more of a zero-sum game since there is a fixed number of supervisory and administrative positions. Recruiting new officers represents no threat to the veterans and may increase the need for more supervisory officers.

In a suit first filed in September, 1977, the DPOA claimed that the promotional practices of the Detroit Police Department resulted in reverse discrimination against white officers in the promotion of patrol officers to sergeants. The DPOA argued that black officers with lower examination scores were selected for promotion over white officers as a result of the 50/50 promotion plan.

In September, James Andary, city defense attorney, called for Judge Kaess to disqualify himself from the DPOA case on the grounds that Kaess had demonstrated a bias against affirmative action programs in law enforcement.[34] No judge likes to be accused of bias. Kaess dismissed Andary's disqualification motion on the grounds that it had been improperly filed. The motion charged that "Kaess repeatedly interjected personal opinions into the trial of the suit, and often acted like he knew more about the evidence than the witnesses and lawyers."[35] Kaess also dismissed a second motion by Andary, again refusing to disqualify himself from the case.[36]

After hearing the city's case, Judge Kaess issued a permanent injunction barring the city from promoting blacks with lower scores over more qualified white applicants. Kaess upheld the DPOA argument that the city's promotion policy violated the equal protection clause of the Fourteenth Amendment, proclaiming, "While the purpose of a quota system is generally compassionate, its effect is intolerable because it denigrates individuals by reducing them to a single immutable birth characteristic, skin pigmentation."[37] Kaess essentially argued that city attorneys had failed to prove a specific history of discrimination against black police officers. According to the judge, the police department had already made every necessary effort, prior to 1974, to attract qualified black applicants. Kaess's ruling stopped short of barring all affirmative action promotions and limited itself to advancement to sergeant.[38]

Administrative reaction to the Kaess ruling was swift. The city announced that it would file an appeal with the 6th Circuit Court of Appeals within twenty days. Kaess refused, however, to delay enforcement of his order pending the appeal. Accordingly, promotions were to be based strictly on seniority and test scores.[39] Did the Kaess ruling signal the beginning of a backward trend in the effort to integrate the police department hierarchy?

Many blacks saw the Kaess ruling as a danger sign, and a new group, the Citizens for Affirmative Action in Detroit (CAADET), was formed by black leaders to combat further erosion of the ground black policemen had so far gained. CAADET included business, labor, and religious community members and was chaired by Larry Washington of the Detroit chapter of the National Association for the Advancement of Colored People. Some members of CAADET filed amicus curiae briefs with the court. CAADET further vowed to mobilize the community and commit to overturning the Kaess decision.[40]

Mayor Young had an equally dramatic response to the Kaess ruling. Young refused to promote additional patrolmen to sergeant in 1978-79, and the policy process was stalemated. It took the action of the courts to start the process rolling again. Judge Damon Keith, a black man, ruled that the city could continue to use affirmative action to promote sergeants to lieutenants. In Keith's opinion, affirmative action was needed to remedy the effects of past discrimination—a view that directly contradicted Kaess's ruling. Keith had been a district judge when the Lieutenants and Sergeants Association suit was originally filed in November, 1975. He had since been appointed to the court of appeals but elected to continue as a district judge to hear the LSA promotions case.[41]

The mayor's affirmative action program was further vindicated and strengthened when the 6th U.S. Circuit Court of Apeals overruled the Kaess decision. The unanimous decision of the three-judge panel was that the city's affirmative action program did not violate the civil rights of white police officers.[42] On 6 December, police chief Hart testified before the Board of Police Commissioners and made the following observation:

> There is no explanation for the drastic underrepresentation of black police officers, sergeants and lieutenants other than the systematic racial discrimination in the hiring and promotional practices of the Department. Therefore, the conclusion is inescapable that many more blacks would have been present in all ranks, including that of sergeant and lieutenant, had nondiscriminatory practices been followed. Therefore, the Board should again acknowledge that racial discrimination in the past has resulted in a present underrepresentation of blacks at the sergeant and lieutenant level.

A promotion plan was immediately developed by the city, but, once again, budgetary limitations brought about restrictions in the scope of the program.

Fiscal Uncertainty and Affirmative Action

Retrenchment had continued to be the overriding reality of city personnel policy since 1978. There were simply no funds to continue staffing at the previous level nor were there funds for new hires. Despite a new federal countercyclical grant for cities with higher than average unemployment, a continuing drop in property tax revenues kept city finances tight.[43] In July binding arbitration began between the city and Detroit's police unions, who had been without a contract for over a year.[44] An arbitration panel ruled in favor of the DPOA because it found that even the city's poor financial condition in no way prevented it from paying the wages the union demanded. This ruling came on the heels of a three million dollar arbitration award to the LSA.[45] Wayne County Circuit Judge Victor Baum upheld the three-year wage award set by the arbitration panel as the city attempted to overturn it on financial grounds.[46] The city appealed, however. The State Court of Appeals gave the city a reprieve when it ruled that the city did not have to make eighteen months of retroactive payments immediately. The appeals court also ruled that the city should begin paying the police at the higher rate until the controversy was settled.[47]

More and more financial pressure was applied, as Wayne County Circuit Judge Patrick Duggan ordered the city to begin paying the higher rate dictated in the LSA arbitration award.[48] Mayor Young remained adamant about overturning the two awards—"Otherwise we're out of luck," he said. "I mean, we're talking about cuts that are unthinkable, like lots of cops and lots of firefighters."[49] In September four hundred police layoffs were announced and attributed to budget deficits.[50] Young announced that unless the courts overturned police and fire arbitration awards, more police would face layoffs.[51]

The battle over arbitration and wages continued in 1980, with the Republican convention as a backdrop. In January 1980, the Young administration took its case against compulsory arbitration to the Michigan Supreme Court, arguing that the arbitration law (Public Act 312) was unconstitutional. Some opponents of arbitration saw it as a crutch used by unions to avoid collective bargaining. Proponents of the compulsory arbitration law viewed it as a guarantee against strikes by municipal public safety employees. Young asserted that he would risk such strikes in order to regain control over city finances. His preference for collective bargaining over arbitration reflects his own labor background and the growing sense that arbitrators were making fiscal policy through labor decisions. Some labor scholars have agreed with him. Levin, for instance, observed:

> The bargaining model reflected in these laws deviates from the industry model rather than parallels it. It assumes that a strike is more costly than any other form of settlement, including compulsory arbitration. Yet one wonders. The arbitrator or impasse panel empowered to decide a settlement is concerned principally with the relationship between the two parties to the dispute and is not directly accountable to the public. Thus the arbitrator searches for a mutually acceptable "solution" that preserves the continuity of services. The cost of settlement is a subordinate objective, particularly in the absence of incentives for labor and management to agree among themselves. So-called "final-offer arbitration" tends to provide those incentives, but relatively few American governments use it.[52]

In subsequent contract negotiations, the mayor asked the police unions to disregard the arbitrators' awards and return to the salary levels proposed by the city in 1977.[53] On 6 June the mayor's attempt at a negotiated compromise received a serious setback when the State Supreme Court upheld the arbitrators' ruling.[54] The impact of the court's ruling on police affirmative action was devastating. With four hundred officers laid off already, the added financial burden of arbitration awards would necessitate additional cuts. In July police chief Hart noted that the proportion of black and women officers would drop by between 26 and 28 percent after the next round of layoffs scheduled for late summer 1980, and this would put minority enrollment back to its 1977–78 levels. In September 1980, 690 officers received layoff notices, of whom three-quarters were women and minorities.[55]

Affirmative action suffered another blow during the fiscal crisis of 1981. In order for the city to pay its bills, it needed to generate more revenues. The mayor asked a blue ribbon committee chaired by Fred Secrest, a retired Ford Motor Company executive, to review the situation and make recommendations. The Secrest Report recommended a tax increase, short-term borrowing, and wage concessions.

Mayor Young called for concessions because of the city's deteriorating economic situation. In April he threatened to lay off as many as 1,050 police officers if municipal unions refused to grant wage concessions. The initial position of the DPOA—refusal to accept either wage concessions or layoffs—brought criticism from black officers, who considered fiscal issues secondary to the prospect of further layoffs. Lewis Colson, executive director of the Guardians, a black officers' association, summarized it: "We can't afford to lose any more black officers." Colson was referring to the black/white officer ratio, which had fallen from 39 percent in 1979 to 20 percent in 1981.[56] Table 9 shows the breakdown of police personnel at the time of the city's fiscal crisis.

This table shows a decline in real numbers of both white and black males. Although the percentage of black males on the force increased, the percentage of female officers increased dramatically. Any progress, in reality, was teetering on the brink, as the city faced the worst budget deficit in its history.

The 1981 Detroit fiscal crisis has been described as a watershed in the city's history. The mayor's blue ribbon study committee forecast a $132.6 million deficit by June 30, 1981, and recommended an increase in the city income tax rate from 2 to 3 percent for residents and from 0.5 to 1.5 percent for nonresidents; the panel also recommended that the city negotiate wage concessions in lieu of layoffs. Mayor Young accepted the recommendations and began to negotiate for wage concessions. Only one union—the Building Trades Council—ultimately refused to accept wage concessions.

Additional police layoffs were avoided when the DPOA and the city agreed to a three-year pay freeze on June 22, 1981. One condition of this pact was that 250 laid-off officers were to be recalled.[57] On 12 August, ninety-seven officers returned to the force.[58] Additional recalls were jeopardized when Young announced on 23 December that cuts in state aid had forced the city to postpone the recalls. DPOA president David Watroba summed up the general feelings of his union members when he said, "When we participated in the Detroit bail out, we were led to believe the budget would be balanced."[59] The fiscal situation did improve eventually, and the city recalled 150 more officers on April 1, 1982.[60]

In March 1983, a panel of the 6th Circuit Court in Cincinnati upheld the 1980 ruling by Detroit district judge Damon Keith, which transformed the voluntary promotion plan into one mandated by court order. Judge Keith had formally upheld the promotion plan as constitutional, thus undermining the LSA's attempt to establish a case for reverse discrimination. In May, however, the U.S. justice department asked the federal appeals court to reconsider its opinion. In its brief, the U.S. Department of Justice argued that a panel of the appeals court erred in its original March 29 decision. Federal attorneys argued that the full court, as opposed to a panel, should review the case.

Table 9. **Racial and Gender Composition of Detroit Police Department, 1981**

Rank	White M	White F	Black M	Black F	Other M	Other F	Total
Superintendent			1				1
Executive Deputy Chief	1						1
Deputy Chief	3		4				7
Commander	10		9	1	1		21
Inspector	32	1	22	2	1		58
Lieutenant	135	10	50	4			199
Sergeant	632	25	161	12	3		833
Officer	1921	117	675	185	33	3	2934
Totals	2734	153	922	204	38	3	4054

Source: Detroit Police Department.

Reagan and Reverse Discrimination

The Reagan administration apparently saw the Detroit case as an opportunity to establish its credentials as the chief opponent of quotas. Federal attorneys asserted that "the right to be free of unlawful racial discrimination in employment belongs to individuals, not groups."[61] In his book *Affirmative Discrimination*, Nathan Glazer made an eloquent statement against quotas.[62] Glazer suggested that middle-class blacks, not inner city blacks, were the chief beneficiaries of the affirmative action policy. The policy only accelerated the job entry of those who would have made it under the old policy of equal opportunity. In addition, the idea of quotas for blacks inflamed white ethnic consciousness and ignited a demand for a distribution of wealth and power based on ethnicity.

The Reagan administration's statement clearly drew the line for those opposed to affirmative action. Mayor Young commented, "The Reagan Administration seems determined to systematically destroy the progress this nation has made toward redressing past wrongs."[63] The Detroit Board of Police Commissioners wrote a letter to Attorney General William French Smith, which pleaded for the support of the justice department in the panel ruling, but it had little effect on the administration.[64] The justice department persisted in its attempts to overturn the ruling. Clearly, the Reagan administration offensive was an attempt to achieve an anti-quota victory in the heart of a liberal, prolabor region. Despite the refusal of the court to permit the justice department to enter an amicus curiae brief on the side of the LSA, the Young administration's efforts to change the court's decision persisted.

In December 1983, the Reagan administration asked the Supreme Court to consider whether affirmative action programs were unconstitutional if they included explicit racial criteria for hiring.[65] The justice department filed a brief before the court concerning the Detroit Police Department plan, with particular emphasis on provisions for equal black and white promotions.[66] But on January 9, 1984, the high court let stand the appeals court's ruling upholding the city's nine-year-old program.[67]

The outcome of *Hanson Bratton v. City of Detroit* confirms the earlier Weber ruling, which upheld voluntary hiring and promotion plans in the private sector. In *United Steelworkers of America v. Weber* (1979) the court found that Title VII does not prohibit private, voluntary race-conscious affirmative action plans as long as they allow for white mobility and retention. Although there was no voluntary agreement by the union, the city clearly met the requirements under *Weber*—that the plan would not result in the discharge of white officers, nor bar them from promotion. The high court rejected the argument by five police sergeants that the promotion plan discriminated against them.[68] The *Bratton* ruling also confirmed the district court's finding that *Weber* is not constrained by union negotiated contracts.

The *Bratton* decision was regarded as a setback for the Reagan administration, particularly since the president had taken such a high profile on the matter. The legal victory solved few of the immediate fiscal problems, focusing as it did on procedure. And it did not offer a way for the mayor to save his affirmative action hires. If new layoffs were indicated, then minorities and women would be the first to go. On September 3, 1983, Mayor Young announced new plans for the layoff of 224 Detroit police officers, for budgetary reasons; of those, 182 were black. Four days later the NAACP petitioned U.S. District Judge Horace Gilmore for a temporary restraining order prohibiting the layoff of the 182 blacks, pending the outcome of a 1980 suit against the DPOA that challenged the "last hired, last fired" policy.[69] Gilmore refused, ruling that the laid-off officers would suffer no permanent harm if the NAACP were successful in its three-year-old suit, which he would begin hearing in September. The legal maneuvers became more complicated when two of the laid-off officers sued in Wayne County Circuit Court to block the layoffs on the grounds that the actions were taken without city council approval. Judge Irwin Burdick gave Mayor Young twenty days to get that approval. Without it, the officers would be reinstated with back pay.

On 2 November, the period expired, and the State Court of Appeals refused to delay Burdick's order pending a hearing. Young then filed a last-minute plea with the State Supreme Court and he refused to rehire the 224 officers. Burdick demanded to know why Young should not be held in contempt of court, but a subsequent stay ordered by the State Supreme Court upheld Young's position that the officers should not be recalled pending the hearing before the State Court of Appeals. In February, 1984, the appeals court overruled the lower court and barred the layoffs.

Then, on 22 February, U.S. District Court Judge Horace Gilmore ruled, in the NAACP suit, that layoffs of more than one thousand officers in 1979 and 1980 were illegal because they were based solely on seniority and discriminated against black officers. Gilmore's ruling held, in effect, that the city's constitutional obligation to uphold affirmative action superseded the collectively bargained seniority rights of police officers. Though the ruling by Gilmore would make a profound impact on the police department, it did not require the city to immediately recall any of the 1,103 laid-off officers. A full trial was to be held in late spring or early summer of 1985 to determine possible remedies in the case. Both union and city officials scurried to defend their actions in the layoffs, which, Young conceded, had had a disproportionate impact on black officers. Young insisted that the city really had no choice because its contract with the DPOA required layoffs to be made by seniority. Union president David Watroba noted that Gilmore's ruling found the city, not the union, guilty of discrimination. Hence, remedies should cost the city financial penalties rather than costing active officers their jobs.[70]

On June 12, 1984, the U.S. Supreme Court found, in *Firefighters Local 1784 v. Stotts*, that seniority rules were valid if negotiated with a nondiscriminatory intent, even when their enforcement would cause adverse impact on affirmative action hires. Justice White, writing for the majority (6-3), stated that the U.S. Civil Rights Act of 1964 "protects bona fide seniority systems and it is inappropriate to deny an 'innocent' white employee the benefits of his seniority in order to provide a remedy for blacks hired under Affirmative Action Programs." White argued, "If individual members of a class demonstrate they have been actual victims of the discriminatory practice, they may be ... given their rightful place on the seniority roster." He and some of his colleagues found no "evidence that blacks have been the victims of discrimination" in the Firefighters' case.[71]

In effect, the court was standing foursquare on the seniority principle of last hired, first fired. In *International Brotherhood of Teamsters v. U.S.* (1977)[72] the court had upheld the seniority clauses for contracts written before Title VII was established. The recent ruling was now expanded to include those written after the 1964 Civil Rights Act. The tenor of the court's argument has been to maintain that, in discrimination cases, the burden of proof is on the individual. The ruling had the effect of insulating most seniority agreements from affirmative action suits. It also made a distinction between individual relief and relief that has the intent of remedying the previous exclusion of some group. After the Firefighters' case, Detroit was left with little flexibility in saving low-seniority affirmative action hires from layoffs or other reduction-in-force actions.

Given the new immunity for seniority systems, future rounds of layoffs are likely to fall disproportionately on minorities and women. In ruling that bona fide seniority systems are both permissible and protected, the court acknowledged the system's adverse effects on minorities, women, and young workers. Conversely, the court strengthened the city's hand in layoffs by eliminating court challenges enjoining strict compliance with seniority rules.

The Court and the DPOA Leadership

On July 25, 1984, Judge Horace Gilmore ordered the city to rehire eight hundred black officers who had been laid off during 1979–80.[73] Granting the black police retroactive seniority, the judge forbade the city to immediately reduce total numbers again by laying off white officers. The judge also ordered the DPOA to include blacks in union leadership within twelve months. Mayor Young responded: "Unless [Judge Gilmore] wrote a check along with the order, we still don't have any means of calling [the laid-off workers] back. The order amounts to an appropriation. The judge is asking me to spend money that he knows we don't have."[74] Although the officers would not receive back pay, Chief Hart estimated that it would cost Detroit fifty thousand dollars to rehire each of the officers, and this could cost the city thirty million dollars.

In his opinion Judge Gilmore cited that the percentage of black officers had declined from 39 in 1979 to 28 in 1980—a change that took place against the background of a city whose black residents amounted to 70 percent of its population. Gilmore's decision was not guided by the *Stotts* case but by the equal protection clause of the Fourteenth Amendment. He opined, "a city does not fulfill its obligations under the Fourteenth Amendment, nor does a union fulfill its obligation to fairly represent its members, by simply giving a difficult problem of redressing racial injustice in our society to the federal courts."[75] His comment was indeed revealing because it signaled the court's insistence upon equal protection of employees during disputes between the unions and the city government.

The DPOA's reaction was to attack Gilmore's references to union indifference toward its laid-off black members. The judge's order regarding the incorporation of blacks into DPOA leadership brought a response from the union's counsel, Walter Nussbaum, who observed, "Not even the Supreme Court has ordered a remedy that predetermines the outcome of an election along racial lines or otherwise destroys the secret ballot, a foundation stone of the democratic process."[76] But Guardian president, Willie Bell, welcomed the Gilmore decision and its clear inference that the DPOA had failed in its duty to provide fair representation.

Conclusions

In *The Politics of Urban Personnel Policy*, I argued that urban personnel policy was a product of a "multidimensional dynamic political process that involves competition, negotiation and exchange among specific interest groups. Participants are engaged in a continuous struggle for dominance, each trying to upstage the others, fighting as if in a game for stakes that include jobs, contracts and political careers."[77] My study of the Detroit Police Department's experience with affirmative action showed that interest groups were prepared to risk public alienation in pursuing their goals. In using the court system, they hoped to add that body's prestige to their struggle. Detroit's police department, like that of many uniformed civil servants, has long resisted mayoral directives that are at variance with departmental practices, and police officers have often viewed their department as a kind of fraternity, one that gives them authority to decide police policy and procedures. Mayor Young's role in the continuing struggle illustrates the growing political clout of black mayors; to his constituency, the test was whether or not he could gain control of the police department.

The case of Carl Stokes of Cleveland was a lesson well studied by black politicians. In his autobiography, *Promises of Power*, Stokes admitted his failure to reform the police department and called it "my greatest frustration and my greatest failure."[78] Many believed that it was his problem with the police department that undermined his political career and forced him to withdraw from politics.

In his own campaign, Mayor Young made it clear that he intended to reform Detroit's police department. The establishment of mini-stations, the promotion of community efforts (for example, of the Blue Pig, a jazz band composed of police, and expansion of the Police Athletic League), the use of foot patrols, and the creation of the Neighborhood Watch Program were all designed to change the image of the police. In many ways the mayor has changed the ethos of the force, though, to do so, he had to assert his leadership against well-organized resistance by white officers, without damaging his political support. His efforts between 1973 and 1983 increased the number of blacks in the department from 18 to 30 percent—a major transformation that also saw women increase their representation from 3.4 to 11 percent. By 1983 an equal percentage of white males, black males, white females, and black females were promoted to lieutenants.

Young's reform efforts were aided by the fact that the police department had lost credibility in the 1967 riot, the Rochester Street Massacre, and again in its STRESS campaign. The fact that the DPOA had been publicly branded a racist organization by black officers also undermined the DPOA's attempts to gain public support. Accordingly, it was possible for the mayor to move aggressively to eliminate STRESS and reorganize the department. Affirmative action became the center of controversy between the mayor and the police department because it was the only issue that the DPOA could possibly use to gain white support. Layoff and seniority issues were easily understood and felt in this city of unions. Whites who supported affirmative action were nonetheless more resolute in their support of seniority as the foundation of unionism.

The black community and its representatives saw the struggle as yet another subterfuge for avoiding implementing affirmative action mandates. For them, the last hired, first fired rule meant they would lose black policemen. Besides, it was essentially the black community's police department, which they had won by voting a black administration into office, and they were outraged that union leaders, some of whom lived outside the city, were openly hostile to the new mayor. In Coleman Young and William Hart, the black community saw some hope of achieving the 50/50 split in the department promised in the 1974 election campaign. They viewed the city's fiscal problems with alarm, because they tended to offset any gains made in integrating the force.

The role of the courts, both state and federal, was also noteworthy. The court found itself making personnel policy after the two parties involved failed in the collective bargaining process. During the ten years examined in this book, the courts reviewed affirmative action plans, voided layoff notices, overruled arbitrators' findings, and mandated that the police union include blacks in leadership. Judge Gilmore went so far as to find the DPOA negligent in its duty of fair representation for its black members. Despite the more than $500,000 in dues paid by black members, the union did little, if anything, to protect them during the rounds of layoffs.

The effects of the city's two fiscal crises exacerbated the normal ethnic replacement process in the city work force. When fiscal crisis became the norm, the opportunity for a negotiated and mutually agreed replacement timetable was lessened. Replacement, a fairly routine matter, became entangled with other issues (for example, race, reform, and residency rules) facing the unions and the city. Detroit's replacement process, which was established during the Cavanagh period, was accelerated during Young's first administration. The fiscal crisis slowed it down, however, and allowed each side to gain political capital from a policy impasse. The DPOA led its members in a confrontation with the mayor, revealing its tarnished reputation on race relations and an alienated black membership. Again, the mayor's opponents had underestimated him. They would do so again in the fiscal crisis of 1981.

8

The Fiscal Crisis of 1981
Detroit's Brush with Disaster

Fiscal Crises and Political Definitions

The fiscal crisis of American cities came to the surface in the mid-seventies, when the nation discovered that cities were not paying their bills out of existing revenues. Although the financial situation of most cities has never revealed great surpluses, their cash flow problems reached a point in the 1970s where it became common practice to sell short-term notes just to keep the city's lights on. The severity of the crisis has prompted a series of questions, such as, How did cities get to this precipice? What factors facilitated and accelerated the mismatch of their revenues and expenditures? Are some cities more vulnerable than others? Are there winners and losers in a fiscal crisis? What can we learn from the history of cities' financial management? What is the role of state government in it? And, finally, what is the proper role of mayoral leadership in running a city's finances?

New York City's fiscal crisis in 1975 produced a plethora of books, articles, and commentary; it became the classic case of municipal financial management. Two scholars, particularly, seem to have keen insights into fiscal problems of the city. Patricia Leeds defined fiscal crisis as "a structural imbalance between revenues and expenditures, a persistent pattern whereby spending outpaces the taxation to support it."[1] She argued that budget deficits, rising taxes, and recurring efforts to enforce economics indicate a fiscal crisis. Leeds distinguishes between fiscal crisis and a financing crisis; she attributes the former to a city's need to engage in extensive borrowing in the bond market, whereas the latter represents the city's inability to continue to market its debt. New York reached the latter stage. The political differences between a fiscal crisis and a financing crisis are significant. Leeds observes, "The politics of fiscal crisis are organized around the distribution of benefits; the politics of a financing crisis are concerned with the equitable distribution of losses and risk of losses."[2]

In an earlier study, I attributed the fiscal crisis to conditions outlined by Leeds and others but saw it too as reflective of the changing guard, or an illustration of interest group succession—that is, who manages the cities. New York's fiscal crisis enabled the new "fiscal managers" to gain hegemony in city politics. This new group of municipal reformers lacks a coherent policy toward civil servants; it seems to be more interested in eliminating jobs through streamlining operations and relying on labor-saving new technology—not creating them. Detroit has not reached this stage, but the 1981 fiscal crisis may be a harbinger of this new class.

In another important city study, Terry Clark and Lorna Ferguson outline a typology of fiscal actors, emphasizing the role of mayor.[3] When faced with a crisis, Democrats tend to employ an attitude of social liberalism, which involves mobilizing organized interest groups and persuading them that certain prescribed fiscal measures are in their best interest. Alternatively, when Republicans are faced with a fiscal crisis, they tend to resort to retrenchment and cutback management. Ethnic politicians, who are characteristically liberal-minded on fiscal matters and socially conservative, employ the same tactics as the Democrats. Another type, according to Clark and Ferguson—the New Fiscal Populists (NFP), who emerged in the 1970s—eschewed the organization of interest group politics and advocated fiscal restraint and a populist ideology. Clark and Ferguson's empirical research found a public preference for fiscally conservative and socially liberal approaches. In other words, the public is prepared to support lower expenditures and taxes and fewer services. Americans are becoming increasingly liberal-minded on issues of personal liberty and tolerance, however, and, hence, the rise of the New Fiscal Populists is a direct response to this contradiction in the data. In analyzing data on 227 mayors and council members, Clark and Ferguson found mixed response to their NFP hypothesis. They found that Democrats generally did not become New Fiscal Populists, although there were some variations.

An equally interesting finding in Clark and Ferguson's study concerns the spending preferences of black citizens. Blacks tended to prefer more government spending than their white counterparts in the same income range. The study also found that black interest groups are declining in saliency, and race has declined as a political issue. Coupled with fewer federal and state resources, there is a trend toward more conservative fiscal policies by black leaders.

Clark and Ferguson's commentary about changes in political culture relates well to the current situation in Detroit. They briefly summarized the Detroit situation:

> Young gained support of the "New Detroiters," an urban coalition of blacks, business, and labor leaders including Henry Ford and Leonard Woodcock. He arranged huge fiscal support programs from Washington in the Carter years for the Chrysler Corporation and a new General Motors plant brought him considerable national attention. A senior statesman with such business leaders and in Washington, Young could also be street-tough enough to recall his background as union organizer. This combination of personal traits and public policies helped him head off more fiscally liberal contenders for the mayorship.[4]

The success of Coleman Young in holding off contenders is much more complicated, however, than Clark and Ferguson suggest. Young has been a fiscal conservative throughout his mayoralty yet retains his concern for social welfare issues. In turn, he has designed all kinds of methods to keep his city solvent. At times he has scaled down department development and skipped replacement cycles for city equipment and vehicles. At other times he has relied on layoffs, freezes, and attrition to reduce operating costs. In 1981 he advocated and won a tax increase in an environment of nationwide tax revolt, acting as he did from a position of electoral strength and drawing from the deep well of support from both his constituency and audience. Thus, a definable financial leadership strategy has emerged and is consistent with his governing style. It includes: interest group politics in the New Deal tradition; a tough bargaining posture with unions; active confrontation with opponents and critics; and maintaining the independence of city management structures, that is, protecting them from what have been called fiscal managers. The plight of Detroit in the thirties provided an example of what happens when a mayor fails in guiding the city through troubled times. The city went into default and fiscal managers took over Detroit's financial affairs.

The Fiscal Collapse of the 1930s

During the depression of the 1930s, as the nation's economy came apart and the market for automobiles disappeared, the fiscal foundation of Detroit collapsed. Detroit had been a victim of unbridled population growth combined with a lack of sound fiscal planning. Between 1915 and 1930, the city's population had doubled—from 673,000 to 1,630,000.[5] City government was forced to expand its services and personnel to accommodate the new residents, yet tax revenue collection procedures failed to keep pace with that other growth, and the city developed severe cash flow problems.

When the economy collapsed, many former taxpayers became relief recipients. Residents simply did not have the money to pay fees or tax bills. Lacking a reserve, the city had to borrow money to keep pace with new expenditures. During the recent period of expansion, the city budget had increased from $10.3 million to $76 million. The city's debt grew from $15.9 million in 1915 to $225 million in 1930.[6] Hence, investors, especially the banks, concluded that the city—overextended and underfinanced as it was, was a poor loan risk.

The size of the city's indebtedness and its growing unemployment forced Detroit to take drastic measures. The common council decided to seek outside assistance to study the problem and make recommendations for solutions in order to restore the city's fiscal reputation and the confidence of bankers and other investors. Since, however, the city is run by elected officials, politics have an inevitable influence on the true course of events.

Charles Bowles was elected mayor of Detroit in 1929, the year the stock market crashed. He never got a handle on the city's problems and was unable to provide the necessary leadership. Relief rolls simply overran all attempts at organization. Bowles's background as a Republican, and his alleged Klan connections, served to undermine his mayoralty. Late in 1930 Bowles became the first Michigan mayor to be recalled, only seven months after he took office. He was the latest of several men who had occupied the post in the preceding decade; James Couzens had resigned the post in 1922, Frank Doremus in 1924, and Joseph Martin in 1924. John Lodge served as interim mayor in 1923 and 1924 and was elected to the office in 1938. This merry-go-round, among other results, caused the common council's leadership function to devolve.

The onset of the depression forced the council to solicit outside advice, and it reluctantly accepted the recommendations of citizens' groups and reform organizations since it had lost its credibility with financial institutions. Ralph Stone, chairman of the board of Detroit's Security Trust Company, was invited to organize a committee to study the fiscal situation. The committee included representatives of the real estate board, the Detroit Board of Commerce, the Business Property Association, the Detroit Automobile Club, the Woodward Avenue Improvement Association, and the Detroit Bureau of Governmental Research, which conducted much of the group's research. The Committee of Industrialists, headed by Alfred Sloan, then chairman of General Motors, later joined Stone's committee, and the common council asked the Bureau of Governmental Research to set up a committee to monitor unethical behavior on the part of politicians and bank employees.

The Stone Committee literally ran the city's financial affairs from 1930 to 1938. Stone, who had been secretary to Michigan governor Hazen Pingree, set city salary policy, recommended budget cuts, approved bond proposals, advocated tax levies, and negotiated with banks. The common council agreed to cut city employee wages by 50 percent, issue scrip, and take collection measures on delinquent taxes.[7] In spite of these measures, the city became technically in default on its interest payments on February 15, 1933.

Modern day fiscal problems, although less apocalyptic than those of the depression era, again have caused elected leaders to call on outside assistance to help them through the fiscal maze. The cash flow problems of the 1970s and 1980s were less complex than those of the 1930s, but this time the problem was not merely the result of a tremendous population increase. This time the city was suffering serious attrition of its population. The problem was not caused merely by white flight to the suburbs—even though that certainly has contributed. The changing demography of industry in this new economic era also prompted statewide population losses, as workers have followed industrial migration to the Sunbelt. The Detroit of the 1980s has more income sources, including an income tax, than its 1930s predecessor. Nevertheless, a sizable gap remains between revenues and expenditures, and the national economic crisis has rudely exposed it.

The Genealogy of the Modern Deficit

Coleman Young took office on January 2, 1974. The following 15 November he was advised of a potential $35 million city operating deficit and took a number of measures to limit the deficit. The first was a total hiring freeze. In January 1975, he approved a layoff of 1,237 city employees and proposed an increase in nonresident income tax rates. Two months later, an additional 243 city employees and 400 special service employees were also put on indefinite layoffs, and all city-operated recreation centers were closed for thirty days. In April another sixty-three employees were laid off. In the city's 1975–76 budget, a total of 4,116 city-financed jobs were eliminated, leaving 21,299 jobs that were funded by the city's own revenues. City automobile replacements were cancelled, which saved $2.3 million. In June, yet another 815 city employees were laid off, including 314 CETA employees. That same month the mayor obtained an agreement with the Detroit Police Officers' Association for reduced pay and hours in return for a commitment to retain 641 police jobs. Four other unions made similar agreements in lieu of reductions in force. Mayoral appointees agreed to forgo all pay increases for a period of one year, which saved the city $300,000.

The result of this monumental effort was that the deficit for the year ending June 30, 1975, totaled approximately $16.5 million, instead of the previously forecast $35 million. Despite all efforts to reduce the size of the deficits, the continuing shortfall in revenue and gradually mounting problems in the national economy made the city's fiscal problems increasingly resistant to intuitive solutions. Attrition had had a substantial effect on the size of the city payroll, but still costs escalated. Despite wage concessions, personnel costs demanded an increasing proportion of city revenues. Even the strategy of delayed maintenance and service of city vehicles began to create more costs than it saved. It became increasingly clear to Mayor Young and his administration that the city would soon face a serious financial crisis if it did not act. Such a crisis could lead the city to default on its obligations, and even if it did not, the city's fiscal reputation would be seriously impaired. It was during this time that New York City was making headlines with its own fiscal crisis.

Detroit resisted the temptation to which New York had succumbed—of borrowing enough money to roll the debt over to the next year. Rather, the city fought valiantly to balance its books. Nevertheless, the city was fast becoming a fiscal leper, and immediate and radical action was necessary. The deficit that was accumulating had several roots, but the taproot was the declining tax base. Many former city residents left Detroit to avoid the high taxes, but as commuters they still enjoyed the benefits of city living (the use of public buildings, street maintenance, and protection at work). Despite the declining population, costs of service delivery remained fairly constant, due in large part to the high national inflation rate.

Detroit's fiscal problems were also complicated by its heavy reliance on the city income tax. Aside from the inequity of tax shares between residents and nonresidents (2 percent versus 0.5 percent) the mere existence of a city income tax tended to accelerate the exodus of residents and jobs; many residents chose to avoid the tax by living and working outside Detroit. Another problem was the inability to accurately forecast revenue from the income tax from one year to the next. As is generally true with cities, Detroit has been unable to produce reliable estimates of corporate income tax liabilities. Since the only taxable corporate earnings are those derived from activities within the city, officials cannot adequately predict Detroit's share of a multisite corporation's earnings.

Income taxes are far more sensitive to economic fluctuations than other forms of taxation and are therefore difficult to gauge in advance. During periods of recession or local industry cutbacks, tax revenues are sharply curtailed. Further, the "ripple effect" of unemployment imparts additional distortions to the revenue forecast picture; unemployment compensation is not subject to income taxes. A report in 1975 by the mayor's special task force noted the problem of tax revenues as a continuing source of fiscal insecurity for the city, stating:

> Despite ... increased tax rates, dollar revenue from the property tax increased by only 28 percent in 15 years, representing a decline in government purchasing power of 40 percent. Total tax revenues increased in dollar terms by 129 percent over the 15 year period, but this represented a growth in government purchasing power over the entire period of less than 7 percent. Over the past four years, total city tax revenues increased by only 16 percent, while the national index of the costs of local government rose 35 percent. Last year total city tax collections actually *declined* in dollar terms, while the national index of local government costs increased by nearly 11 percent.[8]

Municipal governments incur deficits when their income does not match their expenditures. In modern times, short-term cash flow problems have been handled through short-term borrowing on anticipated tax revenues; Detroit has always borrowed money to cover current shortfalls or cash flow problems. Cities also borrow to finance long-term capital investments. It is rare that investment brokers cannot find investors willing to purchase bonds issued to fund the construction of city facilities or additions to infrastructures.

Since the 1975 New York fiscal crisis, however, municipali-

Fiscal Crisis of 1981

Table 10. **Detroit Budget Data, 1970–83 (in thousands)**

Year	Revenue	Current Expenditures and Debt Retirement	Capital Expenditures	Net Borrowing	Retirement Contribution
1970	410,917	332,780	54,209	40,357	56,951
1971	500,727	381,598	82,498	95,810	58,461
1972	481,427	424,746	99,451	34,368	92,903
1973	665,257	461,153	115,789	36,480	91,082
1974	674,112	494,503	90,992	42,665	117,378
1975	661,005	550,709	109,312	26,743	103,626
1976	781,947	597,886	96,515	20,985	111,844
1977	897,023	609,141	119,874	8,895	139
1978	943,589	759,612	170,172	51,610	135,818
1979	1,052,879	875,417	164,990	155,185	160,040
1980	1,170,996	934,267	226,163	49,600	136,305
1981	1,297,814	952,377	265,845	37,295	56,328
1982	1,426,211	1,053,014	175,104	124,097	276,500
1983	1,351,533	1,037,934	362,613	32,158	133,562

Sources: U.S Bureau of Census, City Government Finances; various issues.

ties have had to show that they are not "cooking the books"— that is, borrowing to cover deficits. Table 10 shows that since 1970 Detroit has had surpluses, albeit small ones. Based on U.S. census data, it appears that the city's revenues have always exceeded expenditures. The first column lists revenues (including taxes, grants, and fees). Expenditures are divided into those for operating use and capital, with debt retirement added to operating expenditures. Net borrowing reflects income from short-term notes issued for the fiscal year. The record shows that Detroit has been a prudent borrower for many years. One interesting aspect of this table is the growing increase in the city's contribution to its debt retirement account. An equally notable aspect is the growth rate of both revenues and expenditures. The charts show that the city did not "roll over" any debts. The deficit of $44 million, which appeared in 1975, was the result of a shortfall in current revenues, when the city failed to take in enough cash to meet current expenditures.

Balancing this budget involves two separate actions: first, the city must raise the deficit amount; second, it must implement reductions in the budget to prevent the deficit from recurring. Analysis of the city's 1975 financial statement clearly indicated that cash flow problems would take on the semblance of a revolving door if new revenue sources (taxes) were not implemented. Detroit's crisis, coming as it did in the same year as the Great Fiscal Crisis of New York City, could not escape comparisons.

Mayor Young's task force instead commented on the contrast between the financial conditions of the two cities, saying:

> Detroit's net debt per capita as of June 30, 1975, was $265 compared to $1,500 for New York City. *Moody's*, the investor service that assigns bond ratings to cities, says Detroit's debt load is "moderate" and rates the city "favorable" on debt factors. *Moody's* also notes that much of the city's gross debt is self-supporting and that the retirement rate of the debt is rapid.
>
> Detroit's financial problems are not analogous to New York City's; nevertheless, the city has a real and urgent crisis. Unless immediate solutions to this crisis are found, Detroit will face financial problems equal in gravity to those of New York City.[9]

The obvious question is exactly how is Detroit's money being spent, and can its costs be restrained? The city's budget, like most public budgets, contains controllable and uncontrollable factors. The controllable ones are those that can be delayed, eliminated, or reduced. Uncontrollables are such items as entitlements (for example, pension costs) and payments on debt service.

One of the most visible items in the budget is personnel. By the end of 1975, Mayor Young had already eliminated much of the slack in personnel through his tough attrition policy and layoffs. The city's work force shrank by nearly four thousand employees from its 1973 high. Despite layoffs, union contracts were renegotiated, and wage and fringe increments were made; accordingly, the more significant sources of the city's deficit were personnel and labor costs. The Joint Economic Committee studying New York's crisis had studied the ratio of government employees to city residents and found that Detroit ranked sixteenth among the twenty-four largest cities in the country. The highest ranking city was Washington, D.C., with 418 municipal employees per 10,000 residents, compared to Detroit's 266. Columbus, Ohio, ranked last with 240.5 city employees per 10,000 residents.

While it seems that the number of employees would be reduced by attrition and layoffs, the cost of government continues to rise for several reasons. Unions tend to escalate their wage demands, even while population and union membership decline. A policeman making $20,000 per year could easily be persuaded that he should be making $25,000, and union leaders would rather agree to layoffs than wage concessions. In recent years municipal unions have become increasingly militant and successful in wage negotiations. Detroit, a prolabor city with several elected and appointed officials whose own political careers are based on the labor movement, has produced a very liberal labor policy. Many residents are "true believers" in the labor movement and support the aspirations of city employees on principle. The liberal labor laws of Michigan, especially arbitrations, tend to reinforce the authority of labor leadership. The courts are quite ready to accept suits affecting stalled labor negotiations and have intervened many times during the bargaining process. Short of a total collapse of revenues, the city remains relatively defenseless against its unions.

Immediately upon assuming office, Mayor Young had to deal with labor union job actions. His predecessor, Roman Gribbs, had done little to establish a strong bargaining position for the city, and Young had to deal with a strong set of labor leaders. Many in the DPOA had opposed his election and at first seemed to be seeking a confrontation. The mayor thus spent much of his first two years trying to make reductions that would be acceptable to all parties concerned. Many employees were simply not willing to accept the impact of changing demographics, especially the loss of revenue occasioned by white flight. Some thought the solution to the city's fiscal problem was to spread the city expenditures across the state. If only the state could be persuaded to treat Detroit as it did its other municipalities, then the city could continue to spend at its current rate. This idea continually resurfaced in state and local fiscal relations only to meet a quick death because of outstate residents' unwillingness to support city services on an ongoing basis. Another idea that often gains support suggests transferring some city functions to the state. The problem with this idea is that it also transfers control. A newly empowered black elite was not prepared to give up any of the power it had fought so long to acquire. Detroit was not the empty prize Paul Frema had predicted in 1968, but it was slowly becoming a more costly operation for its remaining citizens.

The mayor's efforts to stem the tide of personnel costs were failing. There were four thousand fewer city employees than when Young came to office, yet, even so, the deficit of $40 million resisted short-term measures. What was needed was an adjustment of city expenditures to match current and anticipated revenues, and what emerged was a blue ribbon committee, consisting of leaders from across the city. These civic, religious, and business leaders would legitimate the mayor's claims that the city had had to make the layoffs it had made and that the deficit was real. The 1975 fiscal crisis had to be communicated as an adjustment decision. The city could not continue to carry its fiscal load unless it was prepared to see annual deficits of $100 million in the near future. It was also clear that the new administration had to polish its fiscal reputation in order to govern effectively.

The 1975 Crisis

In 1975 Mayor Young established a Task Force on City Finances with Alfred A. Pelham, former city comptroller and retired Wayne State University professor, and Douglas Fraser, vice president of the UAW, as cochairs. The task force included Louis Allen, president of Manufacturers National Bank; Tom Banas, director of Community Relations, WWJ-TV; John Cannon, attorney; Emily Gail, owner of a retail store, Emily's Downtown; David Harper, president of First Independence National Bank; George McKean, bond counsel for Dickinson, Wright and McKean; Benson Manlove, owner of L & M Office Supplies; Warfield Moore, attorney; Father William Murphy, director of Education for the Archdiocese of Detroit; John Sagan, treasurer, Ford Motor Company; Frederick G. Sampson, pastor for the Tabernacle Missionary Baptist Church; Hawkins Steele of Hawkins Steele Real Estate Company; Tom Turner, president of the AFL-CIO of Metro Detroit; Marian Wiseman, president of Palmer Park Citizens' Action Committee; Gladys Woodward, community leader; Donald E. Young, vice president, Burroughs Corporation; John B. Cook, assistant treasurer, General Motors Corporation; E. Harwood Rydholm, vice president of civil affairs for Chrysler Corporation; Robert Surdam, chairman of National Bank and Trust; and John Boyd, Detroit Bank and Trust. This heterogeneous group was entrusted with the task of evaluating the city's fiscal situation, identifying revenue problems, assessing cost savings, and recommending ways to meet new revenue needs. The mayor had already taken steps to reduce costs—such as through layoffs, hiring freezes, and maintenance delays. Hence, part of the charge of the task force was to review these steps and decide whether they should be continued.

The budget department had projected a deficit of $44.3 million for 1975 and $103.3 million for the 1976–77 fiscal year. The task force suggested continuing the attrition and hiring freeze strategies that were in place, increasing civilianization of nonpolice-related work, providing better tax collection, undertaking a study of one-man garbage trucks and another of the number of city-owned cars and small police cars. The group rejected the idea of transferring D-DOT operations to SEMTA because of the pension cost of D-DOT's obligations. It noted that a maximum of 8,100 city workers could be legally laid off between February and July. The police contract prohibited layoffs. Employees in self-supporting departments such as water, airport, and sewer would

Table 11. **Sources of Budget Deficit, 1975–1976**

Major Appropriation Deficits	
40% increase in employee hospitalization rates	$ 4,100,000
Unemployment benefits to laid-off city workers	1,900,000
Social Security	1,400,000
Failure to achieve 8% savings in Fire Dept.	1,655,000
Environmental Protection and Maintenance Dept.	1,053,000
Subtotal —	$10,108,000
Major Appropriation Surpluses	
The city set aside $25 million to pay costs above the $10,000 per employee ceiling set by federal government for its share of public employment costs. Fewer public employment grants than expected meant a surplus.	$ 5,550,000
Final totals for previous year show a $16.4 million deficit rather than $17.6 million	1,248,000
Subtotal —	$ 6,798,000
Total Appropriations Deficits —	$ 3,310,000
Major Revenue Deficits	
Nonresident Income Tax—Legislation still pending	$14,000,000
Reduction in City Income Tax collections due to economic conditions	6,300,000
Reduction in State Revenue Sharing—economic condition	7,533,000
Reduction in Federal Revenue Sharing—new census data	4,625,000
Failure to sell farm acreage at DeHoCo	2,700,000
Reduction in Traffic Court revenues	3,000,000
Reimbursement—Criminal Justice Institute	1,000,000
Buildings and Safety Inspection revenues	800,000
Subtotal —	$39,958,000
Total — Major Items —	$43,268,000
All Other Items —	$ 1,032,000
Total Estimated Deficit —	$44,300,000

Source: Secrest Committee Report.

not be involved in a layoff. After 1 July it would be legally possible to lay off police and firefighters. The report stated that laying off the average employee for sixteen months would save the city $22,000. At that rate 47,000 employees, or more than thirty-five percent of the city's non–revenue producing employees would have to be laid off to eliminate the $103 million projected deficit. The task force published Table 11 to outline the 1975 deficit.

Given the size of the deficit and the limits on layoffs, the only alternative was to raise more revenue. The task force supported the mayor's call for an increase in income tax by 1 percent as a last resort. Aside from restoring income rates for residents and nonresidents, it was projected that the new tax would generate $44 million from residents and $28 million from nonresidents. The task force also endorsed a New Detroit, Inc. (NDI) recommendation that $102.4 million be added to the tax effort formula of the Michigan Revenue Sharing Act. This addition could mean $40 million to the city of Detroit. NDI also recommended nuisance taxes on cigarettes, liquor, and beer. Finally, NDI, like the mayor's task force, was opposed to increases in the income tax except as a last resort. The time was simply not right for a tax increase as a solution to city fiscal problems. The task force also suggested that Detroit establish a millage for garbage collection and disposal. If the state granted such authority, the new tax could generate $15.2 million. The task force also urged soliciting state financial aid for the main branch of the Detroit Public Library, the Detroit Institute of Arts, the Detroit Historical Museum, Fort Wayne, the Dossin Museum, and the Detroit Zoological Park, plus reimbursement by Wayne County for indigent services performed by Detroit General Hospital. (In the preceding six years, the city had lost $9.3 million in health care.) The task force also advocated transfer of the Harbormaster Services to Wayne County ($1.4 million cost) and recommended that Huron-Clinton Metropolitan Park Authority assume the full cost of maintaining Belle Isle ($2.5 million per year). It also supported offtrack betting legislation, casino gambling in downtown hotels, and greyhound racing legislation.

Finally, the task force advocated changing the fiscal calendar for the city of Detroit from 1 July–30 June to 1 October–30 September to be consistent with the new federal fiscal years. An extension of the fiscal year would generate approximately $30 million in the first year—a substantial gain. The task force did not advocate the change in order to obtain a one-shot revenue of $30 million, but if Michigan changed its fiscal year, then the city might follow, despite legal and technical difficulties. The task force also made some recommendations to the state and federal governments, suggesting, for instance, that the state reconsider the governor's veto on a bill to reimburse Detroit for the cost of maintaining a crime laboratory—a move that could generate $1.7 million and that would be consistent with state policy in the rest of Michigan. The task force also asked the state to assume traffic enforcement on city freeways, which would save another $1.7 million. In addition, the group suggested that the state treat Detroit as a county for the purpose of distributing health funds. In 1975 the city did not receive such funds, despite the fact that it had a health department. The task force sent a telegram to urge the passage of an anti-recession bill (H.B. 5247) that would have given the city $38 million in the 1976–77 fiscal year. Recognizing its temporary status, the task force advocated the establishment of an Economic Growth Conference Board to advise the city on economic growth and finances. It recommended approximately thirty members, with representatives from the automobile industry, three mayors, the Renaissance Center Corporation, Burroughs, the Medical Center Corporation, the chamber of commerce, New Detroit, Inc., and the Detroit Convention and Tourist Bureau. Many of the task force's recommendations were adopted by the mayor. Nevertheless, the city's problems continued.

In 1976 Young negotiated an equity package with the state of Michigan. Young argued that many Detroit cultural and educational facilities served all residents of the state, not just Detroiters; therefore, the cost of maintaining these facilities should be shared. Under the plan the state would reimburse the city for some of the cost of such institutions as the Detroit Institute of Arts, the Detroit Zoo, and the Detroit Public Library. The mayor's negotiations with Governor Milliken over the cost and shape of the package were some of the toughest in Michigan's history. Many state legislators and some of the public were opposed to the idea of special aid for Detroit, but Young was adamant about the cost sharing plan. Milliken recalled, "We went at it pretty good, the mayor and me. But we came out of it with a respect for each other that we've maintained throughout the years."[10]

The mayor got his equity package but it alone could not solve the city's fiscal problems. As Young approached his first reelection bid, his fiscal maneuvering acted to delay but not prevent a new crisis. He was challenged by Ernest Brown in the 1977 election, but fiscal problems were not stressed in the campaign. After the mayor's reelection, it became clear that more layoffs were intended. The national recession continued to hold the city hostage, and the serious inflation spirals, which started in the Nixon-Ford period, continued under the Carter administration. By 1980 the inflation rate was 18 percent, and the prime interest rate reached a peak of 21.5 percent.

The automotive industry took a nose dive, taking with it concomitant industries, resulting in a ripple effect on all aspects of business in Michigan. Vehicle production was down 33 percent in 1980. The state had an unemployment rate of 12.4 percent (534,000), the bulk of which was located in Detroit. Unemployed autoworkers meant lower tax receipts, less consumer buying (less sales tax), and higher welfare costs. The city of Detroit also had a weak local tax base; only 25 percent of its budget is supported by local taxes, assessments, and fees. The city had become more dependent on external grants-in-aid, and its income tax base was below the statewide average. The yield in Detroit was $70 per capita, one of the lowest in the state. Had it been $85 per capita, as was Lansing's, it would have generated an additional $30 million. By 1979 it was clear that the glue from the first crisis was coming apart. The following year saw the dawn of a new fiscal crisis.

The Fiscal Crisis of 1981

The 1975 fiscal year proved to be only a forerunner of a much more serious problem. The layoffs, hiring freezes, delayed maintenance, switches to smaller cars, and one-man garbage trucks were not enough to offset the revenue problems of the city. The 1975 recession continued in Detroit mainly because of the automobile industry. Gas prices rose rapidly, and the car buying consumers were switching to fuel-efficient foreign cars. American automakers were rushing small models to the production line. The city's financial foundation was eroding, despite a new, friendlier federal administration in Washington. In 1979 the city borrowed $155,185,000, the largest amount since the beginning of the Young administration. It also paid an equally large amount into the pension fund. Clearly, the revenue deficit projected by the city did not reach the $196 million mark, but the Secrest Committee confirmed a deficit forecast of $132.6 million as of June 30, 1981—still a landmark in the city's history that threatened to return it to the dark days of the thirties. The city had exhausted all effects of previous tactics to reduce its deficit. The police force was cut 27 percent between 1977 and 1981. The city's bond ratings had taken a nose dive, from *Baa* to *Ba*. The general work force had been cut to the bone. The city now had a situation where fundamental, not makeshift, changes in the city's revenue structure were necessary. The mayor decided to establish a new blue ribbon committee to study the problem before taking any action.

Decision to Refer

Economic decision making always involves the question, To whom should be delegated what responsibilities? The decision to go outside the established bureaucracy was dictated by events, as well as by the lack of any one staff person prominent enough to engage the confidence of the financial community. As was the case with the Stone and industrial committees of the thirties, politicians appointed to such forums accepted the advice of citizen committees when they were unwilling or found it inappropriate to act alone.

In the case of the Secrest Committee, the mayor had control over output in that he could selectively follow the group's recommendations. The Budget Planning and Stabilization Committee, headed by Fred Secrest, represented a unique cross-section of the community. It included longtime mayoral advisor Alfred Pelham; Roy Williams, head of the Urban League and former aide to Governor Milliken; Stanford C. Stoddard, president of Michigan National Bank Corporation; Robert M. Surdam, chairman of National Bank of Detroit; Donald Davis, chairman of the board of First Independence National Bank of Detroit; Alan E. Schwartz, a partner in Honigan, Mitter, Schwartz and Cohn; Arthur Seder, chairman of American Natural Resources Company; Stratton S. Brown, managing partner, Miller, Canfield, Paddock and Stone; David Rynne, vice president, Burroughs Corporation; Harry Kosins, president of Kosins Clothes; Walter J. McCarthy, Jr., president of Detroit Edison Company; Richard Meisel, managing partner of Arthur Anderson and Company; Dean E. Richardson, chairman of the board of Manufacturers National Bank of Detroit and Manufacturers National Corporation; Rodkey Craighead, chairman, Detroit Bank Corporation; Robert Krestel, chairman of City National Bank; David J. Byrne, vice president of corporate operations for Burroughs Corporation; Raymond Majerus, secretary treasurer, UAW; George Johnson (C.P.A), director of George Johnson and Company; Anthony J. Masters, chairman of the city's General Retirement Fund; Richard L. Measelle, managing partner of Arthur Anderson and Company; Jane E. Moeller, senior vice president of First Federal Savings and Loan Association of Detroit; Otis Smith, vice president and general counsel of General Motors Corporation; Matthew Steckel, chairman of Bank of the Commonwealth; Dennis Green, accounting manager, Ford Motor Corporation; Jack Wood, president of the Greater Detroit Building Trades Council; Janice Shatzman, partner, Peat, Marwick, Mitchell, and Company; Judith A. Mulberg, policy analyst at Ford Motor Corporation; and Carrie Gray, manager, Chrysler Corporation.

The membership of the committees, dominated by bankers, accountants, and corporate leaders, was designed to provide credibility to its findings. Most banks were represented, as were the largest labor unions. Conspicuously absent were representatives from the largest public employee unions, the American Federation of State, County, and Municipal Employees (AFSCME), and the common council. By shifting weight to the financial community, the panel avoided the usual political labels surrounding such special interest groups. The involvement of bank chairmen was meant to impress bond market investors and outside financial observers. In helping to draft the committee's report, bankers become better educated in the city's financial problems. The other financial houses and accounting firms contributed by offering staff and information support. In many ways, Secrest's group amounted to a combination of both of the 1930s committees.

The Final Decision Package

The Secrest Committee studied volumes of documents and hired consultants from the investment community. Its report attempted to describe the economic condition of the city and compare it to other cities. The report recommended that the city address its short-term cash problem by issuing medium-term notes to cover immediate cash flow difficulties. The report also stood foursquare on an increase in the city income tax rate for both residents and nonresidents. Finally, it suggested freezing wages, salaries, and benefits for all city employees and obtaining concessions from them.

Upon receipt of this report, the mayor moved quickly to implement its recommendations. To alleviate the city's deficits, the mayor proposed the following plan: city residents were asked to vote themselves a 1 percent increase in the city income tax rate (from 2 percent to 3 percent for residents and from 0.5 to 1.5 percent for nonresidents); the unions were asked to give up scheduled wage increments for fiscal years 1982 and 1983; the city asked state permission to issue budget stabilization bonds (five-year bonds) for $113 million. The city also eliminated all completely federally funded jobs, such as those of CETA.

In July, 1981, Young was able to get fifty-two of the city's fifty-seven bargaining units to agree to wage concessions. The unions agreed in return for no layoffs to forgo wage increases scheduled for fiscal years 1981, 1982, and 1983. Only the Building Trades Council, which represented construction workers, balked at the agreement and experienced some layoffs. Many city job vacancies were not filled, and all departments were asked to increase productivity.

The Income Tax Mobilization

In mobilizing the vote for the tax increase, the mayor had to contend with several audiences. The state legislature held the key, for its approval was necessary to put the issue before the voters. Within the legislature, there were several possible coalitions. The suburban-rural coalition could stop the plan. Suburban legislators, especially those representing Detroit, were opposed to a commuter tax increase. Outstate Republicans were generally opposed to grant authority for the increase without some concession from the unions and assurances from the cities about budget balancing. The governor had just lost a major battle for Proposition A—a proposal to cut property and income taxes in half in exchange for higher sales taxes. Many journalists and politicians were speculating that his career had reached an end. Several state legislators were seeking visibility in order to run for the Democratic nomination. The pressure was on the mayor to get the legislature to give approval for the city commuter tax proposal. On 1 June the mayor had not yet secured approval. Governor Milliken had endorsed the proposal, but his support was considered by many to be relatively weak. Mayor Young traveled to Lansing to negotiate the contents of the bill and let it be known that he was not happy with the bill's language on mandated wage concessions. Outstate legislators, however, especially the Republicans, were adamant regarding the so-called tie bar language in the legislation (for example, that it proposed flat-rate wage cuts or dollar limits on labor negotiation). The mayor responded:

> The bill will not stand any more political weight. What you have in that case is some people, some very conservative people, trying to write a labor contract into the bill and you can't do that. The freezes and cuts have to be negotiated through the collective bargaining process and that is going on now. That's not my idea, it is not a question of what I could live with, but of what these guys [in the legislature] will vote for. I'll support any damned thing that gives me the three points that I want.[11]

In giving his response, the mayor was able to stand firm on the principle of collective bargaining—anticipating union claims of a sellout and placing the blame for tie bar on nameless and faceless legislators. Simultaneously, he was signaling that he desperately needed the legislature. Suburban legislators were, however, opposed even to that compromise. Ordinarily sympathetic Democrats such as William Faust (D-Westland) opposed the commuter tax, stating that he objected to a continual pipeline from the state to Detroit.[12]

Meanwhile, polls showed a likelihood for passage of the tax. In polls taken by Market Opinion Research and reported in the *Detroit News*, 65 percent of Detroit residents backed the tax increase, while suburbans opposed it 49-43.[13] When Wayne, Oakland, and Macomb counties were aggregated, there was an average of 51 percent overall support for the tax increase. New Detroit, Inc., cited the poll as evidence of "metropolitan agreement," even though the measure was defeated three weeks after the poll was conducted. The polling agency made no such claims for the metropolitan agreement, yet the poll was folded over into the campaign to convince state legislators that votes could be won and that "commuting" suburban residents were not overwhelmingly opposed to an increase in their taxes.

The two leading daily papers joined the debate, posting editorials supporting the taxes. The *Free Press* called the "taxation without representation" issue phony and argued that Detroit should be allowed to tax itself. The newspapers gave little support for a state management agency or the state takeover (or receivership) idea. Thomas Murphy, chairman of General Motors, and Douglas Frazier, UAW president, addressed an unprecedented joint session of the legislature. Meanwhile, the legislature was under intense lobbying by the Detroit Economic Growth Corporation to pass the measure; corporate lobbyists also contributed to the effort.

On 3 June the state legislature passed the Detroit Tax Plan. A joint committee of legislators reversed the position taken by the House and passed the proposal—with three conditions. The $125 million bond must be sold, wage concessions made, and a budget submitted to the State Administration Board. All transactions had to be completed by 15 August.[14]

The city continued the polling strategy. It commissioned a new poll by Martilla and Kiley, a Boston-based polling company, which differed from a *Detroit News* poll.[15] Martilla and Kiley's sample included 483 registered voters in Detroit and found that the views of blacks and whites differed sharply. Blacks supported the tax increase 48-29 percent with 23 percent unsure; whites opposed the increase 48-30 percent with 22 percent unsure. Across the board support was 41 percent in favor, 37 percent opposed, and 22 percent undecided. The poll was taken two days after the defeat of Proposition A. Given its small sample size, the sample error was very high. The aftereffect of Proposition A was setting in, and Mayor Young had twenty-one days in which to win over the undecided.

The bill for the Detroit Tax Plan reached the Senate after getting House approval, and it created a raucous session by all accounts. By the time of the actual vote, tempers were heated and partisan politics had taken its toll. On the first go-round, Bill Faust missed the vote tally, causing an outburst from Basil Brown of Highland Park. Faust finally voted on the third vote,[16] which ended in a 19-19 tie, necessitating a tie breaking vote from Lieutenant Governor James Brickley. Some of the nineteen opposition votes came from Detroit suburban senators. David Plowecki (Dearborn Heights), Kerry Kramner (Pontiac), and John Hertel (Harper Woods) voted for the measure. John Kelly was the lone Detroit senator who voted against the plan. The clock continued to tick. The city now had nineteen days before the vote.

To conduct the campaign for the income tax proposal, it was estimated that a budget of $500,000 would be needed. New Detroit, Inc., was given the responsibility for raising funds. Larry Horowitz, vice president of NDI, was given responsibility for fundraising and making up a campaign budget. NDI developed a quota for industry and labor, relying on a simple contribution formula for the Big Three auto companies whereby for every dollar General Motors contributes, Ford gives eighty cents and Chrysler fifty cents. NDI also pulled together a working committee from twenty-five companies, which raised about $250,000. A birthday party for the mayor raised an additional $100,000, followed with $50,000 to $75,000 from vendors and assorted interest groups and individuals.

The mayor was not only active with the state legislature in Lansing; he was also busy selling the proposal to the people. There was no doubt in anybody's mind that success of the vote depended on the mayor and his influence. His staff said so, and campaigners at Vote Yes Detroit agreed. When asked what was the campaign's greatest asset, Vote Yes Detroit's cochairman, William Beckham, responded, "The straight-up strength of Coleman Young. He will be a very active participant in the campaign. He has to be. It is difficult in this environment to get voters to vote taxes for any reason." Malcolm Dade agreed that "the proposal would rest with the Mayor's popularity and the Mayor's ability to trade on his popularity with city voters."[17]

The Vote Yes Detroit committee was simply a mobilizing vehicle. It had a campaign staff imbued with the responsibility of supplying public opinion leaders and voters with literature supporting the tax increase, but the campaign decision making took place in the mayor's office. Aside from Beckham and Dade, the committee was directed by two young politicians. Conrad Mallet, Jr., scion of a well-known and highly successful black family, directed field operations. Linda Barnes, on leave from the state commerce department, was codirector. Mallet revealed that they intended to raise and spend $500,000 for the campaign and would use the old pyramid approach to reach the voters. This approach entails contacting 50,000 opinion leaders and asking them to contact ten other people. The committee developed and distributed brochures to these leaders. It was also in charge of the day-to-day operation of the campaign.

Opinion leaders were given "survival kits" containing brochures, postage-paid postcards, and lawn signs. The field coordination staff supported the grassroot campaign efforts of the identified opinion leaders. The Detroit community was divided into nine groups: senior citizens, precinct delegates in the 1st and 13th congressional districts, East Side and West Side, block clubs, community-based organizations, black churches, interracial churches, and the mayor's ten thousand people. The latter group was comprised of volunteers who had worked in Young's election and reelection campaigns.

Mallet summarized the official position of the committee, saying that the plan was to "accumulate the positive" and ignore antitax campaigns. "This referendum is on the city," he said, "not on Coleman Young and his performances. The message is simple, Save our City."[18] Despite this disclaimer, everyone knew that Young would be at the center of the campaign, and voters would have to believe him and vote with him or else embarrass the mayor and suffer the consequences of a fiscal collapse.

Meanwhile, the mayor was mounting a massive campaign within the community and the churches. At a meeting of the Council of Baptist Ministers, he asked rhetorically, "Are we going to do what we have to do to guarantee the city continues to move forward and our destiny remains in our own hands? Or will we do what thousands of bigots hope we'll do—vote no and the state takes over?" Although this was a friendly audience, the mayor sounded tough, seeking to portray the vote as "us," meaning "blacks against the bigots." At the same time and since the press was present to relay an appeal to whites, Young stated,

> I don't believe the legislators from the suburbs speak for the people of the suburbs because I can't believe the average person living outside of Detroit is so blinded by hate that he'll cut his own throat to get mine. If Detroit goes in receivership all that progress will be wiped out. Investors will stay away, business will move out, jobs will be scarcer. We stand to lose just about everything. If I believed that most whites in this city or state or nation don't want blacks to live their lives in dignity, I'd quit being mayor and grab my gun to get ready for the next great race war. But I don't.[19]

This speech, widely reported in the newspapers, contained several political messages. Although it was presented in the mayor's folksy style, it contained several significant images. First, he told suburban whites that they are not racist. Second, he created an image of a fiscal fire storm that may engulf everyone. Third, he appealed for support on the grounds of dignity for blacks. Only Coleman Young could have made that kind of speech with its various messages. The groups that were the target of the mayor's subsequent sniping were the unions and ACORN.

The Association of Community Organization for Reform Now offered to support the tax increase if the mayor would agree to use the revenues in neighborhoods. The mayor called their demand "blackmail tactics." ACORN did not have the following or resources to mount a credible threat to the mayor's plan, but the public employees union was another matter.

Bob Johnson, president of AFSCME, met with nineteen local chapter presidents and declared the union's opposition to the tax plan, citing the tie bar language as his reason. "We were not originally opposed to the Tax Plan but the legislature included a wage rollback and we can't buy that approach. Based on that, we have to attack the whole system," he said.[20] The statement was echoed by labor leaders Lloyd Simpson and Tom Turner. For the union the campaign against the vote was one of principle.

At a speech before three hundred community leaders, Mayor Young declared:

> The only possible way we can afford to pay our workers is to get more money. AFSCME's contract is with the city of Detroit. If the state takes us over, AFSCME doesn't have a contract with the state. They must be damn fools. They either deal with us or deal with a state receiver. And the receiver will be appointed by some of the people who are trying to sink this city.[21]

The message was clear; the mayor was prepared to take on the union leadership but only if they wanted a fight. After the speech Young claimed that he did not know the identities of the union leaders. By refusing to name them, he divided the leadership and avoided a personalized campaign. He continued his depoliticized campaign against suburban organizations opposed to the tax increase, saying, "Some people in this state are playing a dangerous, divisive game. What they want is to take over Detroit. They are not after me. They're after us. We're dealing with a bunch of opportunists so blinded by ambition and hatred. These people are so anxious to cut Detroit that they are willing to cut their own throats to do it. It is a damn shame." This was a similar theme and tactic taken in the earlier speech.

The finale to Coleman Young's speaking blitz was a speech broadcast on the three major local television stations. The mayor returned to his theme concerning the need for Detroiters to save the city, and he condemned union leaders who opposed the tax increase. He asserted that they would be "among the first casualties if the city treasury runs dry."[22] The mayor's strategy of attacking unspecified union leaders proved to bear fruit. In a poll of voters with city union connections (a union member in the family), they supported the tax increase 60 to 23 percent. Indeed, 36 percent even supported wage concessions.

The mayor then turned to the dramatic. He held up a scrip issued during the Murphy administration and said, "I would not want to be the second Mayor in the 20th Century to put pieces of paper like this in the pay envelopes of city workers." Although the speech lasted only seventeen minutes, it gave the mayor time enough to sell the package in the living rooms of Detroiters and suburbanites.

Meanwhile, the polls continued their erratic behavior. A 21 June *Detroit News* poll rated the vote a toss-up, finding 36 percent in favor, 30 percent against, and 31 percent undecided (3 percent refused to answer) just three days before the vote.[23] A *Free Press* poll taken twenty days earlier, however, found that blacks were in favor of the increase by a solid margin. Massoglia and Associates of Lansing used both black and white interviewees. In a sample of 497, they found 58 percent supporting and 26 percent opposed, and there were 14 percent undecided. Blacks made up 61 percent of the sample and supported the increase by 72 percent with 13 percent opposing it. Thirteen percent were undecided.[24]

The day of the special election saw a 40 percent turnout, a large one for this type of vote. The proposal won the support of 160,350 (68.8 percent) to 91,135 (36.2 percent).[25] The mayor had won the day, and he celebrated by saying, "There can be no doubt that we have a special kind of city here in Detroit. We have been willing, in the face of a so-called national tax revolt, to step up to the window in Detroit and pay the price to buy a ticket on the train of progress and freedom."[26]

The *Free Press* took a closer look at the support for the tax increase and found the expected racial split. In an analysis of predominantly white precincts at Livernois and Michigan Avenues, the vote was 7-1 against the proposal. In other white areas, such as Fort-Central (southwest Detroit) working-class communities, the vote was 6-1 against the proposal. It had been won in the black precincts. In the Grand River–Joy Road area, the proposal won 9 to 1 with 47 percent voter turnout. Turnout in the black precincts exceeded that in white precincts. The end result was a big victory, with 80 percent of black voters supporting the proposal. It was as William Beckham had predicted—a "straight-up" vote for the mayor. Young acknowledged as much in his victory statement: "There was no question that [defeat] would have been regarded as a rejection of me if it had gone down."[27]

Winning Wage Concessions

The income tax vote gave the mayor momentum. He now turned his attention to winning wage concessions from the city's unions. This task would prove to be tricky and difficult since the mayor, the old labor man, had proved to be a tough negotiator and had alienated many union leaders. Almost every one of them seemed to have some pending labor business with the city during the struggle to save Detroit fiscally. Young's original wage concession strategy was simply to convince the union leadership of the severe fiscal problems facing the city and to rely on them in turn to persuade the membership that wage concessions were necessary. Throughout the income tax mobilization vote, many union leaders remained doubtful about the entire Secrest report, and they often contradicted its recommendations, thus reinforcing doubts among the less informed membership. The leadership adopted a strategy that would make any compromises appear as if workers were caving in to the mayor's demands for wage concessions. Yet, each knew that labor had little or no choice but to support the plan.

The mayor's first victory came with the DPOA's leadership agreeing to wage concession. The DPOA was the second largest and best-organized union. The largest union, AFSCME's District Council 25, seemed amenable initially as the leadership agreed to a two-year wage freeze in return for no layoffs. The agreement was negotiated for over four days with the help of state mediators and was contingent upon the mayor achieving other parts of his "survival plan."

The agreement started to unravel, however, at sessions designed to convince the locals that it was all the leadership could get under the circumstances. Locals began to balk and voted down the agreement. Local number 1023, which included civilian police workers, neighborhood city hall employees, and 911 operators, voted the proposal down 53-47. Although the vote was closer than subsequent votes, it spelled trouble for the plan. A spokesman reasoned, "It reflects a consensus that we already gave. We gave in 1974 and in 1977 when we gave up the Cost of Living Allowance (COLA) and settled for lower raises. The city's problems are not our fault."[28] By 10 July eight more locals joined in rejecting the proposal.

Although the margins of defeat were high in many locals, the turnout remained low for all locals. For example, Local 207 of the Lighting, Water and Sewerage workers, considered by many a pivotal local, rejected the proposal 291-40 but had a turnout of 24.2 percent.[29] Other locals, such as 229, 214, and 2799, had lower turnout figures. In the final tally, the AFSCME locals rejected wage concessions. During the vote, word leaked that the mayor would lay off workers if concessions were not made. It was not enough to stem the No vote. One labor leader concluded, "The members are not accepting the wage freeze because they were not given enough assurance that there would be no layoffs. The Mayor's threat of layoffs backfired."[30] Another allowed, "We have a contract that runs to 1983. If [Mayor Young] wants wage concessions, talk to us, I like the guy personally. If he runs for mayor again I will vote for him, but I am not going to vote to cut my throat."[31]

The failure of the locals to support the mayor's wage concessions plan came as an embarrassment and a mild shock to both the union leadership and the city negotiators. Union leaders blamed the mayor for interjecting layoff scares into the voting process. Bob Johnson, AFSCME's president, asserted that "they said 'Stand up and fight or lie down and take gas.' To hell with you, we'll stand up and fight."[32] The No vote by locals created a crisis within a crisis. It was a crisis for the union because the leaders could not deliver the vote and a crisis for the mayor, coming so soon after his big victory in the income tax vote, which was thought by many to be the most difficult part of the whole plan.

The mayor met with a close advisor at Manoogian Mansion to discuss the crisis. Mark Ulicny called leaders of AFSCME's District Council 25 to suggest another round of negotiations. Robert Johnson, state president of the union, and Lloyd Simpson, its executive vice president, were more than ready to negotiate. They were convinced that the No vote would give them more leverage in dealing with the mayor. Young had decided, however, to play hard ball. The mayor's office also began to draft layoff notices to be sent to 428 AFSCME workers in twenty-nine departments. Young announced a proposed layoff of five hundred city employees, an increase of one hundred by 31 July if the city workers did not agree to a two-year wage freeze. Johnson's response to the mayor's heightened stakes was that "some members feel that they will make out better under the layoffs than under the regular pay scale."[33] Johnson called Young's plan "a shotgun approach" and vowed to fight the layoffs. But two days later the union offered a new proposal when they agreed to accept a pay freeze if the city would give them a twenty-five-year-and-out retirement plan. They also asked for a twenty-five cents an hour increase plus additional vacation days as a "monetary equivalent" to offset another twenty-five-cent raise due under the present contract. They also wanted elimination of attendance programs and a two-year guarantee against layoffs. The city responded in two ways, by escalating the number of layoffs to 597 (a 40 percent rise) and outlining the locations of each layoff—water and sewerage would have 154, public works 83, recreation 57, transportation 49, and 43 would occur among civilian police workers.

The stage was set for confrontation. The union could play brinksmanship or statesmanship, and they decided on the latter. The new negotiations included the presidents of fifteen locals with the mayor in contact via telephone. Young's chief negotiator, Mark Ulicny, expressed surprise at achieving a new agreement after a ten-hour meeting. He stated, "I guess during these negotiations nothing should surprise me."[34] The union dropped the wish list items, such as the twenty-five-year retirement and the twenty-five-cent raise proposals. When AFSCME leaders capitulated, locals began falling into line. Local 1642, clerical workers, voted yes first; the next five to vote in favor included locals 207, 1227, 457, 62, and 836. The mayor responded to this trend by increasing pressure on firefighters and police lieutenants and sergeants. Again, he played the layoff card, threatening one hundred layoffs for firefighters and three hundred demotions of police supervisors. In doing so, initially, he allowed that those numbers were "just a guess at this point."[35] Everyone knew the escalation of numbers could follow. The mayor also used the opportunity to praise Local 207 for its affirmative vote and remarked, "I believe that as 207 goes, so goes AFSCME."[36] He blamed earlier rejection on the leadership's failure to present the fiscal crisis effectively. He now thought they understood the true condition of the city. One member disagreed, however, saying, "I voted yes because we had to. We were blackmailed." Another agreed: "I voted yes because there would have been many workers laid off."[37] Another leader observed, "The Mayor has been in this business for a few years. He knew how to wring the membership. That's what he did."[38] The union representing city accountants would not comply and in fact sued to collect a 6 percent annual wage increase, charging breach of contract. The fight was led by Perry Koslowski, president of the Senior Accountants, Analysts and Appraisers Association. Koslowski would later challenge the mayor in a mayoral race.

The Politicization of an Investment Decision

Young proposed that the state pension funds buy bond issues of $25 million but balked at the state asking price of 17 percent. He also wanted to sell $25 million to each of the city's police-fire and general employee pension funds. The remaining $50 million would be sold to a consortium of local banks. The city proposed selling the bonds through a negotiated "private placement" because the loss of investment grade bond rating the previous fall precluded Detroit from selling them in the open bond market. Selling to the state would also help improve bond marketability. But the sale had several problems: first, the bonds were at higher risk than other risk investments for state pension funds. Loren Monroe, the state treasurer, stated that, because the state pension funds could not benefit from the tax-exempt status of the proposed bond, they would have to carry a rate comparable to the fund's taxable investments "to meet our prudent requirements." The state was paying 15 to 16 percent on U.S. government securities. A conflict arose over whether the city should plan to pay local pension funds 12 percent. Finance director Paul Thompson denied any such proposal.

The Lieutenants and Sergeants Association threatened a lawsuit if trustees did not supply details about the proposed sale. The mayor's Wall Street advisor, Eugene Keilin of Lazard, Freres and Company, called the threatened suit a self-inflicted wound, saying, "You can't expect anyone to buy a lawsuit."[39] The banks then began demanding that the mayor pledge the new city income tax revenues as additional collateral for a $50 million share. In effect, they wanted a first lien on the new income tax and state revenue sharing fund. This would have required the city to establish an escrow account equal to the annual payment of $30 million in principal and interest. Mayor Young concentrated his attention on pension fund trustees. He had spent several hours with municipal bond trustees outlining terms of the sale. Meanwhile, the state investment advisory board instructed the state treasurer to buy the city bonds only if they paid 17 percent. Monroe believed that ruled out the state, since other pensions and the banks were only getting 13 and 14 percent, respectively.

Two questions remained for the bond sale. How could the pension fund buy bonds and not lose its tax-exempt status? Would a threatened suit by police and fire unions jeopardize the marketing of the bonds? The mayor dispatched two aides to Washington to negotiate with the Internal Revenue Service (IRS) on the tax-exempt status problem and personally took charge of negotiating with two local pension funds to offset a suit. He asked that they buy $31.2 million each ($6.2 million more) at 13.5 percent (below the going rate of 17 percent). The banks would buy $62.5 million. Young sold the idea of lower rates as necessary to pay off the bonds in four and a half years whereas a higher rate would take seven. In any case, the two pension funds of $1.5 billion would be jeopardized if the city went into default. The mayor's argument included a plea for a sacrifice by all in the short run and fiscal stability in the long run.

The clock continued to run, however, toward the 15 August deadline. On 11 August the mayor had only four days to untangle the snag in the bond sale, and he admitted then, "We may go down to the absolute deadline Saturday." Lieutenant Governor Brickley told the State Administration Board that "the next 72 hours are sort of a high noon for you."[40] Despite the fact there was still no IRS ruling on the tax-exempt status of the pension funds, the State Administration Board was willing to accept the plan, contingent upon a formal IRS ruling expected in several weeks. The IRS wanted assurances, meanwhile, that half of the total bond package would be bought by independent purchases and not by pension funds. In a three-and-a-half-hour secret meeting, the IRS also sought assurances that the purchases would not violate prohibited transactions in the tax code and that the deal would meet the legal requirements of the pension plans to make investments for the "exclusive benefit of the pension fund members."

As the police unions began to favor an agreement, Earl Berry, Detroit Firefighters president, again threatened a suit if the police-fire retirement system were to buy the bonds. The suit would delay the plans and the city would lose $20 million from income tax monies, retroactively. Berry's threat came two days before the vote on the general retirement system and a day before the police-fire retirement system vote, which was just two days away from the Saturday deadline of 15 August. The union's leaders claimed that their objection was based on the low interest rate. Berry observed: "The interest isn't enough and the possibility that this sale threatens our tax-exempt status is also a real concern. But the most important thing is that the money [Young] intends to borrow from the pension fund is, in all probability, to be used to pay us what he owes us."[41] He continued: "We filed a suit last year and won, and we've filed suit again because they're 30 to 40 days late on the 1981 payment. To lend the Mayor 31.25 million dollars would be unconscionable for the trustees to even consider."[42]

Despite the uncertainties of a union suit, the trustees of the general retirement system voted seven to two to buy their share of the bonds after a bitter debate. The two dissenters, Richard Fleming and Alexander Topalov, gave as their reasons "pensions, pending IRS rulings, and the city's labor record."[43] Meanwhile, the bank balked on buying the additional $125 million bonds; they would only buy $50 million. Finally, the bank decided to split the difference and buy $56.5 million. Young appeared again before the trustees of the police-fire pension beseeching them to buy the bonds at the proposed rate. The mayor also met with Berry to avert a last-minute delay in the completion of the survival plan. The union had several other bones to pick with the mayor, not least of which was their objection to his proposal to take the promotion based on seniority to arbitration. Young hoped to install an affirmative action plan similar to that in the police department. Both the firefighters union and the Amalgamated Transit Workers had earlier rejected the mayor's call for wage concessions.

With these uncertainties still dangling, Mayor Young went to Lansing to convince the State Administration Board of the merits of his survival plan. Without the mayor's presence, the board voted its unanimous approval of the plan, contingent upon IRS approval of the pension fund purchase. The firefighters went ahead with their suit to block the sale of $28.25 million of the city's bonds. Nevertheless, the trustees voted 11-0 to purchase the bonds, contingent on the IRS ruling, even after listening to the union lawyer call the city "uncredit worthy." The seven banks agreed to buy $56.5 million worth and to contribute to a token purchase to be made by the struggling Bank of the Commonwealth. Young, who was not present for the trustees' vote because of last-minute negotiations with the union, hailed the approval. He lauded the banks and concluded: "This is not a short-term plan. This plan seeks to establish the ability for Detroit to survive the next five years. This is not a one year fix."[44]

It had been a long and bitter fight that was not yet over. Detroit bond counsel John Axe praised the banks, saying, "They [banks and pension funds] are doing the city a favor. There is no question that civic pride is involved."[45] Many acknowledged the arm twisting done by the mayor and the governor. The real victor was the city itself, and its champion was Coleman Young.

Budget Deficit and Fiscal Reputation

The fiscal crisis of 1981 came at a crucial moment in the city's history—before a mayoral election and after the presidential election of Ronald Reagan. The newly elected president had run on a platform of fiscal restraint and decreasing social programs. He had criticized Johnson's lasting Great Society programs and aid to cities in general. There was no reason to believe that the new president would not carry out his threats to dry up most CETA funds, revenue sharing, and economic development monies. If the new administration carried out its threats, it would place many city programs and services in jeopardy, since only 25 percent of the city's budget was covered by revenues from taxes, fees, and interest. The remaining 75 percent came from grants-in-aid from the state and federal governments.

The fiscal crisis, in the end interdicted by the mayor, had all the makings of a fiscal collapse. As in most municipal crises, the press sought villains. Could fault lie in the union contracts, which were among the most liberal in the nation? Was the national economy at fault—that is, was Detroit's present trouble the fallout of a prolonged recession in the automobile industry? Was Detroit sending more taxes to Lansing than it was receiving in benefits? Were the suburbs paying their share of city expenses? Were Detroiters undertaxed? Clearly, any fiscal crisis in a municipality is a harbinger of problems for the state. If the city of Detroit defaulted, a ripple effect would be felt on the state's bond rating and fiscal reputation.

Fiscal reputations have become vital to municipalities, which have become extremely dependent upon the short-term market for cash. Bond ratings are based on rating service judgments about whether or not a governmental entity can pay back the loan in a timely manner. As a result, the city had to bring in a fiscal manager, a Lazard Freres representative from New York, to study the problem and clear local officials of charges of fiscal mismanagement. The blue ribbon panel was necessary to impress doubters that old makeshift tactics were no longer effective. Still, in the end it was the mayor's job to sell the package. Even the governor gave the income tax plan only a 50 percent chance of passage.

Many people doubted that the mayor could convince unions to make wage concessions. Young, however, was able to bring all parties to his point of view; there were no other rational alternatives. The mayor's strategy worked because residents believed him when he said that the income tax increase was necessary. An idea that he planted in the midst of the 1975 crisis bore fruit in 1981.

Conclusions

Detroit's fiscal problems started soon after Mayor Young took office. Though he tried to stop the crisis by traditional means—layoffs, attrition, and purchase and service delays—he also established a blue ribbon committee composed of representatives from all sections of the Detroit community to study the fiscal conditions. This group identified areas of potential savings and recommended that the state assume more of the city's financial burden. The city followed many of the panel's recommendations, yet Detroit's fiscal condition continued to deteriorate. Then came the onset of a more serious fiscal problem in 1981, which saw the creation of yet another blue ribbon committee. The Secrest Committee departed from the 1975 Pelham/Fraser committee in that it strongly endorsed an increase in city income taxes and recommended wage concessions from the unions.

The mayor was able to sell the decision-making package to the voters and to convince the unions that concessions were preferable to layoffs. In the past unions had accepted layoffs rather than wage concessions. Their willingness to support the mayor this time enabled him to proceed with the other part of the plan. Young had to go to the people to ask for equal sacrifices. He was demonstrating to his larger Michigan "audience" that the city was prepared to get its house in order to save its fiscal reputation and that his constituency backed his initiative. The mayor's 1981 strategy worked, and city residents, by a 56 percent margin, voted themselves a tax increase. The city rescue mission was completed with a good deal of political fanfare. The Secrest report had the effect of assuaging the mayor's critics and supporting the most important and critical change under consideration—the increase in income taxes. The cooperation of the unions over wage concessions was made possible by the mayor's evenhanded policy of layoffs and the realization by unions that they simply could not push for wage increases when most city residents were feeling the effect of a prolonged recession. The wage concessions also gave the unions an opportunity to build an IOU for the future. Union leaders looked like statesmen—a rare posture for them—and there was a general feeling that the auto industry would bounce back, maybe not to the golden era of the fifties and sixties but enough to fortify the city treasury.

Not everyone took part in the politics of the situation. The Reagan administration could not be expected to rescue the city as the Ford administration had done for New York City in 1975.

9

Conclusions

The preceding chapters have explored Coleman Young's administration with special emphasis on the mayor's role. The study was made from a particular vantage point, which to some readers, might seem incomplete. Not being members of Young's inner circle, we relied heavily on interviews, newspapers, and published data to develop our account. In any case, it is cautious to acknowledge that all the issues raised by this presentation do not lend themselves to one simple explanation. Some issues concerning Detroit's mayor must be left open-ended, their interpretations best left to future historians with the benefits of retrospect. Nevertheless, the present study seeks to provide future researchers with a starting point for their analyses of Detroit politics and the Young administration.

To place Coleman Young accurately into Detroit's history, one must return to the administrations of Hazen Pingree and Frank Murphy in order to find Detroit mayors of equal or greater political influence and impact on the office. Pingree and Young dominated the city's policy agenda as well as the electoral politics of their eras. Pingree, credited with singlehandedly eliminating the political machine, gave the city a new political ethos. Young deserves equal credit for guiding the city through the toughest economic transition it has faced since its inception. The transition to a mixed economy has been a particularly difficult move for Detroit because of the previous investment in local industry and the competition faced by the city's political and economic leaders. The city's human and infrastructure capital resources have been heavily invested in the auto industry. To reverse, control, and redirect this longtime trend has required support from the federal and state governments, and this type of support has been intermittent. Yet, Mayor Young has made considerable headway in putting Detroit on the road to economic diversity despite incredible odds and a host of naysayers.

Far from hindering the mayor's ascendancy, the national economy has on occasion served as a straw man to direct public dissatisfaction and at other times as a rationale for bold economic decisions. The demise of the Carter administration and the advent of Reaganism has meant that the city has had to rely more and more on its own local economic resources.

The visible accomplishments of Young's administration—affirmative action in the police department, economic development downtown and elsewhere, and the successful management of two fiscal crises—represent but the tip of the iceberg of his policy changes. At the surface are the conflicts and apprehensions that have accompanied the transfer of political power to the black elite, an ethnoracial transition. Below the surface is the ongoing impact of critical economic decisions that have already been made and their long-term effects on the future of the city. At the base is the mayor, who has to be a consummate organizer, negotiator, and city promoter.

The building of a new economy has inevitably led to some political and social displacements. Some of the participants in the city's emerging economy are not quite sure where all the policy directions are headed, and many of the consequences of the Young administration's decisions are still in the process of developing. Indeed, it could be argued that the essence of mayoral decision making is the accumulation of nuances. Rarely are definitive actions final. To consider Detroit's case fairly, one must review Young's administration as a multilayered system dissembling under the race issue. Decisions concerning any of these layers are more complex than they first appear. As one unravels a decision package, one finds more conflicts than options; there are few freestanding policy conflicts. Each policy seems to be connected, however tenuously, to other issues. Some decisions snag previously settled issues as they work themselves along the administration's decision tree. Others appear out of sequence and demand immediate attention, forcing the mayor's attention to unanticipated problems. The Young administration has done more, however, than react to the city's problems; it has successfully set its own new agenda and has resisted falling victim to collapse as other cities have done.

Young's Role in the Transformation

The 1973 election of Coleman Young marked a profound transformation in Detroit politics. In defeating the symbol of white police power, John Nichols, Young promoted pride in the black community and apprehension in the white community. The black community knew that they had elected a man with whom they could identify and one who would not defer to whites at their expense. Whites, on the other hand, believed that Coleman Young would treat them like second-class citizens. This misconception among whites came from the belief that a black mayor cannot be evenhanded in his approach to racial issues. Many white Detroiters have consistently voted against Young and his proposals. They consider his rhetoric insolent and himself indifferent to their needs—the trouble is with Young's style. He has always tailored his rhetoric to appeal to his audience in the black community, and his barbs against racism come across as being antiwhite. Thus, he is perceived as being against whites when he talks about racism, yet there is no evidence that he or members of his staff have adopted an antiwhite stance in the administration of city affairs. However, Young has been forceful in pursuing his policies. Having espoused a strong affirmative action policy during the early campaign, Young has attempted to implement major change in the first three terms of his administration, including adding more black and female police officers, firefighters, and department heads than ever before in the city's history. (By 1986 Young had a female deputy chief and two female commanders.) The reforms came, however, during a national recession that left the city with few financial resources. During the first three years of the Young administration, the city's fiscal crisis became more and more apparent, and the new mayor struggled with deficits, layoffs, and union pressures, and he avoided fiscal bankruptcy by obtaining wage concessions and raising taxes. His fiscal performances won applause from the white business community, though they did not win him the hearts and minds of the average white Detroiter.

The fiscal strategies of the Young administration, rising unemployment, and layoffs in the auto industry all played a major role in shaping the attitude of black Detroiters in the 1977 election. V. O. Key would have called this reelection bid a "maintaining election." It proved to be a vote of confidence for Young. The 1981 and 1985 elections involved less formidable opponents, but they came at a time when national attitudes toward cities were changing. More than any of its predecessors, the Reagan administration had a different agenda, one that envisioned less help for cities. Kirk Cheyfitz, an influential local journalist, predicted a decline in Young's political clout with the defeat of Jimmy Carter and the ascendency of Reagan. In "The Survivor," Cheyfitz observed that "in one day, Young was transformed from an insider in national affairs to an outsider."[1] As the title of the essay suggests, however, Coleman Young has been a "survivor." He survived Reagan in part because Congress resisted Reagan's cutback policies and also because he was smart enough not to alienate local Republicans who could help the city.

Probably the most striking aspect of recent Detroit politics is that they have undergone such enormous changes within the span of the Young years. Since 1970 the black population had gone from 44 to 63 percent in 1980. This increase is more than a changing of the races and social class; it is a major change in the way black residents view themselves. They have gone from minority to majority status within a single generation, and they have taken the place of white families in neighborhoods that blacks were previously afraid to enter after dark. Moreover, Detroit's politics have changed. No longer black politics, they are the current politics of Detroit. People who were black leaders are now city leaders.

The social transformation has made certain past behaviors and attitudes obsolete. Detroiters now understand that it takes enormous resources to maintain their city. They have proven willing to vote themselves new taxes for maintaining the city and its schools, and they have done this without the tutelage of the white liberal establishment that once dominated black politics in the fifties and sixties.

The Evolution of the New Clientage Politics

One of the most fascinating aspects of urban history has to do with differences in black leadership recruitment and sponsorship among cities. The evolution of the automobile industry created a black subleadership class composed of clients of the business leadership and the unions. As clients of labor leadership, they were trained differently from their black counterparts in other cities such as Atlanta and Newark. Since few were college graduates, they lacked an alternative professional reference group to the union movement. Yet, over time, they displaced their middle-class rivals. In some cases, they had no community-based constituency prior to their involvement in the labor movement.

Accordingly, their major function was to promote the allegiance of black workers, penetrate the black precincts, and extinguish political fires. While other cities saw rivalries between the black clergy and emerging community organizers, Detroit had a group of polished black labor organizers led by Jack Edwards who had the backing of white labor leaders. Armed with financial resources, printing facilities, and full-time organizers, they were able to fend off challenges from the clergy because they had the allegiance of black blue-collar workers who were well paid and who were the social pillars of the black community. In a review of the role of blacks in UAW history, historians August Meier and Elliott Rudwick suggested that the activity of the Trade Union Leadership Council was a "prelude to the militant agitation of the 1960s."[2] Far from being a prelude to militancy, TULC proved to be to firefighters what some white labor leaders expected it to be.

The labor movement taught these leaders that protest, negotiation, and labor organizing principles were appropriate for uplifting the conditions of blacks. The black leaders also thought that white liberal intellectuals, having great insights into social movements, would help guide blacks past white resistance. If a coalition could be formed between white liberals and progressive blacks, then an agenda could be mounted that would truly be a force in government. Many labor leaders believed that, if properly tutored, blacks could become equal partners of the liberal-labor coalition. Other whites saw the development of black leadership as simple insurance (a premium paying relationship) or as a liaison group to an important segment of the membership (a patron-client relationship). White sponsorship of ambitious blacks in the 1950s and 1960s had its negative impact, since it was one-dimensional—that is, carried out in the purely political realm. Not only did this practice foster dependency, but it herded all black talent into one crowd. Blacks did not gain equality in banking, industry, and professional occupations.

Some black leaders naturally resented the paternalistic and condescending attitudes of white supporters. They were not in a position, however, to extricate themselves from the entangling structures that reinforced these relationships. Some viewed the relationship as an outdated form of plantation politics. Indeed, it was a neo-clientage politics within a fairly benevolent context. By the mid-sixties black leaders had an expected challenge from more militant community leaders. The southern civil rights movement in the sixties, with its militant and confrontational style, made northern black leaders look even more conservative than they probably were. In response, many blacks were pressured to assume more aggressive public postures, to protect their domain and to prove their usefulness once again to their white sponsors.

The new clientage politics can be seen as a political straitjacket for its practitioners. On the one hand, it allows them enough flexibility to disagree with labor's endorsement decisions (Conyers over Austin, Young over Ravitz) but, on the other hand, it does not allow them the freedom to build an independent political structure that covers the entire political spectrum of policy agenda for the city. Of the existing black political groups, TULC comes closest to being a leadership coalition, though it stays close to labor issues. Neo-clientage practitioners have little or no leverage with the corporate or business world, and there is no evidence that it has any influence with whites other than in labor leadership. Indeed, its most important function seems to be to monitor the development of potential rival organizations and politicians, particularly in congressional district groups.

Coleman Young is no appendage of the new clientage politics. The labor movement unintentionally liberated him during the fifties and sixties; after "falling off the edge of the pork chop," he was able to build a personal political organization. His network has grown over the years to include people from every part of the community. Today, the white labor leadership treats him as an equal (and his popularity allows him to insist on it). However, Young is not a man who forgets his friends or who would put down new clientage practitioners; rather, he treats them with respect and as allies. He knows that they must look good to their white patrons, and accordingly, he is not interested in eroding their influence within the labor movement. His magnanimity has earned Young great respect among the community of new clientage practitioners, who are very solicitous and protective of the mayor as an individual.

The other side of the "law of the pork chop edge" coin demands that violaters be treated painfully and quickly. If one falls off the edge, he is quickly fired and accorded little hope of reinstatement. Coleman Young learned early that a staff appointment is an extension of power and is itself not autonomous power. He currently practices what he has learned. As one individual put it, "If a person gets too big, Coleman will cut them down. Coleman divides people into two types, those who helped him and those who he helped."[3] The former are those in the labor movement and progressive community that defended and stuck by him during the fifties. How far can one go toward the edge of the pork chop depends upon which group one falls into.

Young has also been served by the strength of his loose ties with various interest groups. Sociologists distinguish between what they call tight and loose couplings in networks. Those who practice tight coupling—that is, close friendships and alliances—find they cannot easily break from old relationships to make new alliances. The relationships have become personal and as such inhibit development for both parties. Loose coupling in a network allows for many varieties of relationship since it does not involve personal and thus potentially inhibiting commitments. Young has remained flexible in making and participating in networks. He has contacts in all groups, but no single group has his total commitment.[4]

Mayoral Power and Corporate Challenges

In *The Sustaining Hand*, Bryan Jones and Lynn Bachelor analyzed the impact of urban politics on corporate decisions for three Michigan cities. They concluded that Robert Dahl was wrong when he claimed that "industrial society dispersed political resources." Using Detroit as an example, they discovered a concentration of economic and political power in a limited number of large organizations—namely business, labor, media, government, and the church. They offered the term *sectarchy* (rule by multisectors) to explain the interaction of these groups. The city is no longer arbiter but is a power on its own terms. The other sectors in the sectarchy have parallel interests but come together in what the authors call "peak bargaining." In such, "coalition building is stimulated":

> Sectarchy implies that peak leaders are able to dominate elements within sectors on issues where peak bargaining is activated. This is never a forgone conclusion, because organizations within a sector have incentive to reject policy settlements at the peak when their interests are threatened. Hence peak leaders may themselves bargain both with the other peak leaders and with leaders within their organized sector. This is most true of the political sector.[5]

Jones et al. are correct in their conclusion that reformers have removed the structural bases of ethnic politics, leaving Mayor Young to act as a relatively free agent, capable of dealing on par with corporate leaders at the time of peak bargaining. The charter revision of 1974 shifts the fulcrum of city politics to the mayoralty, and the Young administration has succeeded in its new responsibility because of a confluence of various factors, among them white flight, economic transformation, and voter loyalty. Coleman Young's successor's tenure may be influenced by the same factors, but coalition building will be even more difficult, since the internal politics of the city is changing so rapidly. A new generation of Detroit politician impatiently waits in a queue without the political IOUs, experience, or vision of Coleman Young. These leaders may not be able to manage their sectors; if they do not, decisions may never reach the peak bargaining stage.

The future of the automobile industry is crucial to the destiny of Detroit. Coleman Young agrees, but he also believes that the overall interest of the city is not synonymous with that of the auto industry. To him a city is more than the sum of competing interest groups and rivalrous politicians; it is the center of economic exchange and development. People move to cities and stay in cities because of jobs. Detroit cannot keep its residents unless it is able to create jobs for them. The competition for jobs has become an international one. It was for this reason that Mayor Young traveled abroad looking for people willing to invest in Detroit. In some cases, foreign bankers have been more willing to invest in Detroit than local banks. Since the job market does not stop at city limits or international borders, mayors must sell their cities to investors. Detroit has assets, yet they must be carefully packaged; they include an excellent location and a long history as a leading manufacturing city. Coleman Young has been able to sell Detroit's assets to investors. The city has plenty of empty land and access to regional and national transportation networks. There are several choice building sites for housing, but the riverfront area continues to be a center of attraction.

Coleman Young has encouraged investors who regard the city as a potential tourist and convention center. Wisely, he has not attempted to make Detroit a mini version of Route 128 in Boston or a Silicon Valley. In a report to the newly organized Business Attraction and Expansion Council, a regional group studying venture capital possibilities in Michigan, David Brophy urged investors not to follow the Boston and California examples.[6]

The pursuit of a downtown/convention–centered strategy like Young's is not without its critics. Journalists and academics have argued that such development occurs at the expense of neighborhood restoration or growth. Richard Child Hill, a sociologist, calls this strategy corporate-centered. Believing that the "profit logic" cannot save Detroit, Hill warns:

> Bluntly put, Detroit's plight is that of a city which is no longer competitive within the institutional rules of the game. Private

corporations accumulate and reinvest capital, Detroit does not. Capital is mobile, Detroit is not. In the absence of national and regional developmental planning and coordination, Detroit's own strategy has been shaped through bitter rivalry with other governments for corporate smokestacks and skyscrapers. Mobilizing public incentives to leverage private resources, city officials now call themselves "entrepreneurs in the public interest." But in the nature of the case this version of the public interest boils down to the needs of private investors.[7]

Although most of Hill's data are now roughly eight years old, his argument has remained the same in an updated version. Essentially, he argues that disinvestment in Detroit is so massive that nothing less than a national reindustrialization policy can save the city. He is not sanguine about this possibility, however, and suggests the conversion of idle heavy metal industries into light manufacturing shops such as energy hardware products. The venture capital for these enterprises will come from public and private pension funds. Hill calls this plan a democratic-socialist alternative to Young's current corporate-centered strategy.

Todd Swanstrom, a political scientist, also has expressed reservations about a corporate-centered strategy for old industrial cities. In his study of Cleveland's default, he concluded that tax abatements did not work and that the progrowth strategy adopted by the city has corrupted its political process. Swanstrom joined the so-called community elite theorists who believe that a single business elite can conspire to make political decisions by controlling investment decisions. Although there are several references to Detroit in the book, for the most part, the cities are different in politics and opportunities for economic development.

Detroit's business elite have appeared eager to help Mayor Young to turn the city around economically; after all, it makes good business sense to be located in a city with a probusiness reputation. Business leaders volunteered for economic planning groups and mayoral committees, it being good business to know what the city was planning. Detroit business leaders have sat in more meetings with black leaders, self-styled black nationalists, socialists, and labor leaders than their counterparts in other cities. They have heard several socialist development schemes and have themselves been denounced as corruptors of the city's politics. Yet, they stay engaged to city politics. Coleman Young has convinced them that the private-public partnership can make money for them and jobs for his constituency, and they like the way the mayor conducts the city's business. Investors know that if Young looks good, they look good; the mayor knows that they want to make money, and they know he wants them to do so in Detroit. Simply put, the exchanging parties are not aiming at ideological kinship but rather at a mutually self-serving relationship.

Hidden Tensions in Detroit Politics

The transformation of Detroit politics is, in part, a story of the rivalry between the black, white-collar middle class and the black, blue-collar middle class. In producing two versions of the black middle class, the city has accommodated a tangled web of social isolation on the one hand and political cooperation on the other. The predecessors of the white-collar group, the so-called Elites or Cotillion Club types, and small businessmen have evolved into a black professional class. These lawyers, corporate executives, school administrators, and physicians use politics to advance their careers. Unlike their predecessors, they are not content to stay behind the scene or eschew patronage; instead, they want status, power, and visibility. More importantly, this group has isolated itself from its blue-collar counterparts.

The blue-collar middle class, mainly autoworkers and skilled tradesmen, are less educated than their white-collar counterparts but enjoy higher incomes. Many of these individuals are one or two generations removed from the South. They represent the bedrock of Young's political support. They consider their white-collar brethren to be self-serving and indifferent to the plight of the lower classes. William Wilson, a sociologist, hinted at this tension between the two groups in his controversial work, *The Declining Significance of Race*. In it, he observes that black professional politicians have been forced to shift their emphasis from concern over civil rights to the agenda of the poor. With the increased politicization of the black lower class, black middle-class politicians have found it necessary to articulate in a more forceful manner the particular needs and problems of the poor, which reflects a shift from a middle-class–based politics to a lower-class–based politics—a change from the concerns of professional civil rights organizations and that focused primarily on problems of race discrimination to a politics whose issues were defined in response to the urban unrest of the 1960s and focused on problems of de facto segregation, class subordination, welfare state measures, and human survival in the ghetto.[8]

Young's success can be attributed to his attention to the issues facing poor people while simultaneously attempting to rebuild the economic base of the city. Paying attention does not mean that the mayor has been able to change the structural location of blacks in the economic structure of the city, and keeping the concerns of the poor on the city policy agenda is difficult when influential state and federal governments have failed to enact sweeping antipoverty legislation. The city, alone, cannot upgrade the life chances of the poor. Ironically, many working poor agree with the economic elite that the mayor is maintaining a satisfactory holding pattern—or as Max Fisher put it, he is holding things together with the "sheer force of his will and personality." When Mayor Young articulates the economic aspirations of the poor, they appreciate his attention to their situation. Thus, in the 1981 income tax vote, they overwhelmingly supported him. Prudently, the mayor has not tried to overorganize or overpromise this group, yet his care and nurturing of his constituency has also allowed him to safely ignore the criticisms of the white-collar middle class. Young does not govern, however, at the expense of any group.

An equally important tension in black politics has been the continuing struggle between the black church and black labor leaders. In the thirties labor organizers criticized black ministers for being supportive of Henry Ford's antiunion policies and for being the recipients of Ford's largess. In the fifties and sixties, union organizers under the leadership of the late Jack Edwards, the first black UAW executive board member, formed an alliance with the ministers and their congregations. The relationship was marked by joint planning and cooperation.

Currently, new tensions have arisen when ministers enter politics on the behalf of candidates not endorsed by labor. Yet, it is in the interest of all parties involved not to allow these disagreements to leak to the public. The Black Slate, the political arm of the Shrine of the Black Madonna, presents a good example of this rivalry. In claiming partial responsibility for the election of Coleman Young and other black politicians, this group's reputation exceeds its influence. Indeed, the mayor shares some patronage appointments with the Shrine, but the relationship is not one in which the Shrine can dictate policy or appointments to the mayor. Obviously, the mayor listens to members of the Shrine. This, of course, could be said for labor leaders as well. Councilperson Maryann Mahaffey claims that Young intentionally allows certain groups and individuals to think they are his key advisors. She asserts, "it is his style to let each group think that they are the only one advising him. And they are the only one he really listens to. He has continued [to do] that. He watches people fight it out." Mahaffey also claims that the mayor's philosophy can be summarized as: "Don't ever depend on one person. They will get power over you. Keep them all guessing."[9] The rivalry among competing black leaders allows Young to receive multiple suggestions. It is his task to separate the self-serving from objective advice. The tactic does not eliminate tension, but it helps to explain why the mayor has attempted to mediate disputes.

The most obvious tension in city politics is misunderstanding between some of the city's remaining white constituencies and the mayor. The white residents do not support him in his reelection bids, nor do they subscribe to his policies, and this is particularly true of working-class whites. Those who have remained in the city do not think that the mayor is doing enough for them. They dislike his racial references in speeches, and they believe he is driving whites and middle-class blacks out of the city. It is difficult for Mayor Young to reach this group because it is not organized and it has few leaders with whom to negotiate. None of the current white members of the city council present themselves as leaders of the white community. They are instead forced to represent all groups because of the at-large election system, and they cannot afford to alienate black supporters. The white business community, with which the mayor has had good rapport, also has not been spokesgroup for the working-class or middle-class communities. Without such leadership and clearly defined "white issues," it is difficult for the mayor to address residents' feelings of outgroupness and alienation. The misunderstanding therefore continues.

The Twilight of the Democratic Party

The waning of the local Democratic party's influence in elections occurred long before Coleman Young entered politics. The 1918 charter, which institutionalized the nonpartisan elections of city council members and the mayor, helped eliminate the need for strong party identification by candidates and voters. Political activists obligate patronage as a result of their campaign work rather than as contributors in the party. Various city politicians, particularly city councilpersons, have built small personal followings based on community organizations and church affiliations. Candidates still have to present petitions and make rounds to get the proper endorsements, the most important of which remains the UAW. The union maintains its influence by heavily infiltrating the precinct and district organizations. Since its 1969 disaffiliation with the AFL-CIO Committee on Political Education, the UAW Community Action Program (CAP) endorsement leads to visibility, some money, and credibility. The UAW-CAP still operates as the only citywide precinct organization in the city.

The second most important endorsement, aside from the mayor's, at least for blacks, has been the Black Slate, which endorses candidates for local offices. Incumbents who fail to get the Slate endorsement are considered in trouble in the black community. An endorsement means support from a fairly organized group that will publish its endorsements and assist in campaigning. The power of incumbency is solid enough, however, that failure to get the endorsement can be overcome.

Other endorsements include those from reform and civic organizations. The Urban Alliance interviews and endorses candidates and issues. Having begun as a small, loosely organized group of liberal activists seeking to establish some middle-class issues, the group has never had a large active membership, and endorsements have become its main function. In a city in which endorsements from any group matter, even a loosely organized group can get a candidate's attention. In Detroit support from the local newspapers is just as important as from these reform organizations.

The election and reelections of Coleman Young have resulted from selection related factors. First, white residents have lost their registration edge over blacks; second, the extent of white flight and psychological withdrawal from city politics has increased over the years; third, black political activists had a chance to learn several lessons from Austin's previous defeat. Among the lessons was the importance of turning out voters in the inner city election districts; black leaders also learned the unreliability of the liberal-labor coalition. Fourth, the first election involved a realignment in which white labor leaders, investors, and liberals joined the Young coalition. Then, in subsequent elections, it was Young's performance which made the difference in voter behavior. Coleman Young set the agenda and determined the standards by which his administration was to be evaluated. Finally, the incumbent mayor customarily enjoys an advantage in fund-raising. The mayor can glean available financial resources, leaving his opponent little with which to mount a campaign. For these reasons Coleman Young has never needed to create a highly organized political machine to keep him firmly in power.

The Common Council and Public Policy

The emergence of the Young era dwarfs city council activities. Despite the creation of the ombudsman in the 1973 charter, city councilpersons have persisted in burying themselves in excessive casework at the expense of policy development and review. Repeated attempts to hire its own legal and budget staff underline the council's inability to develop alternatives to the mayor's policies. The logical grounds for confrontation or negotiation with the mayor has been the budget, and the council has consistently been unable to override the mayor's veto of budget items. Council members also do not have any unifying mission or a representative willing to risk his/her political career in order to take on Coleman Young. The decision of Ken Cockrel not to run for reelection to the council left it without a flamboyant and articulate black political figure. Although councilpersons have publicly disagreed with the mayor, they lack the hortatory skills of Cockrel. Since the at-large election system has separated councilpersons from specific constituencies, they have been forced to be conservative lest they incur the wrath of Young supporters. More importantly, the at-large elections, once an invention to deny immigrants opportunities to build political machines, have created a bland and formless council politics. The return to a ward system would probably reduce white representation, increase fractionalism, and increase opportunities for establishing a political machine.

Race and Pluralism in Detroit Politics

The most regrettable characteristic of Detroit politics has been the persistence of racism. Race continues to intervene in nearly all evaluations of the mayor's performance. Young has been more widely reported for his faults, or those of his subordinates, than for his accomplishments. Yet, the real problem in the city has been the lack of an effective spokesperson for the various interest groups in the city. There are few, if any, alternative policy agendas, and policymakers have been forced to look toward the mayor's office for guidance on issues; that office simply cannot handle the policy load. Pluralism, once thought by academics to be essential to effective policy-making, is not well differentiated in Detroit. Neither the black church, UAW, nor ACORN, for example, has emerged as a source for policy ideas. They do not function as multiple local veto points or challenges to mayoral policy-making.

Perhaps the single most formidable obstacle to building an alternative to Young's policy is the concentration of power within the mayor's office. Unlike many large cities (New York City, for example) power is not dispersed across city agencies, nor have local politicians been undercut by excessive state interference.

Douglas Yates's *The Ungovernable City* suggests that cities are not amenable to rational governance because of the fragmentation of politics, power, and bureaucracies, which fosters reactive management among cities. The reason cities are so poorly managed is that they are not in complete control of their destiny; they also lack the resources to practice proactive management. Accordingly, Yates is not very sanguine about the future of the fragmented city. In Detroit the 1973 charter ended much of the fragmentation in mayoral agencies and consolidated control in the mayor's office. Under the present system, the mayor can ignore city council attempts at legislative oversight. The office of the mayor, empowered at the expense of the council and the bureaucracy, operates with few institutional checks and balances. In effect, it is possible for a strong mayor to dominate the policy agenda of the city.

Coleman Young has been successful because he has understood the differences between politicking and governing. Traditionally, he has retained three sets of advisors (political, economic, and administrative) on his office staff. The leaders of the first and thirteenth congressional districts are staff appointees and act as his political advisors. Young mixes their advice with that of old friends in the labor movement and the ministers. Economic advisors are an entirely separate group and are also crucial to Young's success. In addition to an in-house staff, he solicits advice from the white economic elite and from corporate leaders. The mayor's administrative staff consists of a separate group of people who relate primarily with the day-to-day operations of city departments. Such an operational procedure allows the mayor to be central in all communications. In keeping these advising groups separate, each group is allowed to become an expert in a particular sector.

In an earlier study of New York City, this author was struck by the the fragmentation of the city's politics. Part of the problem appeared to relate to changes in the ideology of the civil service. New York bureaucrats long thought of themselves as professionals with a right to administer independently from politicians, and this view was reinforced by civil service reformers. In the case of Detroit, strong professional norms (that is, the primacy of professionalism over a lay administration) have allowed bureaucrats to maintain their autonomy from politicians, although bureaucrats have tended to see the struggle as a matter of employee rights rather than professional norms. The difference between New York and Detroit may be a function of city size. Detroit, with its 20,000 employees, could fit inside the New York City police department. Coleman Young's confrontation with the bureaucrats, with the exception of the police, has typically been over rights and benefits rather over the future of the city.

The real rivals, if any, to mayoral power have been the judges, who have served as partners in the management of city policy. Their participation has been intermittent and has lacked the coherence necessary to permanently alter city policies. The courts have been used repeatedly by public employee unions in gaining what they could not win at the bargaining table; the unions have relied on judges rather than on collective bargaining. Accordingly, as they have in other cities, courts have become partners in the collective bargaining process. Litigation has become a particularly entangling and expensive element in the governing of Detroit.

The continuous evidence of racism in the outside suburban community, as exemplified by the recent polling of whites, has served to strengthen the hand of the black elite in building a black consensus. The resulting policy consensus has served as a dam against the flow of opposition groups. There is a need for outside white critics since there are few internal black critics. Because they are usually coopted in the early stages of political organizations, internal critics have not been able to grasp or seize the political agenda. For example, the rising resentments over street crime could have been a potentially powerful organizing political force, yet the mayor has seized the issue and effectively blocked the development of a strictly civilian anticrime interest group.

Another unique aspect of Detroit politics is the relative lack of independent islands of decision making. In Detroit there is no public agency head can who can build a separate and effective consituency to insulate himself or herself from the mayor's influence. Young has taken care to shift officials between agencies to avoid having his appointees do what Herb Kaufman once called "going native"—that is, developing an in-house constituency that could veto the mayor's policies. His policy also prevents appointees from getting lost in the bureaucratic maze. If other cities have islands of influence, then Detroit has its peninsulas with overlapping jurisdictions and portable directors. This is not to say that there are no opportunities for policy sabotage.

Eudaemonism and Public Policy

The risk-taking behavior of Coleman Young has enabled him to perform effectively in the Detroit political context. By taking risks, he has begun to revitalize Detroit. He also shows a capacity to grasp the big picture necessary for city development and projects. His attitude is a teaching one. In order to change his constituency's view of reality, he must gamble for them, and if he wins, they win. He has encouraged his constituents to "think big." For a relatively powerless constituency, teaching by example is perhaps the most effective agent for change.

The role of the mayor in economic growth and change will take years for economic historians to unravel. Guiding the transition from an industrial-based economy to a mixed one has been difficult. Detroit has lost some potential skilled manpower it will never regain, yet the mayor moved quickly to embrace the new economy when almost everyone, including the media, was saying that no one wanted to live, locate, or build in the city. Building Joe Louis Arena when others were resigned to driving to Pontiac to see major sports events was at variance with conventional wisdom. The critics said no one would come downtown because of crime. Nevertheless, the mayor built the arena and had it named after a national black hero, and so far it has been partially successful in finding a place in the sports industry. It was there, for example, in 1985, when the competing Silverdome collapsed.

The entire development of riverfront property should have been started in the fifties, but it took the mayor's vision and his need to have things built—to attract investors—to get projects off the drawing board in the 1970s. Young has moved quickly to show his constituency that Detroit can survive despite corporate relocation decisions—again, a teaching role. He has taken time to reassure his constituency that they retain both economic power and political efficacy at times when Detroit seems to be going under. Young's faith in the city has kept others from deserting it. His belief in the city has persuaded merchants to give their city businesses one more chance and investors the sense that things are moving along. More importantly, downtown merchants now have a tangible vision of downtown as the major entertainment center of the Detroit-Windsor Metroplex.

In an age of entrenched city bureaucracy and militant public sector unions, the Detroit mayor's office remains powerful. It sets the tone of city politics. Despite its accomplishments, Young has not been without his critics, which range from the expected partisan sources such as conservative Republicans to crusading newspaper columnists, ambitious politicians, and ex-supporters. He has faced several major confrontations with labor leaders, party officials, and the media. Yet none of the criticisms has undermined his ability to govern the city or seriously threatened his reelection. He has been able to govern because he has outmaneuvered opponents and anticipated policy shifts in Washington and Lansing. His political reactive skills, including an uncanny ability to anticipate his opponents' attacks, have been matched by his proactive skills. His anticipatory skills complemented by his proactive eudaemonistic behavior have allowed him to avoid many of the administrative problems experienced by other black mayors of large cities. Coleman Young has been a consummate agenda maker, perhaps more than any black politician in this nation. His background as a labor organizer and state legislator has served him well, but more important has been his ability to keep an open mind about the city's future. He has also been able to touch the psychological antenna of his constituency with his continued championing of civil rights and causes affecting poor people.

In America politicians learn their trade from watching other politicians. Young has watched Detroit's mayors, from Frank Murphy to Roman Gribbs. Young has also learned from the stewardship of Richard Reading, Edward Jeffries, Albert Cobo, Louis Miriani, and Jerome Cavanagh. The *Detroit Free Press Magazine* concluded that Young's style represents a "composite of some of his predecessors. He has the social consciousness of Pingree, the political savvy and savoire faire of Frank Murphy, and on occasion, the barbed tongue of Edward Jeffries."[10] Unlike his predecessors, however, Young has been forced to spend time reacting to the racist concerns of whites who have left the city.

Detroit's future will be shaped by Coleman Young's current decisions. If he is successful in transforming the economy, integrating the work force, and revitalizing the downtown and city neighborhoods, then history will rank him among the great mayors of the city. If he does not succeed, then Detroit will be a testimony to the plight of rustbelt cities in the eighties. Currently, the city is served well by Young's eudaemonism and flexibility, but it needs more than one man's resolution. The media must help educate the suburban white readers rather than feed their anxieties. White investors must also help to change the city, and they must continue to support the political elite and dissuade it from turning inward. Politicians who want to succeed Coleman Young should study his vision of the city before they articulate their own. They may not share Young's vision, but they may begin to understand why a mayor needs such a clear vision.

Notes

Chapter 1

1. Jeffrey Pressman, "Preconditions of Mayoral Leadership," *American Political Science Review* 65 (June 1979): 11–24.
2. Peter Eisinger, *The Politics of Displacement* (New York: Academic Press, 1980).
3. D. J. Wurdock, "Neighborhood Racial Transition: A Study of the Role of White Flight," *Urban Affairs Quarterly* 17: 1 (September 1981): 75–89.
4. Richard Neustadt, *Presidential Power* (New York: John Wiley and Sons, 1960), 179.
5. James Q. Wilson, "The Mayors v. the Cities," *The Public Interest* no. 16 (Summer 1969): 28.
6. Wallace Sayre and Herbert Kaufman, *Governing New York City* (New York: W. W. Norton, 1960).
7. Thomas A. Schwartz and Sharon West, *A Report on Media Coverage* (Columbus: Ohio State University, 1984).
8. Reginald Stuart, "The New Black Power of Coleman Young," *New York Times Magazine* (December 16, 1979): 112.
9. John P. Kotter and Paul R. Lawrence, *Mayors in Action* (New York: John Wiley and Sons, 1974).
10. Edward Banfield, *Political Influence* (New York: Free Press, 1961).
11. James B. Cunningham, *Urban Leadership in the Sixties* (Cambridge: Schenkman Publishing Co., 1970).
12. Robert Dahl, *Who Governs?* (New Haven: Yale University Press, 1961).
13. See Gene Fowler, *Beau James* (New York: Viking, 1961) and Arthur Mann, *La Guardia Comes to Power: 1933* (Philadelphia and New York: Lippincott, 1965).
14. Charles H. Levine, *Racial Conflicts and the American Mayor* (Lexington: Lexington Books, 1974), 23–24.
15. Ibid., 41–42.
16. Ibid., 127–41.
17. See Jesse Bernard, "The Eudaemonist," in *Why Men Take Chances*, ed. Samuel Z. Klausner (New York: Anchor Books, 1968).
18. Tom Greene, "Coleman Antes Up," *Monthly Detroit* 7: 7 (July 1984): 58.
19. *Detroit News* "Michigan" (January 19, 1986): 10.

Chapter 2

1. Bernice Grier (Coleman Young's sister), interview with author, October 2, 1987.
2. Joel Aberbach and Jack Walker, "The Meanings of Black Power: A Comparison of White and Black Interpretations of a Political Slogan," *American Political Science Review* LXIV (June 1970): 367–88.
3. Horace Bond, *Negro Education in Alabama: A Study of Cotton and Steel* (New York: Associated Publishers, Inc., 1939), 192.
4. David Davis, "The Decline of the Gasoline Aristocracy: The Struggle for Supremacy in Detroit" (Ph.D. diss., Harvard University, 1976).
5. Ibid.
6. John M. Ragland, "The Negro in Detroit," *Southern Workman* 52 (November 1923): 536.
7. Edward D. Kennedy, *The Automobile Industry* (New York: Reynal and Hitchcock, 1941), 155.
8. Ibid.
9. Shelton Tappes, interview by R. Young. "A Report on Detroit Politics" (unpublished honors thesis, Harvard University, 1974), 24.
10. Kenneth Jackson, *The Ku Klux Klan in the City 1915–1930* (Oxford: Oxford University Press, 1967), 142.
11. David Allan Levine, *Internal Combustion: The Races in Detroit 1915–1926* (Westport, Ct.: Greenwood Press, 1976).
12. Robert W. Dunn, *Labor and Automobiles* (New York: International Publisher, 1929), 69.
13. Bernice Grier, interview with author, October 2, 1987.
14. In Studs Terkel, *American Dreams Lost and Found* (New York: Pantheon Books, 1980), 355.
15. Ibid.
16. Ibid.
17. *Directory of Colleges and Schools 1932–33*, National Catholic Welfare Conference (Washington, D.C., 1932), 243.
18. James T. Cronin, "A Basic Plan for Catholic Curriculum Construction" (Ph.D. diss., Catholic University of America, 1927).
19. Ibid., 357.
20. B. J. Widick, *Detroit: City of Race and Class Violence* (Chicago: Quadrangle Books, 1972), 44.
21. Bernice Grier, interview with author, October 2, 1987.
22. A. J. Stovall, "Before Coleman Young: The Growth of the Detroit Black Elected Officialdom, 1870–1973" (Ph.D. diss., Union College, 1983), 69–70.
23. Aaron Toodle, "The Negro in Michigan Politics," *The Crisis* (July 1943): 213; also cited in Stovall.
24. Horace White, "Who Owns the Negro Church?" *Christian Century* LV (February 9, 1938): 176–77.
25. Widick, 75.
26. T. Arnold Hill, "The Negro and the CIO," *Opportunity* (August 1937): 243–44.
27. Edward Litchfield, "A Case Study of Negro Political Behavior in Detroit," *Public Opinion Quarterly* V (June 1941): 267–74.

28. August Meier and Elliott Rudwick, *Black Detroit and the Rise of the UAW* (New York: Oxford University Press, 1979), 197.
29. William Kornhauser, "The Negro Union Official," *American Journal of Sociology* 57 (March 1952): 443–52.
30. Daniel Thompson, *The Negro Leadership Class* (Englewood Cliffs, N.J.: Prentice-Hall, 1963).
31. Jesse Hougabrook, interview with author, August 7, 1985.
32. Martin Kilson, "Political Change in the Negro Ghetto, 1900–1940," in *Key Issues in Afro-American Experiences*, vol. 2, ed. Nathan Huggins and Martin Kilson (New York: Harcourt Brace Jovanovich, 1971), 167–92.
33. Allison Davis, *Leadership, Love and Aggression* (New York: Harcourt Brace Jovanovich, 1983), 7.

Chapter 3

1. Benjamin Stolberg, *The Story of the CIO* (New York: Viking Press, 1938).
2. See Alfred McClung Lee and Norman D. Humphrey, *Race, Riot, Detroit, 1943* (New York: Octagon Books, 1968).
3. Coleman Young, interview with author, October 9, 1986.
4. Coleman Young, interview with author, October 9, 1986.
5. See Michigan Public Act of 1947, no. 270.
6. Coleman Young, interview with author, October 9, 1986.
7. Coleman Young, interview with author, October 9, 1986.
8. Press release, "New from the UAW-CIO," October 22, 1951.
9. For another view see Sumner Rosen, "The CIO Era, 1935–55," in *The Negro and the American Labor Movement*, ed. Julius Jacobson (Garden City, N.Y.: Anchor Books, 1968).
10. Roger Keeran, *The Communist Party and Auto Worker Unions* (Bloomington: Indiana University Press, 1980).
11. Coleman Young, interview with author, October 9, 1986.
12. Ibid.
13. Ibid.
14. James Q. Wilson, *Negro Politics* (New York: Free Press, 1960), 31.
15. George Crockett (Recorder's Court judge and former union official), oral history, Wayne State University Labor History Archives (February 2, 1968).
16. This interpretation of events is based on interviews with David Moore, November 10, 1987, and Robert Battle, July 7, 1988.
17. For a brief discussion of the TULC see Ray Marshall, *The Negro and Organized Labor* (New York: John Wiley and Sons, 1965), 68–72.
18. See Stovall, 111–12.
19. See Widick, 149–50.
20. Denise Lewis, "Black Political Consciousness and the Voting Behavior of Blacks in Detroit, 1961–1968" (M.A. thesis, Wayne State University, 1969). Also see Oscar Elantz, "The Negro Vote in Northern Industrial Cities," *Western Political Quarterly* XIII (December 1960): 999–1010.
21. Cited in Detroit Urban League, *A Profile of the Detroit Negro 1959–1967* (Detroit, 1967), 14.

22. Herbert Locke, *The Detroit Riot of 1967* (Detroit: Wayne State University Press, 1969), 87.
23. *Observation Balloon* 2: 5 (April 30, 1968): 1.
24. Coleman Young, interview with author, July 10, 1986.
25. Robert Vanderbeek, interview with author, September 28, 1987.
26. See this account in Reginald Stuart, "The New Black Power of Coleman Young," *New York Times Magazine* (December 16, 1979): 101–12.
27. Letter to Mrs. Jessie Wallace, August 26, 1966. The Coleman Young Collection, Box 1, Archives of Labor and Union Affairs, Wayne State University.
28. Coleman Young, interview with author, July 10, 1986.
29. H. H. Gerth and C. Wright Mills, ed., *From Max Weber* (New York: Oxford University Press, 1946), 84.
30. Coleman Young, interview with author, July 10, 1986.

Chapter 4

1. Frederick P. Currier, "Mayor Race Is Too Close to Call," *Detroit News* (November 2, 1969), 1.
2. Coleman Young, interview with author, July 10, 1986.
3. Coleman Young, interview with author, July 10, 1986.
4. Hubert Holley, interview with author, June 25, 1986.
5. Bob Pisor, "Coleman Young," *Detroit News* (October 15, 1973), 3A.
6. Robert A. Popa, "Whither Coleman Young?" *Detroit News* (November 16, 1968).
7. Marcia Van Ness, "Coleman Young Eyes U.S. Senate Seat," *State Journal* (March 28, 1971): A-13.
8. Barbara Cranham, "Foresees Negro Governor in Michigan," *Lansing State Journal* (September 26, 1968).
9. Coleman Young, interview with author, July 10, 1986.
10. Mel Ravitz, interview with author, July 21, 1986.
11. Coleman Young, interview with author, July 10, 1986.
12. Mel Ravitz, interview with author, July 21, 1986.
13. Pat Murphy, "Young / Nichols Trade Barbs on Race Issue," *Detroit News* (1973).
14. Ibid.
15. Remer Tyson, "Nichols, Young Clash Head-On in Round 1," *Detroit Free Press* (October 3, 1973).
16. "Running for Mayor, Two Streetwise Men: Nichols v. Young," *Detroit Free Press* (October 7, 1973).
17. Edward P. Carrier, "Young Retains Lead over Nichols," *Detroit News* (November 4, 1973), 1.
18. For a discussion of this transition, see Robert Hansbury Phillip, "Equal Employment Opportunity and Affirmative Action: Mayoral Initiative and Bureaucratic Responses, The Case of Detroit" (Ph.D. diss., Wayne State University, in progress).
19. Claud Young, interview with author, August 2, 1987.
20. "How Detroit Candidates Stand on Some of the Issues," *Detroit Free Press* (November 1, 1981), 1B.
21. Ibid.

22. Michael Traugott, "Poll Says Young Is Ahead 2-1," *Detroit News* (June 9, 1985), 8A.
23. See Raymond E. Wolfinger and Steven J. Rosenstone, *Who Votes?* (New Haven, Conn.: Yale University Press, 1980).

Chapter 5

1. Kent Robinson, "The Impact of Transportation on Central Business Districts," *Traffic Quarterly* 343: 4 (October 1980): 523–37.
2. Detroit Area Economic Forum, *1984 Economic Fact Book*.
3. Ibid.
4. Andrew McGill, "Metro Detroit. A Look Ahead," *Detroit News* (January 6–20, 1985).
5. William Haber et al., *Michigan in the 1970s: An Economic Forecast* (Ann Arbor Bureau of Business Research, University of Michigan, 1965).
6. H. Browning and J. Singlemann, *The Emergence of a Service Society: Demographic and Sociological Aspects of the Transformation of the Labor Force in the U.S.A.* (Springfield, Va.: National Technical Information Service, 1975).
7. Ibid.
8. Thomas Stanbeck, *Service: The New Economy* (Totowa: N.J.: Allanheld, Osmun, 1981).
9. James Kenyon, "Robert L. Millender—meet the Kingmaker for black candidates," *Detroit News* (November 1, 1977), 3A.
10. See "New Detroit and the (Negro) People, 1967–1977," prepared by the Coalition of Black Trade Unionists (CBTU) (July 23, 1977).
11. Max Fisher, interview with author, September 9, 1987.
12. Charles Reich, "The New Property," *Yale Law Journal* 73: 5 (April 1964): 733–87.
13. Kenyon, 3A.
14. William Milliken (former governor of Michigan), interview with author, September 5, 1986.
15. Coleman Young, interview with author, October 9, 1986.
16. Alvin Toffler, *Future Shock* (New York: Random House, 1970), 119.
17. Emmett Moten, interview with author, October 13, 1986.
18. See Lynda A. Ewen, *Corporate Power and Urban Crisis in Detroit* (Princeton: Princeton University Press, 1978).
19. Floyd Hunter, *Community Power Structure* (Chapel Hill: University of North Carolina Press, 1953).
20. Clarence Stone, *Economic Growth and Neighborhood Discontent* (Chapel Hill: University of North Carolina Press, 1976).
21. Steven S. Cohen and John Zysman, *Manufacturing Matters: The Myth of the Post-Industrial Economy* (New York: Basic Books, 1987), 50.

Chapter 6

1. Theresa Tuohy, "Detroit OKs Plan for Arena Stadium," *Detroit News* (October 20, 1976), 10A.

2. Ibid.
3. Theresa Tuohy, "Riverfront Area Plan Cleared," *Detroit News* (October 28, 1976), 1B.
4. "Tiger Stadium Deal Gets a Rogell Assist," *Detroit News* (October 28, 1976), 6A.
5. Tuohy, *Detroit News* (October 28, 1976), 1B.
6. *Detroit News* (October 28, 1976), 6A.
7. "$5 Million Detroit Arena Grant OK'd," Washington Bureau, *Detroit News* (January 4, 1977), 6A.
8. David Ashenfelter, "State Bars $1.5 Million for New Arena Study," *Detroit News* (February 9, 1977), 13A.
9. "Young Won't Give Up on Arena," *Detroit News* (February 15, 1977), 1A.
10. Theresa Tuohy, "Rogell Fears Arena Would Be a Bust," *Detroit News* (February 10, 1977), 1A.
11. D. Ashenfelter and C. Willcox, "Detroit Taxpayers May Pay for Arena," *Detroit News* (February 16, 1977), 3A.
12. Ibid.
13. "Young Won't Give Up on Arena," *Detroit News* (February 15, 1977), 1A.
14. Ibid.
15. Ibid.
16. Ibid.
17. C. Willcox, "We Don't Need You, Young Tells Wings," *Detroit News* (February 19, 1977), 6A.
18. Theresa Tuohy, "Detroit Eyes Arena Options," *Detroit News* (February 17, 1977), 6A.
19. C. Willcox, "Council OK's New Arena 5-4," *Detroit News* (March 9, 1977), 1A.
20. C. Willcox, "Arena Approval a Victory for Young," *Detroit News* (March 10, 1977), 4A.
21. C. Willcox, "Detroit to Fight Court Ban on Sale of Arena Bonds," *Detroit News* (March 29, 1977), 1, 13A.
22. C. Willcox, *Detroit News* (March 29, 1977), 1A.
23. C. Willcox, *Detroit News* (March 24, 1977), 6A.
24. C. Willcox, "Detroit Arena Fund Still Alive," *Detroit News* (April 8, 1977), 8A.
25. Ibid.
26. "Pistons Are Also Interested in Proposed Pontiac Arena," *Detroit News* (April 2, 1977), 1, 8A.
27. C. Willcox, "Young Threatens Suit to Block Olympia II," *Detroit News* (April 20, 1977), 10A; "Detroit Sues to Halt Arena," *Detroit News* (April 30, 1977), 1A.
28. C. Willcox, *Detroit News* (April 29, 1977), 1A.
29. Steve Kaufman, "Friend of Young Gets Bank to Reject Loan for Olympia II," *Detroit News* (April 11, 1977), 12A.
30. D. Ashenfelter and C. Willcox, "Court Gives Detroit OK to Start Riverfront Arena," *Detroit News* (May 20, 1977), 1A.
31. Peter R. Lochbiler, "Red Wings OK Riverfront Arena," *Detroit News* (August 3, 1977), 1A.
32. Ibid.
33. *Detroit News* (August 3, 1977), 1A.

34. Lochbiler, Meagher, Tuohy, and Wells, "Inside Story on Young's Coup on Red Wings," *Detroit News* (August 4, 1977), 9A.
35. Ibid.
36. Richard Willing, "Arena Plan a Hot Issue," *Detroit News* (August 31, 1977), 11A.
37. James G. Tittsworth, "Police Union Chief Rakes Funds Switch for Arena," *Detroit News* (August 3, 1978), 2B.
38. Chester Bulgier, "Louis Arena Bonds Find Rough Sailing," *Detroit News* (May 24, 1979), 1, 4A.
39. Chester Bulgier and Stephen Cain, "Union Deal Keeps Arena on Time," *Detroit News* (June 6, 1979), 1B.
40. Susan Martin Taylor and Stephen Cain, "Bond Cost Likely to Rise for Arena," *Detroit News* (October 11, 1979), 1A.
41. Joan Walter, "Detroit Defends Its Plan for Arena Loan," *Detroit News* (November 27, 1979), 1E.
42. "Loan Sought for Louis Arena," *Detroit News* (November 25, 1979), 6B.
43. "Loan Sought for Louis Arena" *Detroit News* (November 25, 1979), 6B.
44. Joan Walter, "Detroit Defends Its Plan for Arena Loan," *Detroit News* (November 27, 1979), 1E.
45. Walter, *Detroit News* (November 28, 1979).
46. Walter, *Detroit News* (December 13, 1979), 1, 15A.
47. Charlie Cain, "Detroit Gets U.S. Loan for Louis Arena," *Detroit News* (March 1, 1980), 8A.
48. Nolan Finley, "Council Approves Plan for Arena Loan," *Detroit News* (March 11, 1980), 4B.
49. Nolan Finley, "Arena Loan Risk Stirs Worries on Council," *Detroit News* (March 12, 1980), 1B.
50. For a discussion of this point see Arthur F. Schreiber and Richard B. Clemmer, *Economics of Urban Problems* (New York: Houghton-Mifflin, 1983), 11.
51. *Poletown Neighborhood Council v. City of Detroit*, No. 80-039-426, testimony of Coleman Young (December 1, 1980), 3.
52. Ibid., 4.
53. Michael Robinson, "GM Plans to Merge Two Cadillac Plants—Seeks Detroit Site," *Detroit News* (June 24, 1980), 1A.
54. Ibid., 4.
55. Michael Robinson and Nolan Finley, "East Side Leads as GM Plan Site," *Detroit News* (June 25, 1980), 1A.
56. Ibid.
57. Ibid., 16A.
58. Michael Robinson, "Estes 'Sure' GM Will Stay in Detroit," *Detroit News* (June 28, 1980), 8A.
59. Ibid., 1A.
60. Ibid., 8A.
61. Michael J. Trojanowski, "Two Cities Join to Lure GM," *Detroit News* (July 1, 1980), 1A.
62. Ibid.
63. Ibid., 4A.
64. Ibid.

65. Rebecca Powers, "GM Plan Offers Hope," *Detroit News* (July 7, 1980), 3A.
66. Robert Roach, "Loan Aid Drives for GM Plant," *Detroit News* (July 16, 1980), 1B.
67. Powers, *Detroit News* (July 7, 1980), 3A.
68. Michael Robinson, "Group Threatens Suit on Proposed GM Plant," *Detroit News* (July 22, 1980), 1.
69. Ibid.
70. Nolan Finley and Robert Roach, "City May Finance GM's New Plant," *Detroit News* (July 31, 1980), 1.
71. Ibid.
72. Robert Roach, "Council Says Go on GM Plant," *Detroit News* (August 7, 1980), 1.
73. "The Man Behind the Project," *Detroit News* (July 2, 1985), 1.
74. Robert Roach, "GM to Ask for Tax Break on New Plan," *Detroit News* (October 7, 1980), 2B.
75. Robert Roach and Michael Tucker, "GM Offers Site Deal, Insists on Tax Break," *Detroit News* (October 11, 1980), 1.
76. "GM Plant Won't Add to Job Rolls," *Detroit News* (October 22, 1980), 1.
77. Robert Roach, "New Plant Won't Get State Fund," *Detroit News* (October 24, 1980), 1B.
78. "Cadillac Project Gets Funds," *Detroit News* (October 25, 1980), 9A.
79. Neal Pierce, "Why a Special City Tax Deal Is Not Needed to Get the Cadillac Plant," *Detroit News* (October 31, 1980), 9A.
80. Robert Roach and Michael Tucker, "Young Assails Nader for Backing Poletown," *Detroit News* (February 1, 1981), 1.
81. John Broder, "GM Plant Site Grant on Way, Milliken Told," *Detroit News* (February 12, 1981), 1.
82. Douglas Ilka, "Courts Halt Poletown Evacuation," *Detroit News* (February 21, 1981), 1.
83. Barbara Doerr and Karl Blankenship, "'Mention GM, Nader Foams,' Young Claims," *Detroit News* (March 12, 1981), 1, 11A.
84. See *Poletown Neighborhood Council v. City of Detroit*, 410, 616, 304 N. W. 2d 455 (1981).
85. Pat Shellenbarger, "State Court Clears Way for GM's Poletown Plan," *Detroit News* (March 14, 1981), 1.
86. Robert Roach, "GM Cuts $5 Million from Cadillac Plant Tax— Relief Request," *Detroit News* (March 17, 1981), 1.
87. Robert Roach, "Detroit Keeps Hoping on Grant for Poletown," *Detroit News* (March 19, 1981), 5B.
88. Robert Roach, "City Grants a Tax Break to GM Plant," *Detroit News* (April 16, 1981), 1B.
89. Louis Mleczko, "Mayor's Shovels Start Work on Cadillac Plant," *Detroit News* (May 2, 1981), 8A.
90. Albert Martin, interview with author, July 29, 1987.
91. David Kushma, "Detroit to Take Over People Mover," *Detroit Free Press* (October 2, 1985), 3A.
92. David Kushma, "Young Accuses SEMTA of Diverting DOT Aid," *Detroit Free Press* (August 29, 1985), 11A.

93. David Kushma, "Young: City Will Finish, Run Mover with or without State," *Detroit Free Press* (September 27, 1985).
94. Ibid.
95. Peter Brown, "Blacks on Racism," *Detroit Free Press* (September 9, 1984).
96. David Kushma, "Young: City will Finish, Run Mover With or Without State." *Detroit Free Press* (September 27, 1985).
97. Colin Buchanan, "Urban Transportation: The Scope of the New Technology," cited in *The Political Economy of Urban Transportation*, ed. Delbert Taebel and James Cornelius (Port Washington, N.Y.: Kennikat Press, 1977), 90.
98. Tony Snow, "The Great Train Robbery: Twenty Years of Mass Transit Have Bilked Taxpayers," *Policy Review* 36 (Spring 1986): 44–49.
99. Bryan Jones et al., *The Sustaining Hand* (Lawrence: University Press of Kansas, 1986), 113.
100. This term belongs to Jeffrey Pressman and Aaron Wildavsky; see *Implementation* (Berkeley: University of California Press, 1973).

Chapter 7

1. James Q. Wilson, *Varieties of Police Behavior* (New York: Atheneum, 1976), 283.
2. Joseph Fink and Lloyd G. Sealy, *The Community and the Police—Conflict or Cooperation?* (New York: John Wiley and Sons, 1974).
3. Hans Toch, "Cops and Blacks: Warring Minorities," in *The Police*, ed. Gerald Leinwald (New York: Pocket Books, 1972), 128.
4. Michael J. Falvo, "Affirmative Action Considerations in Police Professionalism" (Master's thesis, Wayne State University, 1978).
5. Dan Georgakas and Marvin Surkin, *Detroit: I Do Mind Dying* (New York: St. Martin's Press, 1975).
6. Ibid., 20.
7. Percentages taken from "The Detroit Connection," *Washington Post* (August 31, 1981).
8. Coleman Young's first months in office are reviewed in "High Goals of Detroit's Black Mayor Foiled by Recession," *New York Times* (January 22, 1975).
9. "Tannian Fights Hatred to Keep His Job," *Detroit News* (December 23, 1974).
10. Stephen Leinen, *Black Police, White Society* (New York: New York University Press, 1984), 267–68.
11. Prior to this ruling, the 1974 "unisex" hiring order of the Michigan Civil Rights Commission mandated that women could not be limited to working in the women's and juvenile divisions; they must receive the same training and duties as men. See *Shaeffer v. Tannian*, E.D., Mich. Civil Number 39943 (1974).
12. "39 Police Absent in Protest," *Detroit Free Press* (October 23, 1974).
13. For a detailed discussion of the Tannian/Blount relationship, see Patrick James Ashton, "Race, Class and Black Politics: The Implication for the Election of a Black Mayor for the Police and Policing in Detroit" (Ph.D. diss., Michigan State University, 1981).

14. "Deputy Put on Sick Leave," *Detroit Free Press* (August 21, 1976).
15. "Tannian Maintains He's Right," *Detroit News* (September 29, 1976).
16. "Equal Employment Opportunity Program 1978–1979," memorandum.
17. "Police Back Seniority Layoffs," *Detroit Monitor* (May 9, 1975).
18. "Black Officers Picket Police Union Headquarters," *Detroit Free Press* (April 4, 1975).
19. "Mayor Renews His Bid for Pay Deal," *Detroit Free Press* (May 9, 1975).
20. "All Police Jobs May Be Saved," *Detroit News* (May 15, 1975).
21. The Lieutenants and Sergeants Association (LSA) accepted the agreement on May 28, 1974.
22. "DPOA Rejects Jobs Compromise," *Detroit News* (May 30, 1975).
23. "Police Accept No-Layoff Plan," *Detroit News* (June 11, 1975).
24. Connie Hager, "Residency Requirements for City Employees: Important Incentives in Today's Urban Crisis," *Urban Law Annual* 20 (1980), 199–222.
25. "DPOA Set to Appeal Residency," *Detroit Free Press* (September 9, 1975).
26. "Nonresident Police Face Hearings," *Detroit News* (October 17, 1975).
27. *McCarty v. Philadelphia Civil Service Commission*, 424 U.S. 645 (1976).
28. "Nonresident Police Face Trial," *Detroit Free Press* (April 9, 1975).
29. Residency rules were part of the city's regulations since 1968, but their enforcement was delayed by a legal challenge from the DPOA. A three-member arbitration panel ruled in September 1974 that officers must live within the city until the DPOA contract expired on June 30, 1977. The State Supreme Court has ruled that residency rules are legal but subject to collective bargaining.
30. "Later Rehiring Likely," *Detroit Free Press* (April 18, 1975).
31. "Black Police Ask Others to Join in Refusing Pay Raises," *Detroit News* (March 26, 1976).
32. "City, U.S. Head for Clash over Police Layoffs," *Detroit Free Press* (June 20, 1976).
33. For information on rulings, see "Detroit Police Torn by Layoff Decision," *New York Times* (July 3, 1976); "Protest Seems to Be Waning," *Detroit News* (July 2, 1976); "Detroit to Rehire 450 Police," *Detroit News* (August 12, 1976).
34. "Kaess Won't Remove Himself from Bias Case," *Detroit News* (September 29, 1977).
35. "Kaess Dismisses Disqualification Motion," *Detroit News* (September 24, 1977).
36. "Kaess to Hear Trial," *Detroit News* (September 28, 1977).
37. "Police Ordered to Halt Minority Promotion Plan," *Detroit News* (February 28, 1978).
38. Ibid.

39. "Kaess Refuses Delay," *Detroit News* (March 4, 1978).
40. From *CAADET Bulletin* (March 28, 1978).
41. "Federal Court Victory for City," *Detroit News* (October 2, 1979).
42. "Detroit Police Antibias Plan Wins on Appeal," *Detroit News* (October 13, 1979). See *Baker v. Young*, 483 F. Supp. 930 (D.C. Mich., 1979), 23 EPD, para. 30, 313. *Detroit Police Officers v. Young*, 608 F. 2d 671 (CA-6, 1979).
43. "Young Gets Windfall," *Detroit News* (April 21, 1978).
44. "Showdown on Police Wages," *Detroit Free Press* (July 11, 1978).
45. "City Shows No Hardship—So Police Win," *Detroit Free Press* (December 22, 1978).
46. "Court Orders Back Pay for Officers," *Detroit News* (February 14, 1979).
47. "Court Orders Higher Police Pay," *Detroit Free Press* (February 28, 1979).
48. "Court Orders Higher Police Pay," *Detroit Free Press* (March 13, 1979).
49. "Young's Gamble on Police Pay," *Detroit Free Press* (April 16, 1979).
50. "Detroit Police: The Long March," *Detroit Free Press* (May 25, 1979).
51. "More Police Layoffs Likely," *Detroit Free Press* (December 22, 1984).
52. See David Lewin, "Collective Bargaining and the Right to Strike," in *Public Employee Unions*, ed. A. L. Chickering (San Francisco: Institute for Policy Studies, 1976).
53. "Detroit Wants Police to Take Pay Cut," *Detroit News* (April 4, 1980).
54. "Supreme Court Upholds 1978 Police Pay Raises," *Detroit Free Press* (June 7, 1980); see *City of Detroit v. DPOA*, 408 Mich. 410, 294 N.W. 2d 68 (1980). "Women, Blacks Hurt Most by Police Cuts," *Detroit Free Press* (July 8, 1980).
55. "Police: Fewer Men, More Efficiency," *Detroit Free Press* (November 10, 1980).
56. "Black Police Fight to Save Jobs," *Detroit Free Press* (May 24, 1981).
57. "City, Police Agree to 3-Year Pay Freeze," *Detroit News* (June 23, 1981).
58. "A Comeback for 97 Officers," *Detroit Free Press* (August 12, 1978).
59. "Recall of Police May Be Delayed," *Detroit News* (December 23, 1981).
60. "150 Laid-Off Police Officers Recalled," *Detroit News* (April 2, 1982).
61. "U.S. Assails Ruling on Detroit Police," *New York Times* (May 3, 1983); see *Van Aker v. Young*, 541 F. Supp. 448 (D.C. Mich., 1982) 29 EPD, para. 32, 902.
62. See Nathan Glazer, *Affirmative Discrimination* (New York: Basic Books, 1975).
63. "Cop Plan Challenge Angers Young," *Detroit News* (May 3,

1983). "U.S. Urged to Back Off Hiring Case," *Detroit Free Press* (May 17, 1983).
  64. "Black Cops Attack Hike in Union Dues," *Detroit News* (May 18, 1983).
  65. "Police Racial Quotas Taken to Top Court," *Detroit Free Press* (December 3, 1983).
  66. "U.S. Joins Lawsuit Opposing Detroit Police Promotions," *Detroit News* (December 3, 1983).
  67. "High Court Backs Police Promotions," *Detroit Free Press* (January 10, 1984).
  68. *Hanson Bratton v. City of Detroit*, 712 F 2d 22 (6th Cir., 1983); also see *Baker v. Detroit*, 483 F. Supp. 930 (E.D. Mich., 1979).
  69. *National Association for the Advancement of Colored People (NAACP), Detroit Branch v. DPOA*, U.S. Eastern District, 591, F. Supp. 1194 (1984).
  70. *Firefighters Local 1784 v. Stotts*, docket nos. 82–229 (June 12, 1984).
  71. Ibid.
  72. *International Brotherhood of Teamsters v. United States*, 431 U.S. 324.
  73. *NAACP v. Detroit Police Officers Association*, 591 F. Supp. 1194 (1984).
  74. David Kushma, "Call Back Black Cops, Judge Rules," *Detroit Free Press* (July 26, 1984), 1.
  75. *NAACP v. DPOA*, F. Supp. 1195 (1984).
  76. David Kushma and Tim Kiska, "Union Must Add Blacks as Leaders," *Detroit Free Press* (July 26, 1984), 15A.
  77. Wilbur C. Rich, *The Politics of Urban Personnel Policy: Bureaucrats, Politicians, and Reformers* (Port Washington, N.Y.: Kennikat Press, 1982).
  78. Carl Stokes, *Promises of Power: A Political Biography* (New York: Simon and Schuster, 1973).

Chapter 8

  1. Patricia Giles Leeds, "City Politics and the Market: The Case of New York City's Financing Crisis," in *The Municipal Money Chase*, ed. Alberta Sbragia (Boulder: Westview Press, 1983), 114.
  2. Ibid., 115.
  3. Terry N. Clark and Lorna Ferguson, *City Money* (New York: Columbia University Press, 1983), 34–36.
  4. Ibid., 141.
  5. Egbert S. Wengert, *Financial Problems of the City of Detroit in the Depression* (Detroit: Detroit Bureau of Governmental Research, 1939), 1.
  6. Ibid., 2.
  7. Ibid., vii–viii; see also Committee on City Finances, *A Progress Report: January 8, 1930 to September 14, 1931* (Detroit: Detroit Bureau of Governmental Research, September 1931).
  8. "Task Force on City Finances," memorandum submitted to Mayor Coleman Young (1976), 4.

9. Ibid., 26.
10. *Detroit News* (January 19, 1986), 16.
11. Luther Keith et al., "Politicians to Study Tax Plan," *Detroit News* (June 1, 1981), 1.
12. Ibid.
13. Cynthia Lee, "Disowned Poll Raises Tax Hike Hopes," *Detroit News* (June 3, 1981), 1B.
14. David Kushma, "Detroit Tax Plan Revitalized but with Strings Attached," *Detroit Free Press* (June 4, 1981), 1.
15. Ken Fireman, "Dual Tax Would Win," *Detroit Free Press* (June 4, 1981), 1.
16. David Kushma, "Detroit Gets Approval for Vote on Raising Income Tax Rates," *Detroit Free Press* (June 6, 1981), 1.
17. Ken Fireman, "They're Counting on Coleman Young to Get a 'Yes' Vote on Tax Hike," *Detroit Free Press* (June 7, 1981), 1.
18. Susan Pollack, "Yes Committee Opens Drive for Tax Increase," *Detroit News* (June 9, 1981), 1B.
19. Robert Roach and Susan Pollack, "Young Pushing Absentee Vote," *Detroit News* (June 10, 1981), 5B.
20. Ken Fireman, "Income Tax Hike Opposed by Major City Unions," *Detroit Free Press* (June 13, 1981), 1.
21. Ken Fireman, "Young Rips Tax Hike Opponents," *Detroit Free Press* (June 4, 1981), 3A.
22. Ken Fireman and Tom Hundley, "Young Goes on TV to Push Tax Raise," *Detroit Free Press* (June 19, 1981), 3A.
23. "Detroit's Tax a Toss Up," *Detroit News* (June 21, 1981), 1.
24. Ken Fireman and Tim Kiska, "Blacks Provide Solid Margin for Tax Plan," *Detroit Free Press* (June 21, 1981), 7A.
25. David Kushman, "Racial Split in Tax Vote," *Detroit Free Press* (June 24, 1981), 1.
26. Joanne Firestone, "Young Scores Triumph: Detroit Passes Tax Hike," *Detroit News* (June 24, 1981), 1.
27. Ken Fireman and Tim Kiska, "Young Wins First Piece of Rescue Plan by 3-2 Vote," *Detroit Free Press* (June 24, 1981), 1.
28. Robert Roach, "Survival Plan Suffers Wages, Bond Setbacks," *Detroit News* (July 7, 1981), 1B.
29. Robert Roach, "Union Rejects Freeze on Pay, Layoffs Loom," *Detroit News* (July 10, 1981), 1A.
30. Ibid.
31. Ibid.
32. Ken Fireman, "City Tough Tactics Blamed for AFSCME," *Detroit Free Press* (July 1981), 1B.
33. Robert Roach, "AFSCME Counters with 25-and-Out Bid," *Detroit News* (July 17, 1981).
34. David Grant, "City-Union Pact Will Avert Layoff," *Detroit News* (July 21, 1981), 1A.
35. Robert Roach and Michael Tucker, "3 More Locals Agree to Wage Freeze Plan," *Detroit News* (July 24, 1981), 2A.
36. Ibid.
37. Ibid.
38. Ken Fireman, "Union-City Pact Near as 5 Locals Vote Yes," *Detroit Free Press* (July 1981), 3A.

39. Robert Roach, "Young Asks State to Buy City Bonds," *Detroit News* (July 27, 1981), 2B.
40. Robert Roach and Luther Keith, "Survival Plan Nears Deadline," *Detroit News* (August 11, 1981), 1.
41. Robert Roach, "Firemen to Battle Sale," *Detroit News* (August 12, 1981), 1A.
42. Ibid., 12A.
43. Tom Hundley and Ken Fireman, "Pension Unit OKs Buying City Bond," *Detroit Free Press* (August 13, 1981), 3A.
44. Luther Keith and Robert Roach, "State Approves Young's Plans to Rescue Detroit," *Detroit News* (August 14, 1981), 10A.
45. Don Tschurhart, "Civic Pride Was Key to Bank Bond Buy," *Detroit News* (August 14, 1981), 10A.

Chapter 9

1. Kirk Cheyfitz, "The Survivor," *Monthly Detroit* 4 (February 1981): 43.
2. Meier and Rudwick, 221.
3. Interview with a political activist, who wishes to remain anonymous.
4. Mark S. Granovette, "The Strength of Weak Ties," *American Journal of Sociology* LXXVII (May 1973): 1366–80.
5. Jones et al., *Sustaining Hand*.
6. David J. Brophy, *Venture Capital Financing Opportunities and Needs in Southeast Michigan* (Detroit: Metropolitan Affairs Corporation, 1983).
7. Richard Child Hill, "Crisis in the Motor City: The Politics of Economic Development in Detroit," in *Restructuring the City*, ed. Susan S. Fainstein et al. (New York: Longman, 1986), 116.
8. William J. Wilson, *The Declining Significance of Race* (Chicago: University of Chicago Press, 1978), 138.
9. Mahaffey, interview with author, September 24, 1987.
10. Tom Jones "Princes of the City," *Detroit Free Press Magazine* (January 1986): 17.

Index

Aberbach, Joel, 41
Action clusters, 143, 145–46
Affirmative action: in Detroit Police Department, 212–13, 219–21, 225–28; and the fiscal crisis, 222–24
American Motors Corporation, 107, 109
Austin, Richard, 94–96, 98; as first black mayoral candidate, 94–96
Association of Community Organizations for Reform Now (ACORN), 180, 253, 277

Bachelor, Lynn, 270
Banfield, Edward, 31
Barrow, Thomas, 116–17, 125, 199
Battle, Robert (Buddy), 63, 76, 79, 97
Beckham, William, 15, 100, 108, 173, 251, 255
Black bourgeoisie, 56–57, 59
Black Slate, 82, 274, 276
Blanchard, James, 196
Blount, Frank, 214
Bowles, Charles, 26, 46, 52, 235
Brophy, David, 271
Brown, Basil, 85, 251
Brown, Ernest, 60, 109, 110–11, 119, 120, 125, 245
Browning, H., 132
Buchanan, Colin, 201

Caldwell, Manly, 45
Callahan Act of 1947, 66
Caretaker mayors, 36–37
Carter, Jimmy, 18, 150
Cavanagh, Jerome, 22, 26, 29, 31, 77–78, 81–82, 91, 99, 207, 281
Central Industrial Park (CIP), 29, 38; development of, 180–92
Cheyfitz, Kirk, 267
Chrysler Corporation, 51, 210
City Charter of 1918, 44, 275
City Charter of 1973, 19, 108, 369
City of Detroit: changing demography of, 23–25; economic conditions of, 37–39, 126–35; economic elite of, 138–40; economic growth policies of, 136–37; fiscal crises of, 232–63; underclass of, 135–36
Clark, Terry, 234
Cleage, Albert, 79, 82, 138
Cobo, Albert, 31, 74–75, 281
Cockrel, Kenneth, 75, 82, 180, 183, 188, 277
Cohen, Stephen, 151
Congress of Industrial Workers (CIO), 63, 65–68, 74
Conyers, John, Jr., 78, 97
Cotillion Club, 56, 59–60, 273
Crockett, George, 65, 77, 79, 82
Cunningham, James B., 31

Dade, Malcolm, 15, 100, 251
Dahl, Robert, 31, 270
Daley, Richard, 31, 36, 91–92
Davis, Allison, 59, 89
Davis, David, 43
Democratic party and blacks, 54–55, 57–58
Detroit Economic Growth Corporation (DEGC), 190
Detroit Free Press, 102, 104, 117, 250, 254, 281
Detroit News, 104, 110, 116, 174, 191, 250, 254
Detroit Police Officers Association (DPOA), 174, 205, 215, 217, 237; and black officers, 215–16, 219–22, 225–28
Detroit Renaissance, 139
Diggs, Charles, Jr., 50, 60, 73
Diggs, Charles, Sr., 50–51, 76
Dionysian personality, 33
Douglass, Frederick, 59
Du Bois, W. E. B., 59, 70
Dunn, Robert, 47

Edwards, Nelson Jack, 78, 97
Eisinger, Peter K., 21–22
E lite, 57, 60
Equity package, 245
Eudaemonism, 33, 279

296

Index

Eudaemonists, 33
Ewen, Catherine, 149

Ferguson, Lorna, 233–34
Fink, Joseph, 207
Fiscal crisis of 1981, 246–62
Fiscal crisis of 1975, 242–46
Fisher, Max, 139, 149, 150, 198, 274
Ford, Henry, 45, 62
Ford, Henry, II, 108, 130
Ford Motor Company, 44
Fraser, Douglas, 67, 211, 242, 250

General Motors Corporation (GM), 29, 128, 183, 185
Germer, Adolph, 67
Gilmore, Horace, 227–28, 231
Glazer, Nathan, 225
Great Man theory, 32
Gribbs, Roman, 22, 37, 95–96, 208, 210, 241, 281
Griggs v. Duke Power Company, 211

Hanson Bratton v. City of Detroit, 226
Harrington, Michael, 135
Hart, William, 213–14
Hill, Charles, 51, 83
Hill, Richard Childs, 271–72
Hogan plan, 78
Holley, Hubert, 76, 77, 79
Hood, Nicholas, 99
Hougabrook, Jesse Thomas, 56
House Un-American Activities Committee (HUAAC), 71–72, 99
Hudson, Joseph L., 81
Humphrey, Norman, 64

Ivory, Marcellus, 63, 102

Jackson, Jesse, 40, 115
Jackson, Kenneth, 46
Jackson, Murray, 97
Jeffries, Edward, 54, 281
Joe Louis Arena, 35, 38, 169–80
Jones, Byran, 203, 270

Keeran, Roger, 69
Keith, Damon, 106, 216, 218, 219, 221, 224
Kennedy, Edward, 44
Key, V. O., Jr., 266
Kilson, Martin, 57
Kornhauser, William, 55
Koslowski, Perry, 113–14, 119, 125
Kotter, Milton, 31
Ku Klux Klan, 42, 45–46

Lansing State Journal, 99
Lawrence, Paul, 31

Leadership model, 33
Lee, Alfred McClung, 64
Leeds, Patricia, 232
Leinen, Stephen, 212
Lewis, Denise, 80
Locke, Hubert, 81, 87, 94
Long, Norton, 199

McCarran Act, 71
Mahaffey, Maryann, 174, 274
Mallet, Conrad, Jr., 251–52
Martin, Albert, 195, 199, 200
Martin, Louis, 54
Mason, Hodges, 63, 65
Mayoral audiences, 25, 27–28
Mayoral constituencies, 25, 27–29, 30
Meier, August, 268
Michigan Chronicle, 54
Michigan Constitutional Convention (Con Con) 85
Millender, Robert, 77–78, 90, 93, 97, 137
Milliken, William, 143, 150, 175, 191, 245, 249
Miriani, Louis, 74–75, 281
Moten, Emmett, 145, 182, 186–87, 192
Move Detroit Forward Committee, 139
Murphy, Frank, 26, 31, 281

Nader, Ralph, 191, 202
National Association for the Advancement of Colored People (NAACP), 52–53, 70, 207
National Negro Congress (NNC), 70, 83
National Negro Labor Council (NNLC), 70–72
Neustadt, Richard, 27
New Bethel incident, 82
New clientage politics, 55, 57, 267–270
New Deal, 52, 55
New Detroit, Inc., 81, 138, 244, 251
New Fiscal Populists, 233
Nichols, John, 104–5, 209, 266
Norris, Bruce A., 176–77

Obie Wynn incident, 210
Ohio State University Journalism School, 28
Old clientage politics, 45, 57

Patrick, William, 93, 138
Pelham, Alfred, 176, 242
People Mover, 121, 192–201, 203
Personality model, 32
Pincus, Max, 150, 178
Pingree, Hazen, 26, 33, 37, 236, 265

Poletown Neighborhood Council, 185, 189
Power-broker model, 31
Pressman, Jeffrey, 19–20

Race riot of 1943, 64
Race riot of 1967, 81–82
Ragland, John, 44
Randolph, A. Phillip, 53, 70, 76
Ravitz, Melvin, 77, 97, 98, 101, 102, 109, 110
Reagan, Ronald, 18, 225, 261
Red Scare, 68–72, 88
Reich, Charles, 141
Republican party and blacks, 45
Reuther, Walter, 55, 64, 67, 79, 80–81, 88, 94
Risk-takers, 34–35
Robeson, Paul, 70–71
Robinson, Kent, 127
Romney, George, 78, 81, 84, 86
Rostow, W. W., 126, 136
Roxborough, John, 56
Rudwick, Elliott, 268

Sealy, Lloyd, 207
Scholle, Gus, 85
Secrest Committee, 112, 247–48, 262; Fred Secrest as chair, 247
Sectarchy, 270
Service economy, 132–34, 135, 151
Sheffield, Horace, 63, 76, 79, 80
Shrine of the Black Madonna, 274
Singleman, H., 132
Snow, Tony, 201
Southeastern Michigan Transit Authority (SEMTA), 117, 196–99, 203, 242
Stanbeck, Thomas, 132
Stanley, Ralph, 195, 198
Stewart, Reginald, 28
Stokes, Carl, 95, 229
Stolberg, Benjamin, 63
Stone, Clarence, 149
Stone, Ralph, 236
Stop Robberies, Enjoy Safe Streets (STRESS), 94, 104–5, 119, 207, 208–9
Stoval, A. J., 50
Stroh, Peter, 140, 149
Swanstrom, Todd, 149, 272
Sweet, Ossian, 46

Tannian, Phillip, 108, 211, 213–14
Tappes, Shelton, 45, 63
Taubman, Al, 130, 149
Terkel, Studs, 47
Thompson, Daniel, 55
Thompson, Wilbur, 131
Toch, Han, 207
Toffler, Alvin, 144
Toode, Aaron, 50
Trade Union Leadership Council (TULC), 76–77, 79, 268
Turner, Tom, 195, 243, 253

United Automobile Workers (UAW), 62, 68–69, 75, 85, 275
Upson, Lent, 44
Urban Alliance, 110, 276
Urban Mass Transit Administration (UMTA), 194–95, 196, 198, 201, 203

Vanderbeek, Robert, 85
Vaughn, Jackie, 80

Walker, Jack, 41
Wallace, Henry, 67
White, Horace, 50–51
Widick, B. J., 45, 57, 64
Williams, G. Mennen, 82
Wilson, James Q., 27, 29, 206
Wilson, William J., 273

Yates, Douglas, 277
Young, Claud, 109
Young, Coleman: as airman, 53; as Con-Con delegate, 84; as economic decision-maker, 143–49; as first black mayor, 105; as labor organizer, 62–68; as 1973 mayoral candidate, 98–108; political socialization of, 40–41, 61–62; and Red Scare, 68–76; and relations with economic elites, 138–41, 270–73; school years of, 48–49; as state senator, 85–88, 99; youth of, 42–43, 47–48
Young, Ida Reese, 42, 58, 83
Young, William C., 41, 43, 46, 47

Zysman, John, 151

Wilbur Rich received his Ph.D. from the University of Illinois Urbana-Champaign. Currently associate professor of political science at Wayne State University, Dr. Rich is the author of *The Politics of Urban Personnel Policy.*

The manuscript was edited by Elizabeth Gratch. The book was designed by Elizabeth Hanson. The typeface for the text is Trump. The display types are Belwe Bold and Trump. The book is printed on 60-lb. offset paper and is bound in ICG's Arrestox Vellum.

Manufactured in the United States of America.